CHRISTIANITY
in European History

CHRISTIANITY

in European History

WILLIAM A. CLEBSCH

New York
Oxford University Press
1979

Library of Congress Cataloging in Publication Data

Clebsch, William A.
  Christianity in European history.

  Includes index.
  1. Christianity—Europe. 2. Europe—History.
I. Title.
BR735.C57   209'.4   78-19033
ISBN 0-19-502471-0
ISBN 0-19-502472-9 pbk.

Printed in the United States of America

PREFACE

This is a book of history. All the events it relates have actually happened. Of course, to relate all the events that have actually happened in the history of European Christianity would overflow all the books in the world. This book, then, ungrudgingly departs from the style of history that tries to tell something about as many important people and happenings as possible. Instead, it tells a good deal about the few people and happenings that best exemplify the various ways that European humanity has expressed itself through the forms and patterns of the Christian religion. Instead of bemoaning selectivity as a grim necessity, the book turns selectivity into a cheery virtue. Only by so doing can one write a little book of history about a big subject of history.

Readers who know little or nothing about Christianity in European history will find plenty to learn and think about here. Much more can be studied in the sources and the more specialized interpretations that the notes cite. Readers who are already experts in part or all of the subject will no doubt be surprised to find favorite persons and episodes slighted or even left unmentioned. Each expert, to be sure, might have selected a different set of "best cases"; but then each would have written a different book. Recent works on the topic seem insistent on treating very many *more* cases, and they are very different *kinds* of books.

Beginners and experts alike can broaden their perspectives on life by imagining themselves sharing the circumstances and the humanity, the hopes and the fears, of the wide range of Christian experiences and styles of life here narrated. Whether the effort thus to stretch their own personhood points readers toward or away from regarding themselves as more or less Christian men and women is, to be blunt, none of this book's business.

Its first concern is to demonstrate that changing cultures and differing aspirations produced a variety of Christianities, evinced in various manifestations of Christ, over the centuries of European history. Perhaps a more accurate and certainly a more cumbersome title would have been, "The Christs and the Christianities of European History."

Its second main concern is to invite readers to participate vicariously in the experiences and lives of these "best cases." Students who empathize with strange styles of human (and particularly of religious) experience stretch their own human capacities. By sensing the ways that others have sensed the way it was we enlarge our own sensibilities. But the enlargement takes place only if we are ready and able to try on for size others' worlds and not just their ideas or perceptions or opinions—their world views and not just their points of view.

In those main interests the book tells how exemplary men and women encountered their Christs and lived out their Christianities in Europe from the era begun by Augustus Caesar to the era ended (we may hope) by Adolf Hitler. The several less insistent but rather more complicated concerns are detailed in the opening chapter. The story begins with Chapter II.

As the first chapter explains, this story belongs to the genre of religious history in the context of the humanities rather than to the genre of church history in the context of theology. It is worth noting briefly that there is also a far wider context. The study of religion has come into its own during the last one hundred years as part and parcel of the second Renaissance of the humanities.

The justly famous and well-recognized first Renaissance was the great eruption of intellectual energy that ended the Middle Ages and made way for the Modern Age, an unprecedented novelty in which Europeans recaptured from classical antiquity a kind of humanity very different from, although antecedent to, their own. The means of recapture were literary, historical, and philosophical modes of thought; with later refinements, they abide as the intellectual coinage of the humanities.

But when the great mental midwives of the European Renaissance lived, religion was becoming divisive all over Europe. They were far too Christian to appreciate the distinctly religious expressions of pagan antiquity and they were far too irenic to emphasize a social force that in their own day everywhere stirred dissension. The religious dimension of human experience therefore held a weak place, indeed a diminished place, in their purview.

Only recently (about 1875) did the western imagination begin, at once critically and without negative prejudice, to comprehend the non-western humanity of Asians, Africans, pre-Columbian Americans, and Islanders. These ways of being human so pervasively exhibited religion that it could not be overlooked or minimized. Moreover, in the western world of this recent Renaissance religion was more nearly a neutral than a divisive force. Suddenly these newly discovered ways of being human were appreciatively comprehended, religiousness and all, and were taken to be no less magnanimous for being varied and strange.

For all the similarities in method and outlook of the two Renaissances, they differed significantly in appraising religion—both western and non-western. The European Renaissance that turned the sacred epics and dramas of pagan antiquity into profane classics also neglected the European religious tradition itself, save as it had early embraced the literature and ideas of the Greeks and Romans. Such scholars as allowed Christianity to be more than revealed theology tended to reduce it to a set of abstract doctrines or political institutions. Its varied and profound articulations of people's hopes and hurts, often inhumane but always human, went mostly by the boards.

The recent Renaissance made the humanities worldwide or ecumenic, welcoming all discoverable forms of human expression and all identifiable aspects of human experience. The ecumenic Renaissance recovered the sacrality of the pagan classics. Employing the vast data about the European past that the prior century's scholars had accumulated, this ecumenic perspective created both a new esteem for non-western forms and a reappraisal of western forms of humanity. In particular, Europe's own religious expressions were opened to recovery and reassessment; the Christian religion became a human achievement. In the context of this ecumenic Renaissance this book places itself.

It is indeed bold to reappraise European Christianity in the setting of the ecumenic humanities as a way of recovering that tradition's variety of magnanimities—some admirable, some offensive, all fascinating. Thereby, divinity becomes the book's concern only so far as the gods have been encountered by men and women. Religious history, distinguished from church history, becomes the book's context writ small. Ecumenic humanities, distinguished from European humanities, becomes its context writ large.

I will explain a point or two about the text to ease the reading. Certain significant dates as well as certain references to sources are given in parentheses. Parenthetical citations of sources always fall at the ends of sentences and only numbers are given. Parenthetical dates, always accompanied by a word or two, fall medially within sentences. As far as possible, the year of birth and where appropriate the year of death of persons named in text and footnotes have been inserted following the full name in the index. A few biblical references, also parenthetical in the text, are self-evident, indicating citations from the Revised Standard Version.

Wherever possible, sources are cited from the editions or translations that are at once most readily available and most reliable. As a general rule, translations have been checked against standard texts, but translations of Coptic, Aramaic, and Arabic sources have perforce been accepted on faith.

The very nature of the book calls for more acknowledgments of assistance than I could possibly detail. I have been studying the history of Christianity since my earliest training in church history during the mid-1940s. Over the last two decades I have tried to rethink and to relearn this field in the interest of religious history rather than church history—a delicate distinction drawn explicitly in the introductory chapter and repeatedly exemplified in the text. My profoundest debt is owed to the many fine teachers with whom I have studied and to the host of fine students whose teacher I have been. Worthy of special mention among the latter are the graduate students at Stanford University who have worked with me as teaching interns or research assistants for my courses on Christianity.

A fellowship for independent study in 1976-77 from the National Endowment for the Humanities made possible the writing of this book. Visiting professorships during the same academic year at the University of North Carolina in Chapel Hill and at Duke University made the writing pleasant. I am grateful for the libraries and librarians at these universities as well as for those at Stanford; special thanks are due the library staff and the excellent collection of the Duke Divinity School. Typists at the Institute for Research in the Social Sciences at UNCCH and at Stanford helped cheerfully and efficiently to put the book into editable and printable form.

Colleagues who encouraged the project by criticizing and discussing drafts include, at Chapel Hill, Giles Gunn, Charles H. Long, Jouett L. Powell, and John H. Schuetz; at Duke, Robert C. Gregg, William H. Poteat, and Jill Raitt; also Sacvan Bercovitch of Columbia, Hans W. Frei of Yale, Amanda Porterfield of Syracuse, and David Tracy of Chicago. My colleague at Stanford, Lee H. Yearley, read and improved by criticism every chapter, some in more than one draft. Editing in the Oxonian style was done by Elaine Koss, Charles W. Scott, and Caroline Taylor. Susan Kwilecki helped read proof and make index. I thank each and all for many improvements, but none can share my blame for blemishes. For the nonce, the book is better for their help.

Permissions to quote currently copyrighted material were kindly granted by the following:

Oxford University Press for citations from *The Acts of the Christian Martyrs,* ed. and tr. Herbert Musurillo (1972).

Scholars Press for citations from *The Life of Pachomius (Vita Prima Graeca),* tr. Apostolos N. Athanassakis (1975).

W. A. Clebsch

Stanford University
October 1978

CONTENTS

I

INTRODUCTION

History and European Christianity

The Christian religion has been primarily, although by no means exclusively, a European religion, and the principal religion of European civilization has been Christianity. It is generally agreed that to study the history of Europe involves studying the history of Christianity and vice versa. Consensus rapidly fades when one asks how the two stories are related: How much did religion and culture influence one another? Which was the independent and which the dependent variable? This book tries to bring the crises of European culture and the exemplars of the dominant European religion to terms with one another in mutual and equal interdependence. The experiment involves taking religious expressions with greater seriousness than cultural historians usually do. At the same time it involves paying more careful attention to cultural crises and changes in humanity than church historians like to do.

Historians who study European culture tend to place Christianity in a role subsidiary to that culture. Even those who avoid reducing Christianity's significance to, say, economics or philosophy tend to make it ancillary instead of constitutive. Historians who study Christianity typically assume a reverse dependence, holding secular or cultural history to be the vestibule of sacred or church history. For church historians, church history is continuous and meaningful, while cultural history is discontinuous and finally insignificant.

In this study the sacred and the secular always modify and are being modified by each other. They are distinguishable for the sake of discussion but are never really separable dimensions of the human enterprise. It proposes that religious historiography and cultural historiography are viable in combination. Its brevity signals that no attempt has been made to mention everything other histories of Christianity have mentioned—or even all those aspects other histories have stressed. This book, in short, complements and corrects the insights both of cultural history and of church history with the insights of the history of religiousness. It places Christianity in mutual interaction with European culture, not beside or beneath it, not above and beyond it.

The relation of this book to cultural and secular history is simple and straightforward: it shares their method and their aim, while emphasizing certain data that cultural studies tend to neglect or minimize, namely the actors' claims and the eyewitnesses' testimony to the actuality of salvation and of the savior's presence to the saved. In fact, the accounts and testimonies that the historian of religiousness uses as evidence affirm such actualities and not only the apprehensions of them. The testimony affirming real encounters with deity and actual salvation refer to something that may well be unknown or alien to a historian's own experience, but that fact does not alter the other fact that deities and salvations have been central to past actuality. So far as historians are held accountable to "tell it the way it was" for those in the past, their narratives will be replete with strange and wondrous episodes. Truth *is* stranger than fiction. And a license to rule out, as illusion or mere apprehension, everything testified to which lies outside the historians' own experience would collapse their narratives into little more than autobiography.

The historian of religiousness must take such strange testimony with great seriousness when it attests the actuality of salvation and must refuse to reduce what happened to some mere apprehension of salvation. Sufficient testimony, otherwise held reliable, that persons have met the deity and been saved goes far beyond reporting apprehensions or opinions. So does testimony that deity and salvation have lost their transcendence and mystery and have been assimilated into human consciousness and volition— have become apprehensions rather than actualities.

The point is simply that a profound and effective change in human sensibility becomes for the historian of religiousness a change in the way the universe was. No available historical method can distinguish the way men and women personally and socially understood their universe from the way their universe actually was then and there. For the only then-and-there universe to which the historian of religion has access is the universe as it was for those who were there. That holds for pre-moderns who did not make sharp distinctions between actualities and the apprehensions of them, just as it holds for moderns who do drive such wedges. Fundamental changes in apprehension constitute shifts in world view, and world view frames the way things actually were for those who participate in the world.

For example, this book describes how Bernard of Clairvaux and Christ in heaven participated in a mystical embrace. We have no evidence that Bernard merely apprehended such an embrace. Granted, no available historical method can tell who the embracing Christ actually was and how the embrace may or may not have affected him. For Christ, whoever or whatever he may have been, has left us no testimony. In the encounters with Bernard he was the divine savior. What Bernard experienced and attested, so far as he was neither deluded nor lying, is how things actually were for him then and there. His companions added their testimony, and the episode established itself in a historiographic tradition. To deal critically with all that testimony is certainly not to take it gullibly, at face value, but to respect it and to convert it into evidence for our own historiography. Nevertheless, critical history issues no warrant for changing what happened into an apprehension of what happened.

The secular historian whose work leaves little or no room for such strange testimony lands on other but not really more solid ground. There is every reason for such a historian to interpret human affairs in great terms like war, revolution, rise and decline of culture, renaissance, or whatever. But their use does not make those terms accord with identifiable objects, nor does it make them become in themselves the givers of testimony. What the terms refer to are quite analogous to Bernard's embrace with Christ or to Bernard's salvation. Those terms do not refer to realities in themselves apart from human experience, but they do refer to the actuality of things for men and women in their own times and places. The case is the same for the historian of religiousness using such interpretive terms as salvation, mystical union, magic, mana, avatar, deity, or whatever. They do not refer to realities apart from human experience, but they do refer to the way people thought things were. As much as war, these terms "tell it the way it was" for human beings, and, in that sense, they refer to what actually happened.[1]

This study's relation to sacred or church history is somewhat more complicated. It is, in short, a relation of largely shared data, but of different methods and aims. Church history undertakes to narrate the believing community's past in ways that will conserve and encourage that community and its belief. The task is to establish historically organic connections that identify present believers both with past believers and also with the unchanging deity and savior who were orthodoxly believed in by the community. For church history, in a word, "Jesus Christ is the same yesterday and today and for ever" (Hebrews 13:8). This book, on the other hand, undertakes to narrate the past appearances of new and changing forms of humanity as they christianly expressed themselves. It identifies the emerging of these forms of human existence through cultural changes, and it identifies the religious expressions that "took," those that became exemplary. (Not that they all became commonplace or widely imitated, since some of the most influential involved elites such as martyrs.) It then delineates the appearances of Christ as adopting those forms of humanity and functioning as a model savior for the different religious exemplars.

The task of this narrative, in a word, is to make sense of the mutually dependent relation between the Christian religion and European culture by illustrating how the culture has been religiously shaped and how the religion, including its deity and savior, has been culturally conditioned. More simply, European church history shows how Christendom, or some part of it, drew various people into the true church with its true creed and cult centering on a forever-the-same Christ and deity. This history of Christianity in Europe shows how successive people exhibited differences that changed the deity and the Christ who became manifest to them.

Church history must strive for comprehensiveness, while this history of Christianity thrives on selectivity. Church history's concern for continuity and constancy spurs efforts to fill all the gaps with successions of bishops or popes, prophets or believers, and to show that what appear to have been innovations were really the unfolding of implicit traditions, or the developing of the pristine form of the religion, or the recapturing of what had fallen into disuse. This book's concern for the most interesting permutations sends it searching not for such continuities, but for persons and movements that exemplify ingenuity in developing religiously novel expressions for culturally novel situations. What Dionysius of Halicarnassus reported that Thucydides said—that "history is philosophy learned from examples"—applies to this history of Christianity. Church history is theology learned from continua.

Church history typically builds around fortunes of the faithful, particularly of their priestly functionaries. Familiar turning points are the "peace of the church" under Constantine (in 313), the christological definition made at Chalcedon (in 451), the "Great Schism" (of 1054) between Latin catholicism and Greek orthodoxy, the Reformation (in the 1500s), and (since the 1700s) secularization. Each of these events or movements in fact belongs to a different order—one an imperial decree, another a technical formula of theology, then ecclesiastical anathemas, the breakup of massive institutions, and finally a cultural disenchantment. What in fact is measured by them in church history is not a historical process, but simply the boon or the bane of the church. The histories of individual sects or of particular churches typically follow suit—boon and bane—or, in modern times, ecclesiastical reactions to political-military events. In denominational histories, to paraphrase Milton, new presbyter is but old priest writ small.

In contrast, this history of Christianity in Europe builds around events initiating and signaling changes in human capabilities and aspirations, in the fundamental sensibilities of men and women, in world views—indeed, in the very modalities of being human. These changes in European humanity are both economically and adequately symbolized by basic shifts in modes of imperium or sovereignty, understood as the embodiment of divine order and therefore of divine reality—in a word, sacred kingship. The shape of imperium gives clues as to how human beings reached for and grasped order and reality, which in turn indicates, with reference to Christians, what kinds of Christs and deities they were capable of recognizing and accompanying. Those signs in their turn signal typical religious expressions that shaped cultures and eventually helped prepare for still other forms of humanity to emerge.

SELECTION VERSUS COMPREHENSION

Both the comprehensiveness for which church historians properly strive and the selectiveness that this history of religiousness properly takes as its aim are matters more of emphasis than of opposition. Of course, any history that included every available shred of information about Christianity in the European past would be interminable. And a history that left out everything that anybody ever thought unimportant might well end a few pages after it began. Still, church history tends to emphasize comprehension, and the history of religiousness needs to be as selective as possible.

Church history's task is to provide enough information to convince the critical reader that wherever true Christian salvation has been experienced, it was the same—single, continuous, unvarying. That task is frustrated by a call to omit any detail that might bolster this conviction. By contrast, the history of religiousness needs to give examples, both of the cultural crises that evoked new forms of humanity and of the new modes of spirituality that came about when these forms of humanity expressed Christian salvation, just enough to be persuasive. Its task is frustrated by the call to include any detail that might distract attention from the decisiveness with which two or three most convincing exemplars exhibited each kind of religiousness.

While choosing what to include and what to exclude is an inescapable aspect of any historian's work, every sort of history leaves out whatever is immaterial to its genre. Virtue attaches to selectiveness and to comprehensiveness only in relation to the kind of narrative that is appropriate to a particular story of the past. Some kinds of stories require the inclusion of each detail that might be significant, while others need to omit everything but the most telling examples. Examples of fictional narrative may clarify the point.

The moral complications and compromises into which individuals are plunged whenever they engage in the values and customs and institutions of their societies are the themes of many novels. One kind of novel may set out to show the intricacies and the inescapability of this predicament. Another may tell of the poignant, typical, human responses to social involvement. The first kind of story was told unsurpassably by Feodor Dostoevsky in *The Brothers Karamazov* with such fullness of biographical detail for each of the multitude of characters that the reader needs a list of persons and their kinships in order to progress through the initial reading of that marvelous, comprehensive novel. Here is what might be called organic narrative, seamless in its tracings, which recounts every incident and reflects every mood, its inclusiveness being limited only by the reader's capacity to hold all the details within the compass of a single story. Even so, many readers find the book replete with independent stories—for example, "The Grand Inquisitor" has often been separately published. Plot summaries abound.

At the other extreme one might place Mark Twain's *The Adventures of Huckleberry Finn*, a story of extraordinary economy yet one that exemplifies the wide range of possible tensions between individual freedom and social constraint; ingenious strokes of humor deepen the novel's seriousness. Each character's personal liberty and its compromises with social convention arise starkly and in as exemplary a fashion as possible. Here the changes are rung by emphasizing the major variants and by excluding whatever detracts from the most telling examples. Excerpts out of context distort the story, and plot summaries fall flat.

Comparing these two novels should not by any means invite readers to measure the present study by the high literary attainments of Dostoevsky and Mark Twain. The allusion only suggests that narration varies as to detail and may purposefully be inclusive or exclusive. Narration can tellingly exclude many ordinary matters and thereby improve the exemplary character of what it includes. Simple questions, taken in their own right, become silly when raised with reference to *Huckleberry Finn.* For example, Who invented the steamboat? For that matter, Who invented the raft? Who was the governor of Missouri? Who was the President of the United States? For that matter, Who was the judge whose court might have reenslaved Jim? Important as these points would be to a social history about Huck's generation, it was crucial for Mark Twain to omit them for his story's own sake.

Not only church history but other kinds of history have clung to the fully detailed form of narration that was the favorite of classical novelists (in the 1800s), especially in Europe. This kind of organic narration continues to set the pattern for much history, even though other narrative forms have long proved themselves salient for certain purposes. In fact, the most arresting modern novels, from the pens of geniuses like James Joyce, Vladimir Nabokov, and Lawrence Durrell, or even the less famous but extraordinarily gifted Ken Kesey, have no need to begin at some natural, chronological starting point and move step by step toward their denouements. Instead, authorial voice often changes from event to event or from section to section. Time becomes no mere sequence, but a flexible device to be accelerated or retarded or otherwise manipulated at the author's command.

The predicament of historians in choosing between the traditional, inclusive narrative and the traditional, analytic monograph was aptly noted by Richard Hofstadter, who foretold the emergence of a historical genre that would be at once as sparse and as telling as caricature. He disavowed the invidious connotations of that label. "Unlike caricature, good history does not attempt to portray through wilful distortion. But caricature has this in common with history, that its effects must be achieved in broad and exaggerated strokes that cannot render all the features of the subject. And in good caricature the subject is instantly recognizable."[2] This book accepts Hofstadter's challenge to avoid simply retelling a well-known story but instead to caricature, by exemplification and selection rather than by distortion, the Christian religion through its career in European history. It does not discuss many of the "great" figures of church history who did not clearly exemplify the distinctive kinds of religiousness that their particular forms of humanity brought to expression.

In fact, many of these "greats" command much attention in most church histories by virtue of the fact that their religiousness was inimitable and therefore *not* exemplary or expressive of their times. It will be shown below, for example, that Augustine of Hippo was the last great pagan Roman intellectual to accept the authoritative religion of the Catholic church. For that very fact he came to be admired as a thinker, revered as a saint, studied as a writer, and valued as a cataloguer of pagan learning. But that very same fact made his religiousness inimitable by people who were no longer Roman pagans. Perhaps none of his contemporaries, at least in the Latin tradition, had more influence on Christian pessimism about the moral capabilities of men and women; he must therefore loom large in any history of Christian doctrine, particularly the doctrine of sin. But the religiousness that he expressed as a learned pagan encountering Christian salvation had already been decisively exemplified by figures like Justin Martyr and Tertullian and Cyprian and Ambrose. And as a writer of theodicy, Augustine provides a less clear-cut example than Boethius, his successor. Although the Renaissance scholar, Francesco Petrarch, emulated Augustine's self-portrait in the *Confessions,* Petrarch himself was a Christian embracing Roman paganism, while Augustine was a Roman pagan embracing Christianity. This difference betrays the folly of making Augustine the exemplar of Petrarch's religiousness.

Although that line of reasoning controlled the decision that this study should pay little attention to Augustine and to many other "greats" of church history, a subsidiary reason should be admitted. Augustine and Aquinas, Luther and Calvin (in fact many of the fathers and doctors, and most of the reformers), have received so much attention from church historians that their roles and reputations stand firm, hardly to be budged by any brief, general history of Christian religiousness. They are so strongly typed, if not stereotyped, that reconsiderations must be either very detailed or ineffective. Were this book to give them sufficient notice to place them in its story of religiousness, each would require a work that in turn would engage a whole library of interpretive scholarship. Only by eradicating deeply etched impressions of these great men's traditional fame and then by resketching them with respect to their special religiousness could they be placed meaningfully in the history of changing salvations, varying appearances of Christ, and culturally conditioned deities that this work relates.

Such an undertaking might eventually bear fruit, for each of these "greats" in fact entered distinctive relations with a particular vision of Christ as a particular kind of savior granting a particular version of salvation. But the books would take more than one lifetime to write and perhaps nearly a lifetime to read. More important, the variety that Christianity in European history has expressed with reference to salvation, savior, and divinity can in fact be exemplified *better* by the figures who are stringently selected for treatment in this work than would be the case were the "greats" embraced under a principle of even cautious comprehensiveness. In a word, to discuss more than cursorily the "greats" of church history would greatly lengthen but would not significantly illumine this history of Christian religiousness in Europe. It is only fair, of course, to mention the most famous of these "greats" by way of placing them in their historical contexts.

CHRISTS

The history of Christianity is haunted in every period with concern for understanding the personhood and personal identity of the religion's savior. Yet only moderns have been interested in the details of the life and career of the Palestinian teacher from Nazareth named Jesus. Despite a number of ingenious theories explaining how and why and by whom that figure must have been invented, there is little reason to doubt that such a person lived there and then. But this question of Jesus' so-called historicity has only recently (since 1835) been of concern to his followers. Nor, in fact, did a "Christ of faith," detached or detachable from the actual "Jesus of history," hold much interest or influence until the same date. These questions and the further question of the relation between the two, as the last chapter in this work will indicate, bear on the historical study of the religion only as theological problems of the modern period. As such, they have muddied rather than clarified historical issues.

Nevertheless, it is true that the figure who furnished the history of Christianity with its fundamental continuity has been Jesus Christ. Always and everywhere Christians have named him their savior and have made him the model for their religiousness. But that name has always referred to one who appeared to them in so many and such different roles and with so great a variety of salvation-experiences that one properly speaks of the many Christs to whom the Christians have referred. The substantive chapters of this book will indicate the main identities—as it were, the typical Jesus Christs of Christianity. This chapter tries only to show that the actual variety of Christs has been appropriate and necessary in order to bestow salvation upon changing patterns of human existence—as it were, upon the typical humanities of European history.

The earliest record of a manifestation by Christ is found in Paul's accounts of his encounter with his resurrected savior. Paul did not simply apprehend or conceive of a Christ who had risen from the dead and who saved people. His own claim and the testimonies of those who knew him and knew about him point to something else—to Christ as living in Paul's own time and place, indeed in Paul's own life, and as saving Paul and others in a distinctive way. Christ's own self-manifestation, or Christophany, is what the accounts say actually happened to Paul and his converts.

These testimonies, far from being naïve, presented the significance of divine-human encounters with greater seriousness than was shown by those theologians (since 1835) who have differentiated between apprehensions of the Christ of faith and some hypothetically "more factual" Jesus of history. "Any attempt to break up the mystery of the divine-human participation," wrote Eric Voegelin, "as it occurs in a theophanic event, is fatuous. On the subjective side, one cannot 'explain' the divine presence in the vision by a psychology of Paul. And on the objective side, 'critical doubts' about the vision of the Resurrected would mean that the critic knows how God has a right to let himself be seen."[3]

That, of course, is precisely what moderns do with considerable success—set the limits on "how God has a right to let himself be seen." They have every right to do so *for themselves.* But for them to set limits, particularly their own uniquely won limits, on how pre-moderns received manifestations of the divine is surely fatuous. One of the more considerable gains accruing from moderns' tendency to limit the divine's appearances to them is their ability to comprehend in its full force the spirituality of pre-moderns who did not set such limits. Similarly, when moderns insist on distinguishing their consciousness, or apprehension from the actualities of which they are conscious, they gain the ability to imagine what it was like for other people to live with sensibilities that did not include any such distinction.

The more the pity if the very stance that allows moderns to discern different forms of humanity across time and space should lure us into thinking everybody everywhere was always just like us in this respect. Before people began to set the rules for admitting a Christ-savior to their sensibilities, he in fact appeared in a grand variety of ways to various kinds of human beings. In fact, he is most clearly identifiable as the sum total of the miscellaneous ways he has appeared to and been recognized by those to whom he has been present.

In the Gospels, which moderns tend to mistake for biographies, Christ was at every juncture a strange and mysterious person. He claimed very little for himself, although in the Gospel of John he claimed much for the role that God had assigned him. He was repeatedly curious to know who men and women took him to be, as though he were keeping secrets about who he really was or trying to pass himself off for who he really was not. The Gospel of Luke, probably the most artful of the four narratives, almost overwhelms Jesus' claims for himself with instances in which the mystery of who he was is referred again and again to what he did. "Handsome is that handsome does," wrote Oliver Goldsmith; just so, savior is that savior does. The stress on intention-action identity and the underplaying of self-ascriptive identity serve to reinforce the narrative's climax and denouement. So does the fact that the only beings who get a clear reading on Christ before he died are the demons, and vicious demons at that. Very soon after he died, his identity became for the first time crystal-clear to the two men on the road to Emmaus whom he taught and with whom he ate. Having died, he could convince them that he was the one their scriptures predicted would savingly live and die—and live.

For a person's identity to be decisively revealed by particular events is neither unusual nor magical nor even religious, but rather commonplace. It is accurate, for example, to say that Harry Truman was an unsuccessful haberdasher whose business failed and a Kansas City "machine" politician and county judge and a Senator and a Vice President and a President of the United States. But those statements do not say who he most characteristically *was;* they do not reveal his personal identity. In April 1951, however, he consulted his trusted advisers over General Douglas MacArthur's defying the President's policy of containing the Korean War. They counseled that MacArthur had become too popular to be disciplined or reprimanded. But Truman quickly and quietly terminated the discussion by phoning the Pentagon and firing MacArthur. That is who Truman *was,* one who acted out, against powerful advice, his own favorite motto, "The Buck Stops Here." What is different about Jesus Christ is only that the events most distinctly revealing his identity took place post mortem.

Christ in the Gospels was most characteristically himself when, having died, he made himself present as savior to those who believed in and followed him, especially on the occasions of their eating and drinking together in remembrance of him. This point is so strong that its opposite holds: the Gospels accord him no reliable identity prior to the episode of his death, but offer only a series of mistaken identities; even Peter, who called him the anointed one, later denied knowing him. In the accounts of the resurrection and its aftermath he did not take on or certify a previously established identity. In them he first came into his own, he became who he most characteristically was, a savior who after death savingly accompanied those whom he saved, especially when they gratefully ate and drank together, mindful of him. In the Gospels' retrospect only this identity made narrative sense of all the previous guesses and misidentities. All the previous actions on his part could be referred after his death to this intention. After death he *became* what in living and dying he had been *doing.*

Nevertheless, it is unfair to assume and impossible to demonstrate that these "post-resurrection appearances" defined or limited the manners in which he was able afterward to appear. For he was no more genuinely and no more savingly present in these early Christophanies than in the one that occurred (about 1400 C.E.) to a South Indian Sufi Muslim who, wading in a waist-deep lake, met a divinely beautiful girl of fifteen; she, like the other waders, was naked below the waist. She beckoned. He approached like a bridegroom approaching a bride. A cloak was thrown over the two of them. He suddenly became as beautiful as she when there arose between them Jesus, crying, "I am the Son of God." The man and girl argued over whether Jesus was his or her child, and Jesus then jumped around and denounced them both, saying, "I am neither your son nor hers, I am only myself." The girl said again, "Jesus is mine." The man responded, "I find myself to be just like him and just like that water; I am everything."[4] The fascinating details and nuances of the story need not detain us. It nicely illustrates, in its own rather strange way, the double emphasis—first on Jesus' refusal to yield his identity to others and second on his imparting what is valuable about his identity to others.

Those intertwined themes come to the fore in Christophany

after Christophany—he is the savior that he is in order to give others the salvation that he has to offer. He manifests himself in the full sense of the term. He shows himself plainly. He makes himself appear distinctly. He displays himself beyond question or doubt. He becomes recognizable in his own identity by becoming like those he shows himself to—even half-naked waders in a shallow lake in South India. This recognizability pervades the recorded Christophanies. Whatever identity he manifested, he made it accessible.

Irenaeus of Lyons early (about 180) put the transaction of Christian salvation in a phrase that he called "the only true and solid teaching"—that Jesus Christ "became as we are that we might become as he is."[5] The formula is axiomatic. Attention will soon turn to its first phrase, "He became"; his recognizability lies in the words, "as we are." As human existence in Europe has been repatterned by cultural crises and resymbolized by changes in sovereignty, Christophanies represented Christs resembling those humanities.

Otherwise the rest of the axiom is nonsense, for he must have taken on the identity of various people in order to make some of them like himself, namely dutiful and loving daughters and sons of a divine father. His filiality and that of others differed in that others presumably had once been prodigal children in revolt against their father, while he presumably had not. But the difference was not enough to prevent his becoming enough like them to make them become like him.

Granted, the divine word, or logos, that orthodox dogma held to have become incarnate (in the teaching of Athanasius of Alexandria) differed from plain people in quite remarkable ways. They were creatures and he was not. They were mortal, he eternal. Their substance was dust while his was deity.[6] Important as that dogma may be to church history, Christians throughout European history have received salvation from and attributed salvation to the more creaturely Christ clung to by Athanasius' enemies the Arians, a Christ who "made it" to divine sonship in a way analogous to the way ordinary people with his guidance and assistance "made it" to that sonship. He became as they were to help them become as he was.

Irenaeus' formula is useful in pointing to the significance of Christians' tendency to assign Christ the initiative in Christophanies. "He became. . . ." It is worth repeating that historical investigation cannot find any testimonies or monuments made by Christ himself to the effect that he initiated the manifestations of himself; that is not what is meant by the phrase, "He became." The witnesses of those manifestations, however, bear practically unanimous testimony to this effect—again, not that they had some apprehension of him as one who appeared, certainly not that they apprehended him *as though* appearing. Their testimony is simply that to them *he appeared,* recognizably and savingly. Such is the explicit claim of the Gospels' accounts of what happened after he died on the cross. Indeed, in such instances as the story of his transfiguration this characteristic is read back onto events recorded as having taken place before his death. The point is not therefore to reconstruct how it actually was *to Christ* for him to initiate appearances, but rather to recount how it was *for those to whom he appeared* for his appearances to bear the mark of his having initiated them.

The meaning of the history of Christianity in Europe lies in the experience of a series of differing Christophanic events. What is significant about this history, entwined as it inseparably is with events both cultural and cultic, is that new appearances of Christ have occurred to and have confirmed the salvation of new forms of humanity. That significance can be approached only by using modern critical methods of dealing with evidence. Those methods in the hands of the historian of religion must credit otherwise reliable and careful testimony when it testifies to the occurrences of war. (The common way of speaking, to the effect that war occurs, emphasizes the point, since we thereby say that war appears or presents itself.) Voegelin showed that what can be said significantly to have happened in human history is the differentiation of human consciousness by the divine appearances that he calls theophanic events.[7] This book shows that what can be said significantly to have happened in the history of Christianity is the differentiation of the European consciousness by Christophanic events. Included among them is the Christophany that evoked the modern consciousness, a manifestation so complete that moderns took over Christ's traditional functions, yet an event that still belongs to the class of Christophanies.

Has there been *anything* constant about all these various Christophanies? Yes. They refer almost univocally to one who lived in Palestine and died by crucifixion, one who ate and drank with his followers and taught them (often in riddles or *koans*). But what he most characteristically has been in the self-manifestations is what he became *after* so living and eating and dying, the one who made himself savingly present to those who believed in him, particularly as they ate bread and drank wine in his memory. If to a Sufi Muslim he became a young wader, naked from the waist down in a lake, jumping around and denying that he belonged either to the man or to the woman to whom he was so recognizable that both claimed him for a son, and if his appearance made the man become like him and like the water—like everything—then is not the sky the limit? The point is not that there have been no Christophanic constancies, but that constancies have been unimportant in Christophanies.

PREVIEW

In the era since the beginning of Christianity there have been five fundamental, pervasive forms of European humanity. Two exemplary ways of being Christian have arrestingly expressed each new set of human capacities and yearnings. Each religious expression was formed by and referred itself to a distinct manifestation of Christ. Bearing in mind this pattern, the innovations may be sketched in five paragraphs that preview the chapters following.

1. Coincidentally, or nearly so, with the origin of Christianity as a Palestinian sect spreading through the Mediterranean world, Caesar Octavianus and his successors embodied sovereignty over that world in a way that initially turned Romans into world citi-

zens and eventually turned the "world's" citizens into Romans. Imperial rule sacralized the Caesars and their Rome in a distinctive way. Participation in the benefits of this ecumenic, sacral society required tribute in the form of material taxes to Rome. Participation also required spiritual obeisance both to the gods of Rome, who were the source of order, and to the genius of the Caesar, who was the agent of order. Christians enjoyed those benefits and paid their taxes. But they claimed a heavenly citizenship under a deity who transcended the Roman gods and the Caesars. The martyrs exemplified Christian allegiance to Caesar and Christ by drawing the line beyond which loyalty to Caesar should not reach. When Constantine reversed the situation and used the Christians' deity to sanction his sacral rule and to hallow his new capital, the two citizenships tended to merge into one. Then the early monks, retiring from the world to their religious enclaves, assumed the role of the martyrs so they could keep Christians aware of their supreme loyalty to Christ. To the martyrs Christ became present as the one who died with them and welcomed them into heaven. To the monks he appeared as the god-man who overcame all passions and who both preserved in himself and imparted to them the perfection of original human nature.

2. When the western provinces of the Roman Empire culturally and politically disintegrated (after 476), sovereignty in the west shifted from Caesars to Germanic kings. Those kings' reliance on customary laws instead of codified laws and their plural expression of governance, together with the friction and fusion of Roman and barbarian ways, epitomized a humanity preoccupied with chaos and zealous for order. Two religious responses met these concerns. The first was that of theodicy, the demonstration by wisdom that calamity in the long haul delivered benefits. To his own personal as well as to social calamity Boethius applied the gist of Robert Browning's epigram, "God's in his heaven: / All's right with the world." In a circumstance of even worse social decay but one of personal success Gregory the Great developed the theory and practice of exercising an explicitly Christian governance in ordering the world. Taken together, these expressions

of theodicy and prelacy interpreted the failure to achieve social order as a divine blessing and sanctioned the undertaking of ever new efforts to bring order out of chaos. To this fail-safe religion Christ was alternately the incarnation of divine reason dispensing the wisdom of God's providence and the emperor-bishop ruling the universe.

3. The appearance (in 962) of a ruler, Otto I, powerful enough to make and unmake popes, together with the rise of absolute monarchies in the westernmost nations, launched Europeans on their quest for a culture sufficiently unified to harmonize the dissonances symbolized by paganism, by heretics, by the Muslims, by Greek Christendom, by revived classical learning, and by rivalry between church and state. The unifying ideal involved the embodiment of universal but limited power in the popes and of absolute but localized power in the Holy Roman emperors and the great kings. The religious expressions of these new sensibilities were the mystics' absolute acquaintance with deity, exemplified by Bernard of Clairvaux (among others), and the theologians' universal knowledge about God, exemplified by Anselm of Canterbury (again, among others). The mystics' Christ was a heavenly bridegroom mating with the loving believer's soul, while the theologians cherished a Christ who imparted information about deity—a pedagogue-savior.

4. In the epoch between the abdication of Charles V from imperial office (in 1556) and the rise of Napoleon Bonaparte (in 1804) as self-crowned emperor, sovereignty over European peoples was divided among territorial princes, and the religion of European Christians was splintered into territorial churches. Personal life, like the map of Europe, marked off the human endeavor into territories. Science, music, painting, architecture, poetry, drama, the crafts—all became vehicles for attaining and articulating the genius of individual persons. Religion was among these arenas in which practice led to expertise and sufficient practice made perfect—not flawless persons but champions in being religious. The twin paths leading to Christian virtuosity were piety and morality, the one being the way of warm-hearted reli-

gious feeling and the other the way of doing things with a religiously clean conscience. Exemplars of both abounded. Chapter V pays special attention to the moralism of Jeremy Taylor and the pietism of Nikolaus Ludwig von Zinzendorf. By the end of the period, in fact, a few persons had attained Christian perfection in both these areas of skill at once—for example, the Catholic Alphonsus Liguori and the Protestant John Wesley.

5. The modern sensibility of human and cultural autonomy stretches from Napoleon to Hitler (and maybe beyond). Each of these men conquered most of Europe and appointed himself dictator over it. The traditional functions of the Christian deity in creating and redeeming people, in guiding history and judging the nations, came to be assimilated as human functions. Autonomous humanity developed optional stances to Christianity. Some rejected it, while others reconstructed its authority around infallible popes or scriptures. But everybody became to some degree autonomous, and to that degree their choice regarding the religion was take-it-or-leave-it, not be-taken-by-it. Disenchantment, in a word, left open the possibility that one might deliberately renew one's interest—a far cry from simple, undisturbed enchantment. Modern apologists identified dimensions and arenas of autonomous existence and culture that they could christianly analyze in ways that left these areas calling for fulfillment by Christianity. For example, Søren Kierkegaard autonomously construed human existence to lead to a despair that prepared for the authentic existence of being Christian. His Christ was an autonomous god-man who unmasked human pretensions and conferred human authenticity. Activists likewise accepted modernity and identified certain causes that, usually benefiting common folk, could be served christianly. For example, Dietrich Bonhoeffer's Christ was a man for others who showed Bonhoeffer how to live for others, even by participating in plots to assassinate Hitler. Activists might do almost anything so long as they did it christianly.

So run the five substantative chapters and their ten religious exemplars. Why five? And why ten?

SCHEME

The great shifts in the forms of humanity in Europe and in the forms of the sovereignty by which they were ordered make five periods fall into place. Other possible schemes for organizing this study have been found inadequate to account for the data.

To divide the story into two equal periods would mark the first millennium as a time of waiting and the second as an epoch of managing. Voegelin referred to "Augustine's symbolization of . . . [his own] present, post-Christ period as the *saeculum senescens*, as the time of waiting for the Parousia and the eschatological events," and Henri Focillon recalled "the brief and terrible phrase of the Merovingian writer, *mundus senescit"* (the world grows old).[8]

This waning age, when the world waited and became decrepit, differed markedly from the second millennium, the time of building the world's future, which might be called the *saeculum tractans,* or the managing age. During the time of waiting, Europeans built relatively little, and during the time of building, they waited relatively little. Paradoxically, while they were waiting for the end, the future seemed secure (not progressive, but unthreatened), and while they were building the present, the future became more and more uncertain. This division, although simple and neat, is also gross and unrefined, inadequately attentive to the details both of cultural change and of religious expressions.

The five periods of this book arrange adequately all the actual, historical detail and variety, partly because each consists of integral parts. Constantine divides the early period, Charlemagne the next, Innocent III the middle, and perhaps Louis XIV the early-modern. This refinement illumines the history of sovereignty, yet each subdivision represents an attempt more to renovate a bygone form of sovereignty than to invent a new one.

Historiography of all kinds, perhaps particularly the historiography of religion, tends to fall into *some* pattern, which is rarely the only possible pattern. For while the critical historiographer must be held accountable to reconstruct what actually happened, the historian can only reconstruct and interpret, never simply record events themselves in an undifferentiated causal flux. A pattern of reconstruction tries to answer more questions than it raises and to settle more issues than it stirs, not to render alternatives implausible.

The five-period scheme, then, marks the changing forms of European humanity that have been symbolized by shifts in sovereignty. In addition, Christianity has been a broker of European civilization in five major transactions. In the first period the religion bore the apocalyptic and prophetic elements of Palestinian culture into the Hellenistic world under the claim that it could make those elements useful to fulfill the aspirations of the ecumenic empire. In the second period the church preserved and conveyed the ideals of Roman order and organization to the Germanic, pagan societies; in the process the church reshaped those ideals by carrying them in Christian containers. In the third period this cultural transaction, less directly from one tradition to another, brought to terms the universal aspiration of the church and the absolute aspiration of the state, merging into one society city of God and city of earth. Also in this period the church acted as broker by introducing classical learning and some features of Muslim culture to medieval Europe. In the early-modern period Christianity assisted in transferring the basis for social cohesion from religious conformity to monarchy; later, it helped base that cohesion in the popular principle of modern nation-states. In the most recent period it was the Christian deity whose functions were assimilated by autonomous humanity. This brokerage of one culture in itself makes a fivefold pattern of Christianity in European history.

Two characteristic religious exemplars expressed each of the five distinct forms of humanity and their cultural transitions. The ten types, of course, were selected according to their congruence with innovations in the forms of humanity or their giving Christian expressions to new human ways of hoping and rejoicing. The principle of selection accords with the book's attempt to demonstrate that the history of a religion and of its culture account for mutual dependence between the sacred and the secular.

In fact, a considerable body of church history and a not insignificant literature of secular history endorses certain selections as characteristic of their respective epochs. That is particularly true of martyrs and monks for the early period and of pietists and moralists for the pre-modern epoch. It is less obviously applicable to medieval mystics and theologians.

This study, however, avoids an appeal to these authorities for two simple reasons. First, this work must stand or fall on its own criteria, principally the accuracy with which it depicts cultural crises and religious expressions and the congruence of those that it selects. Second, the interpretation of these expressions under the principle of sacred-secular interdependence differs markedly from the interpretations of the same expressions in other historiographic traditions.

For example, the selection of martyrs and monks for the early period might be certified by reference, say, to the work of William Frend and Robert M. Grant, but in each case somewhat self-defeatingly since Frend subsumes the secular under the sacred and Grant tends to do the opposite.[9] Precisely because the selection of theodicy and prelacy for the period of the barbarians and of activists and apologists for the modern period do not readily and obviously accord with the traditional historiographies of those periods, these instances should illustrate most clearly how this book's own criteria operate.

TRUTH

This history of religiousness stands with the nonquantifiable humanities instead of with the quantifiable social sciences. It does not ask, for example, whether Bernard's statement that his mystical raptures lasted a half-hour specifies an amount that is the average or the mean of the duration of n raptures. Rather, the statement is taken as indicating brief (but not fleeting) experiences.

It has become familiar to think of these two modes of study in terms of metaphorical opposites—hedgehog versus fox or soft versus hard, etc. If it can be granted that the data used by humanistic history are softer and more hedgehoggish than those used by social sciences, it is also true that the epistemological procedures used by the humanities are harder and foxier than those of questionnaires and quantifications. The humanities at least avoid the risks of presupposing that responding subjects understand, with a precision that admits of quantifying, exactly what the questioner asks and that those same subjects can analyze and report in the questionnaire's terms their own experience (if any) of what is being inquired about. The humanistic historian's non-responding object of inquiry consists of lives, individual and social, already lived and testified to in testimonies of interpretation that themselves stay put under questioning—granted that the questioner is not absolutely constant from question to question.

Thus the book holds itself accountable to actualities. Its criteria, its identification of cultural crises and religious expressions, its selection of the most exemplary crises and expressions, its juxtaposition of them as congruent, and its depiction of how the figure of Christ changes with changing forms of human society— all are held accountable to the narrative reconstruction of how things actually were for persons in past times and distant places. These "hard" results must be gained, to be sure, from "soft" or seldom quantifiable testimony about the nexus between the sacred and the profane and about the encounter with each in the context of the other. This study affirms that these connections and experiences and encounters have been the "hard" stuff of the history of Christianity in Europe—the actual, lived-out lives of men and women, singly and in groups.

This book, in conclusion, explores how Christophanies and salvation were actual, and, in that sense, *true,* for Europeans through the course of the cultural-religious interactions. No doubt some people who read about Christianity in European history bring to their reading another question—not how it was actual, but whether it *is valid,* whether this salvation is available to them, even whether they can by study assure themselves that they have it and it is in this sense *true.* That, as the saying goes, is an entirely different question—one that would require an entirely different book as well as an entirely different author.

II
CITIZENSHIP

Martyrs and Monks

in the Roman Empire

27 B.C.E.-476 C.E.

Christianity dawned soon after the emperor and people of Rome had newly ordered the civilized world. And an enormous world it was. From the ecumenic empire of Alexander the Great, Rome inherited Macedonia and Thrace, Asia Minor and Palestine, Egypt, and, for a time, also Armenia and Mesopotamia. To those eastern regions Rome added Italy and the lands connecting it with Greece, as well as North Africa, Spain, Gaul, and Britain. The Romans justly called the Mediterranean "our sea," for their world embraced all the peoples of that basin and more. (They might also have called the Nile, the Danube, the Rhine, and for a time the Tigris and the Euphrates "our rivers.")

Octavianus and his great-uncle Julius, who assembled this world, bore the family name of Caesar. All Roman emperors inherited that name as a title, as did later the Russian czars and the German kaisers. Octavianus called himself simply "first citizen" (*princeps*) until the senate (in 27 B.C.E.) accorded him the title "Augustus" (consecrated, holy, majestic, divinized). Just before he died (in 14 C.E.) he recorded his great deeds, emphasizing how, after he had put down the civil wars, he received this title. "I transferred the republic from my own control to the will of the senate and the Roman people. For this service on my part I was given the title of Augustus by decree of the senate . . . in recognition of my valour, my clemency, my justice, and my piety. After that time I took precedence of all in rank, but of power I possessed no more than those who were my colleagues in any magistracy."[1]

In fact, those colleagues bowed to his will because he was the commander-in-chief of all the armies. They looked to him to exemplify the stability, the security, and the virtue that he labored to spread abroad in the world. On his own personal nobility (*aretē*) rested his imperium. To that personal and official genius and to Rome's spirit he required both citizens and subjects to bow in reverence, thus submerging local and provincial to central loyalties. In Octavianus Caesar Augustus for the first time was consecrated a single, Mediterranean-European imperium.

Octavianus at once restored and extended an older, less far-flung Pax Romana. To the military might of his predecessors, which ensured order, he joined respect for the privileges of Romans and Rome, which guarded his authority. Without compromising his own rule, he genuinely took counsel with the senatorial class. "On this condition Italy was prepared to accept and support a military ruler who was almost an autocrat," wrote Mikhail Rostovtsev, and "The provinces were ready to acknowledge any authority that secured them peace and order."[2]

The Romans built a grander world than Alexander's. Their rule, at least in theory, was subtler. For the oriental model of absolute, unquestioned, fully divine monarchy based on archaic, sacred kingship they substituted the model of a ruler whose own nobility would prompt him to serve the public good. Such a Caesar exercised maximum power with a check against arbitrary tyranny. Octavianus himself was able, in Charles Norris Cochrane's phrase, "to associate the notion of power with that of service and thus, at one and the same time, to justify the ascendancy of Rome in the Mediterranean and that of the Caesars in Rome."[3] Those interlocking ascendancies required that Rome be the empire's holy place and the Caesars its holy men. Perhaps to make Rome eternal within time and living Caesars divine overstated the necessary sanctity. Nevertheless, the ecumenic endeavor needed to accord to the bearer and the locus of imperium a supramundane sacrality because they embodied an essentially supernatural order.

The very act of Octavianus in handing to senate and people his unchecked powers and single military command demonstrated his worthiness to have those prerogatives returned to him as duties and responsibilities. The senate readily bestowed a title redolent of dignity and deity. Men and places that embody an order grounded in the gods naturally command regard as divine. The early Christians enjoyed Rome's order and security, claiming that these blessings sprang from a deity above and beyond the empire's gods. When the earlier empire demanded conformity to its symbols of divinity, the ideal Christian response was martyrdom; when the later empire adopted the Christians' symbols of divinity, their ideal response was monastic withdrawal. Each response adapted the figure of Christ to itself. Martyrs and monks and their Christs, responding to the cultural crises of the sacred Roman Empire, provided the story line of early Christianity in European history.

But the Romans' way of divinizing their rulers is not to be confused with the Christians' way of incarnating and humanizing their deity. If there is a touch of the sublime in deifying a noble ruler like Octavianus, there may be a mite of the ridiculous in having a remote Jew synthesize the divinity of the Israelites' Yahweh, Plato's Intelligence, Aristotle's First Mover, and the Rabbis' Abba (Father). The early Christians were at once followers of such a god-man and citizens and subjects under such a man-god.

Their favorite story about Jesus' birth has Joseph and Mary in Bethlehem because Octavianus ordered everybody to their native cities for an enrollment of the imperial population. Of such a census at this time (4 B.C.E.) there is no other evidence, and it is hard to imagine how such a registration could have been administered. In Luke's account it serves to juxtapose the majesty of Octavianus in issuing orders to the whole world against the lowliness of Jesus in being born in a manger. By Luke's day the two figures symbolized different citizenships. One centered in Rome and spread law and order through the provinces into all the world. "One of the chief tasks of the empire in its civilizing mission," according to Rostovtsev, "was to spread the urban method of life in places that knew nothing of it until they were conquered by Rome."[4] The places already civilized needed to be drawn into the Roman patterning of the world. The baby born in Bethlehem became to many the god-man who conferred on his followers a heavenly citizenship that assigned them tasks of loyalty and uprightness in this life and promised them eternal bliss. Thus Christians belonged at once to Caesar and to Christ.

To these two imperia Jesus later referred, in a phrase portending the tensions between Christians' double citizenship, tensions that shaped their religion down to the decay of the Roman hegemony. Asked whether it was lawful to pay tribute or taxes to Caesar, Jesus responded with an enigma that for centuries would hound his followers who at once welcomed and resisted both the Roman world and their heavenly allegiance: "Then render to Caesar the things that are Caesar's, and to God the things that are God's" (Luke 20:25). The coin under discussion bore Caesar's image. But precisely what loyalties belonged to the man-god who was the Christians' lawful Caesar and what allegiances should be saved for the god-man who was their savior? The perplexity led many early Christians to cherish martyrdom, if not for themselves then for others who kept clear the religion's priorities. Later (but still early) Christians found themselves driven by the Caesar-Christ predicament to lonely lives in desert places where they received adulation from fellow believers for setting things straight between their citizenships.

The first generation of Christians had no such problem because they belonged to the Roman world as Jews, enjoying exemptions from observing the state cult and from military service. At first, probably very few held legal Roman citizenship. The most famous of those who did was at once a Jew and a Roman and a Christian. Paul's encounter with the resurrected Christ came to define the religion universally, and his gentile mission began to spread Christianity through the whole empire. His three loyalties —to Torah, Caesar, and Christ—conflicted in ways foreshadowing both the Christians' rejection of Jewish ethnicity and their adoption of Roman ecumenicity. Thus the story (in Acts 24-28) of Paul's triple "identity crisis" typifies the new religion's encounter with its origin and its destiny.

Jewish leaders denounced Paul before the Roman governor, Felix, for agitating Jews everywhere, for being ringleader of the Nazarene sect, and for trying to profane the temple. Paul pleaded innocent. As a Jew, not twelve days since, he had made his pilgrimage to Jerusalem. As a Christian he clung to the law and the prophets while holding also to the resurrection of the dead. Felix indecisively detained him for two years, and Festus, the new governor, found him imprisoned in Caesarea. As a Roman citizen Paul repeated his innocence to Festus and appealed the case to Caesar himself. King Agrippa later interrogated Paul and told Festus, "This man could have been set free if he had not appealed to Caesar" (26:32). After a troubled voyage, Paul arrived in Rome, where he stayed two years under house arrest, "preaching the kingdom of God and teaching about the Lord Jesus Christ quite openly and unhindered" (28:30). There the story ends. Presumably, Paul died in Rome (about 67) when Nero executed some Christians accused of arson.

Such accusations by Jews, together with Paul's offering salvation in Christ to gentiles, prompted Christians to reject Jewish identity and with it the ethnic exemptions from Roman cultic observances. When the Palestinian Jews rebelled against Roman rule (in 66-69 and again in 132-35), Christians denied responsibility for the uprisings. Vespasian destroyed the Jews' temple (in 70) and Hadrian converted Jerusalem (in 135) into the pagan colony of Aelia Capitolina. The Christians were recognizable (by 100) as people with their own religious identity.

Increasingly, the Caesars made the privileged Romans into world citizens and the world's citizens into Romans. Distinctions between the citizens in Italy and the subjects in the provinces steadily eroded until Caracalla (in 212) extended official citizenship, with very few exceptions, to the entire population. The sense of being world citizens by virtue of belonging to the empire spread early and widely. Increasingly, everybody made obeisance to Caesars, who more and more admitted or proclaimed their own divinity. Citizenship in the ecumenic empire thrust upon the early Christians a system of civic duties. The only one they were loath to perform was worship of state gods, for citizenship conferred privileges, none of which they were loath to enjoy.

The martyrs who rendered their lives to God rather than render worshipful loyalty to Caesar were relatively few but very important. Their solution to the predicament set examples for their fellow believers (before 313), not in that all or even many yearned to share their death, but in that they drew the line of loyalties where all believed it belonged. When Constantine based his imperium on Christian as well as pagan deities and when Theodosius I (in 380) made Christianity the sole official religion, ecumenic (world-wide) and uranic (heavenly) citizenships merged into a single instrument. To preserve the distinction the early monks fled civic obligations and privileges to find austere lives, whether solitary or communal, in freedom from human passion and single-minded devotion to heaven.

This chapter, then, first surveys the cultural crises that brought the Roman world in turn to prosperity and trouble, to division and (in the west) to decay. Then it analyzes how the earlier crisis created tension between the Christians' twin loyalties. In some detail it describes the martyrs' way of life—some would say way of death—as the heroic affirmation of heavenly citizenship. The events that brought the religion to favor next call for brief attention. Then the chapter describes the pattern of life adopted by pre-Benedictine monks as surrogate martyrdom. In dealing with both martyrs and monks, and, indeed, with the Christians who raised them to the status of heroes, the chapter shows how the figure of Christ functioned in and for their exemplary responses.

TWIN CITIZENSHIP

Cultural crises are events by which historians organize the past. Typically, church histories narrate the period down to Constantine in terms of persecutions under emperors from Nero through Diocletian's immediate successors and describe the period after Constantine around definitions clarifying and elaborating the church's official, orthodox doctrine. Such a success story at best holds holy water. Only Diocletian, and he very briefly, tried to force all Christians to declare their loyalty to the holy empire and the sacred emperor. And Constantine quickly discovered the deep disunity that prevented Christianity from effectively serving as a new principle of social cohesion. After Theodosius a divided empire coexisted with a dividing church. The councils that emperors convoked to unite the Christians in fact publicized and deepened their rifts.

A brief summary of the imperial policies that tested loyalty to the empire and then a quick survey of the emperors' efforts to unite their realm around a unified church follow. The traditional interpretive keys of persecutions and creeds fail to account for the early Christians' responses to the cultural matrix of their religion. Records show that (by 100) the empire had "a tradition of suppressing various kinds of foreign religions," but they reveal no specifically anti-Christian policy.[5] Nero executed some persons accused of arson, among whom were Christians. Domitian purged his palace administration and killed some named persons whom Eusebius mistook for Christians. Trajan instructed a provincial governor to treat Christians like everybody else, applying the death penalty for refusal to certify loyalty, giving the accused every chance to conform, and not hunting out people to accuse.

This simple policy held for a century. Under Trajan a bishop of Antioch wrote fellow Christians asking them not to save him from the martyrdom he sought—hardly persecution! A bishop of Rome named Telesphorous died under Hadrian. The tolerant Antoninus Pius' underlings thought the Christians' superstition dangerous, and under him (in 156 or 157) the old bishop of Smyrna named Polycarp and eleven of his flock were executed. Under Marcus Aurelius Antoninus local officials executed the teacher Justin and a few of his pupils in Rome (between 162 and 168), as well as Bishop Carpus and his deacon Papylus and a woman named Agathonicē in Pergamum; Christians in Lyons (in 177) suffered awful tortures as scapegoats. Yet Marcus Aurelius held to Trajan's policy, and Christians loyally served in his twelfth legion in Cappadocia.

Commodus' officers seem to have actively looked for Christians in order to test their loyalty. So did those of Septimius Severus (early 200s), and after an interval the same happened under

Maximinus. When Decius briefly (in 249-51) required citizens to sacrifice to the gods, uncompromising Christians in many places died. Valerian had trouble enforcing Decius' policy. Then Gallienus gave Christians full freedom of religion (in 260), a policy lasting into the next century. Diocletian (in 303) sought systematically to force Christians everywhere to evidence their Roman loyalty, but he asked his officers to avoid bloodshed. After he declared victory for the restored empire and abdicated (in 305), his successors in the east sporadically renewed the program. Toleration under Constantine and his sons (begun in 313) was revoked briefly (in 361-63) by Julian, who tried to reinstate the pagan religions.

In a nutshell, such was the era of the Roman persecutions. Hardly had Constantine, out of complex motives, legalized Christianity than he summoned western church leaders to Arles (in 314), charging them to heal their schism and unify their religion. They failed. For Christianity had adapted itself to the diverse peoples, thought-forms, traditions, and religions of the empire's various regions. Church organization had become generally standardized (by 300), but emphases of belief and modes of worship differed, at some points rather sharply, from province to province. Constantine wanted the religion to help provide the common, unifying experience that his program of building social cohesion required. He assembled bishops and other dignitaries (in 325) from the entire empire at his own expense to settle on a single date for Easter and to compromise differences about the nature of the divinity that Christ bore. Nearly unanimous consensus at Nicaea only fueled further disagreements back home. When the rivals agreed to use the same words with different meanings as the only practical solution, new controversies arose about the godhead. Theodosius I, in outlawing all religion except trinitarian Christianity, urgently needed a definition of what was legal, but the bishops he summoned to Constantinople (in 381) adopted a creed that stirred up further dissension. The person of Christ came under debate. Two worldwide councils (in 431 and 451) failed to command church-wide consensus.

For social cohesion the emperors looked to a religion riddled with doctrinal confusion. Later tracings of a line of orthodox teaching through this maze of dispute cannot erase the record of contention and disunity.

The importance of martyrs and monks to the early Christians can hardly be debated, but their role must be kept in clear perspective. Far from being leaders and symbols of revolt against the empire, the martyrs attested the Christian commitment to earthly citizenship by specifying the point at which that allegiance began to clash with loyalty to Christ. The monks took over a parallel function when Christians themselves came close to identifying the cause of Caesar with the cause of Christ. Monks modeled their lives after martyrs by dying daily to worldly concerns such as food, shelter, sex, family, wealth, education, even organized religion, as a reminder that the privileged church still bore the marks of divine salvation and must make its worldly success serve that spiritual cause.

Many Christian writings before Constantine pleaded that emperors should value the support and prayers of their loyal Christian subjects, indeed, should promote this religion; almost none pits Christ against Caesar and church against state. When Constantine suddenly agreed with these pleas, the empire inevitably tamed the church that it favored. Then the monks arose to exemplify the church's calling to heavenly service. In a word, the Christians made martyrs and monks heroes in order to reassure themselves of their dual citizenship, not because emperors were trying to wipe out or subvert their religion. By definition, a hero can hardly be commonplace. Because of the Christians' consistent and profound endorsement of the established order they needed exemplars to draw lines at the ideal limits of that endorsement. With this context in mind it is instructive to review the cultural crises of the period.

Between Caesar Augustus and Romulus Augustulus (from 27 B.C.E. to 476 C.E.), the first and last rulers bearing the title Augustus, passed half a millennium. Put very simply, the main task from Augustus through Domitian (died in 96) was to consolidate the newly assembled world. From Nerva through Marcus Aurelius (died in 180) the effort was to unify Roman culture and civilization. Emperors from Commodus through Diocletian were trying to stave off catastrophes and to shore up frontier fortifications through despotic rule that shunted the imperium from the Capitol to the camp. Constantine and his successors through Theodosius I (died in 395) struggled to regenerate and reunite a fragile society around a new center at the eastern capital of Constantinople. From Arcadius to Zeno in the east the Greek empire was flourishing, while from Honorius to Romulus (from 395 to 476) in the west the Latin empire was decaying. The old united world was splitting into two new worlds.

The great hope and achievement of the Romans was to associate into one world the disparate cultures coexisting around the Mediterranean and in Europe west of the Rhine. Association necessitated their establishing some worldwide, common experience. The assimilating instrument became citizenship, increasingly the badge of association. The older Hellenistic cities preserved their character and traditions even while they were being Romanized. The new colonies and towns copied and spread Roman ways. Thus the ominous turn of events for the Augustan dream was less the dearth of good emperors after Marcus Aurelius than it was the uprisings on the northern and eastern fronts that forced him more and more into military activities and, both actually and symbolically, from palace to barracks. The trend continued under the military emperors (of the 200s), when the army made and broke rulers virtually at will. Septimius Severus advised his successor sons to pay the soldiers and stall everybody else. Those rulers wielded the coercive, military might lent them by the generals and the troops—a far cry from the earlier Caesars who, even if they were weak or mean men, had embodied and conveyed the grand authority infused in them by world sovereignty.

Diocletian, the last military dictator, energetically tried to renovate an empire too fragmented to order the world and too enervated to harvest its citizens' loyalty. He astutely made Nicomedia in the east his own capital. By installing his co-Augustus in Milan he sacrificed the sacral power of Rome to political and military practicalities. Constantine built New Rome on the site of old Byzantium and called upon all religions (especially Christianity) to suffuse both this Capitol and its emperor with divine authority. He and his sons united the world but they could not unify the church. After Julian briefly tried to reinstitute the old Roman religion, the two halves of the world were ruled separately. The Greek half culturally bloomed and the Latin half wilted before barbarians. Theodosius, who decreed that orthodox Christianity would be the only official faith of the realm, for a moment rejoined the two halves, but after his death the parts went opposite ways. Such were the main changes of fate for Augustus' vision of the ascendancy of the Caesars in Rome and the ascendancy of Rome over the world.

Human existence under the Roman Empire expressed itself dually. It was ecumenic, or worldwide. It was also urban and located, localized, locateable, locative. Human beings became both cosmopolitan and, to coin a word, politico-cosmic. Universal order mirrored itself in the places men and women lived, and they in turn took part in ordering the world. The city of Rome sanctified the world of space, simultaneously drawing to itself the allegiance of the tribes in the form of tribute and radiating back from itself to the regional cities the tribes' protection and security. In terms of spatial sacrality Rome became every city writ large while every city became Rome writ small. Such was the new, universal civilization of the Mediterranean basin and the European continent.

The early Christians endorsed this civilization because it articulated their form of humanity. At the same time, membership in their own congregations symbolized an otherworldly civilization that they also endorsed as a divine bestowal. In their worship they re-enacted their civic duties toward Christ and one another. "The 'sacrifice' of alms," wrote Peter Brown, "was quite as much part of the sacrificial offerings of the Christians as was the Eucharist. . . . Thus blessed, the wealth of the community returned to the members of the community alone, as part of the 'loving-kindness' of God to His special people."[6] In their public service, called liturgy (*leitourgia*), they paid taxes to and received services from Caesar. In their Christian worship, called by the same word, they paid oblation to and received benefits from Christ who accepted and blessed and returned their alms to relieve the believing community. Thus their special security in earthly citizenship and their confident hope in heavenly citizenship mirrored one another. Not only between the two citizenships but also within the boundaries of each lurked a tension between security and hope, between accomplishment and expectation.

This tension also stretched between their politico-cosmic, local, traditional embodiment and their cosmopolitan, ecumenic, proleptic fulfillment. Roman Christians no less than Roman pagans, Dodds showed, yearned for a cosmic ordering of their partly checked chaos and for an incorruptible eschaton that would purify the corruption of temporal existence. Both shared the form of human awareness epitomized by Voegelin: "In the Ecumenic Age, the process of reality is discovered as a spatially and temporally open field, with man's existence in eschatological tension as its center of consciousness."[7] What distinguished the Christians from most of their neighbors was their sensibility of living in the presence of a resurrected lord whose lowly career on earth and glorious career after death gave them a taste now, before the full repast, of the peace that would overcome this tension.

Their sacred thanksgiving meals eaten in Christ's memory proclaimed their sense of his being spiritually among them, and at the same time it declared their yearning for him to return into their experience. They prayed, "Come, Lord," to one who had already come to them and yet would come again. As one of them wrote, "But our commonwealth [*politeuma*] is in heaven, and from it we await a Savior . . . who will change our lowly body to be like his glorious body by the power which enables him even to subject all things to himself" (Philippians 3:20). He would return to their realm in order to transport them into his realm. For they were already members of his body, and they became his body by eating and drinking the symbols of it. Cleared of the mystical submetaphors with which piety has surrounded this figure of speech, their religion, like their earthly citizenship, corresponded to a common classical analogy between the physical body and the body politic.[8] They were members of the body that he headed. Nobody put the parallel tensions in this metaphor better than the unnamed author who wrote (in the 100s or 200s) to an unknown inquirer what is known as *The Epistle to Diognetus:* "For the distinction between Christians and other men, is neither in country nor language nor customs. For they do not dwell in cities in some place of their own" nor have their own language and way of life. They follow no human dogmas. "Yet while living in Greek and barbarian cities . . . and following the local customs, both in clothing and food and in the rest of life, they show forth the wonderful and confessedly strange character of the constitution of their own citizenship [*politeia*]." These Christians "dwell in their own fatherlands, but as if sojourners in them; they share all things as citizens, and suffer all things as strangers. Every foreign country is their fatherland, and every fatherland is a foreign country. . . . They pass their time upon the earth, but they have their citizenship in heaven." The world that cannot understand them cannot conquer them. "They love all men and are persecuted by all men. They obey the appointed laws, and they surpass the laws in their own lives. They are unknown and they are condemned. They are put to death and they gain life."[9]

This peculiar religion grew quietly while emperors from Claudius I through Domitian were consolidating the world. From Palestine to every provincial capital and to Rome it spread along the empire's roads and waterways. Like several rival religions it actively sought converts and tended to harmonize attractive foreign features with its central promises. For adherents it made sense of this life and turned death into another life. Its god-man, with his virgin mother and his resurrection, resembled certain other religions' saviors. It freely adopted the heaven and hell, the angels and demons, of other sects. Most insistently it laid claim to universality. All might enroll. All should enlist.

Paul's early, far-flung missionary endeavors concretely defined Christian apostleship. The descending spirit at Pentecost enabled the gathered apostles to speak all languages, according to a story that based its astrological geography on the zodiac.[10] Another account assigned the gentile territories to Barnabas and Paul, giving Peter authority over the mission to Jews conducted by John, James, and himself (Galatians 2:9). The teacher Origen of Alexandria (in the 200s), and the historian Eusebius of Caesarea (in the 300s), distributed the apostles ecumenically: James the son of Joseph to Jerusalem, Thaddeus to Edessa, Philip to Samaria and Ethiopia, Mark to Egypt, Paul to the whole world, Thomas to Parthia, Andrew to Scythia, John to Asia, and Peter to the dispersed Jews and others in many places including Rome.[11] These assignments helped to explain the varieties of Christianity current by Origen's time. More important, regardless of these accounts' traditional and legendary lore, they indicate how self-consciously Christian spokesmen espoused an ecumenic religion.

Under the unifiers of Roman culture from Trajan through Marcus Aurelius leading Christians published their commitment to the Roman world in letters to emperors pleading their religion's value to social order and world peace. The clear majority of early Christian spokesmen known to us professed deep but not total loyalty to the empire. Prominent spokesmen borrowed heavily from the regnant Graeco-Roman philosophical and historical sensibility to ask that emperors be tolerant; some pleaded on Christian grounds that they be converted. Only the followers of the Phrygian prophet named Montanus set Christianity against the dominant culture as alien. These radicals looked for heaven to come soon and wipe away earthly existence. The Christian Gnostics tended to separate spirit from matter and spirituality from everyday life. Both groups were quickly read out of church as heretics—although verbal condemnations did not end their attractiveness. Main-line Christians admired and honored orderly culture and noble emperors but could not bring themselves to hallow the culture or venerate the emperor until both were at least nominally Christian.

An influential teacher named Justin tested the leading pagan philosophies before settling in Rome (in about 150) to teach that Christianity captured the broadest possible synthesis of wisdom and goodness. To explain creation and the cosmos he harmonized the cosmology in Plato's *Timaeus* with the myths of Genesis. To link God with man he identified the Stoics' Reason (Logos) with Christ, who fulfilled Greek yearnings for wisdom and Jewish quests for morality. Because symbols on the Roman legions' banners seemed to resemble the cross, Justin asked that Antoninus Pius convert and ground social unity in Justin's religion. When required to sacrifice to the Roman gods Justin explained his religion and its value, but in the end he met a martyr's death. His commitment to the rational and beneficial culture in which he lived is entirely consistent with his willingness to die for the faith that he took to be best for that culture. Although other writers in the same vein, such as Aristides, Tatian, Athenagoras, Theophilus, Melito of Sardis, and Irenaeus, were not known to be martyrs, each or all might be called to second Justin's endorsement. A man named Apollonius was martyred under Commodus; he argued that the Christians' prayers for the emperor were assets not to be squandered. Tertullian appealed (about 197) to the triumphant Septimius Severus, echoing those approvals and conceding that the Christians could call the emperor "lord" if the title signified less than fully divine majesty.

Under the military rulers (of the 200s) came a revival of local traditions and loyalties, particularly in the older cities in the east. Rome's importance, both actual and symbolic, shrank even before Diocletian shifted the main seat of government to Nicomedia. Meanwhile, the western territories began to lose contact with Greek culture and language. While Christian writers in both tongues looked forward to the time when their religion would dominate, the influential Latin expressions of that hope differed remarkably from Greek statements. The mystical, spiritual, speculative, diverse religion of Clement and Origen in Alexandria caught the Greek imagination, while the penitential, moral, practical, precise religion of Tertullian and Cyprian in Carthage captivated the Latins. In both regions adherents were multiplying, especially in major cities. Western church leaders were attending regional meetings to deal with a variety of problems, and their eastern counterparts were refining their theologies to distinguish orthodoxy from heresy. The Latin catholic church was taking form, with the church in Rome holding primacy over congregations throughout Italy, Gaul, and North Africa. Parallel patterns of church administration developed in the east around the cultural center of Alexandria and later around the imperial capital of Constantinople.

MARTYRS

From Christianity's first encounter with the empire until its finding official favor under Constantine the martyrs grew in prominence and gained their fellow believers' reverence. The story of Stephen's being stoned to death by Jews for preaching about Christ stood near the beginning of the first history of Christianity. Early traditions had both Peter and Paul dying for the faith at Rome. Letters from Ignatius of Antioch to congregations in several cities of Asia Minor were cherished in part because of his eagerness to be martyred. The story of Polycarp's execution (in 156 or 157), widely copied and prized, became the prototype of many martyr-stories.

To be sure, all our accounts of martyrs belong to the genre of hagiography. Moderns by instinct are suspicious of stories about visions and miracles and similar wondrous doings.[12] One handles this problem not by literalizing the accounts but by realizing that they conveyed their own veracity to Christian readers over many centuries. The wonder-workings undeniably give evidence that the wonder-workers were being highly regarded by those to whom their wonders were quite real. The same supernatural marvels pervade the stories about the early monks. Miracles, whatever else they meant, signified that those to whom they happened knew how to keep the right proportion between their citizenship on earth and their citizenship in heaven. They accepted the benefits of Roman world-citizenship, often insisting that the power structure would benefit from their being Christian. This affirmation restrained Christians from actively seeking martyrdom at times when stubborn defiance would have brought sudden death. Instead, most of them awaited the accusations that they considered unjust in the hope that the state would come to its senses and tolerate their religion.

The question of seeking martyrdom raised subtle issues. Suicide was to be shunned. Nevertheless, old Ignatius begged not to be rescued. The story about Polycarp mentions a Phrygian named Quintus who turned himself in, but "when he saw the wild animals he turned cowardly" and was persuaded "to swear by the gods and offer sacrifice"; it went against Gospel teaching for Christians to "come forward of themselves" (5). The Christians who faced execution in Lyons rebuked friends who prematurely hailed them as martyrs (83). A woman named Agathonicē received divine orders to throw herself, unaccused, on the fire burning Carpus and Papylus in Pergamum (29). Two condemned Christians named Donatianus and Primolus at Carthage under Decius yearned to be martyrs but failed to achieve that status when they died (about 215) in prison. Yet from that time on there are indications that in some places persons imprisoned for being Christian gained regard as martyrs.

Origen exhorted two friends imprisoned under Maximin Daja (in the late 230s) to accept the fate of martyrdom. Cyprian wrote that "Among the confessors of Christ, martyrdoms deferred do not lessen the merit of confession, but show the greatness of the divine protection."[13] A senator's wife, according to Eusebius, fearing that Maxentius would rape her, drove a sword through her own breast, and at about that time other Christian women killed themselves for fear their captors would violate their chastity.[14] A merchant of Egypt felt so moved by the execution of the noble son of one of Diocletian's generals that he voluntarily professed his loyalty to Christianity.[15] Yet the bishop of Alexandria named Peter judged (in 306) in detail how Christians who had lapsed during the recent persecution might recover full membership in the churches, laying down the law that "voluntary martyrs were not true martyrs at all."[16]

The martyrs' loyalty to Rome in fact impressed their fellow Christians, who believed that they should not be punished under the Caesars' own standards of justice. Their transcendent loyalty to Christ immunized them to human tribunals. They did not renounce one citizenship for another. They kept the two in a relation that Christians in general deemed proper and that magistrates in particular found unacceptable.

The vast majority of Christians throughout the period never faced the test of martyrdom, but rather enjoyed their double citizenship even when rigorist Caesars demanded fealty to their own genius. Decius first required loyalty oaths of everybody; except for his untimely death, he might have brought the church to heel. Letters and tracts about how the church should deal with Christians who had compromised attest to widespread lapses. Some took the oaths with mental reservations, others paid to have certificates of having sworn oaths forged, and still others bribed officials to misrepresent their loyalty. The honorable compromise of flight commended itself to Bishop Cyprian of Carthage. Even more honored were the confessors who went to prison but escaped execution. Yet the shining examples of rectitude in dealing with the double citizenship were the martyrs who in dying were born into heaven.

They received rich rewards. Christ became their companion and steadied them in their sufferings by reliving his own death in theirs. Their souls sped directly to heaven while other modes of dying put souls into a half-sleep to await the general resurrection. At their tombs their Christian survivors celebrated the anniversaries of their deaths—rather, their heavenly birthdays. Their names identified the congregations to which they had belonged. Written exhortations encouraging them to hold fast to the faith depicted the patriarchs and the prophets, the apostles and the angels, even Christ and the rest of the trinitarian deity preparing festivities to welcome their arrival in paradise. By their victories they won special privileges to dispense favors to the faithful. On a comparative scale of divinization, to put it bluntly, the best of the martyrs outranked the godliest of the Caesars.

Polycarp, hero of the earliest, authentic, extant account of a Christian martyred for refusing ultimate allegiance to Rome, won just these rewards. "The church of God dwelling in Smyrna" recorded his story for "all the communities of the holy Catholic Church everywhere" (3). During a time of loyalty tests, their bishop fled for safety. He had a vision of being burnt alive. Then began a series of coincidences. One Friday evening in an upper room Polycarp was betrayed to a police captain named Herod. After praying for two hours, he rode a donkey into the city and was commanded to sacrifice to Caesar. When he refused to do so, even under threat of being thrown to wild animals, the authorities decided to burn him. They bound him to the pyre like a sacrificial ram. Facing cruel death, he calmly prayed. The flames did not hurt him. When he was stabbed to death, his gushing blood extinguished the flames. Christ, whose dying he imitated, was seen to be present conversing with him and his fellow martyrs (3).

Then Jews petitioned the governor not to surrender the body to Christians lest they worship the dead bishop as though risen. The Smyrnan church's report emphasized that they reverenced Christ alone as son of God and savior, "whereas we love the martyrs as the disciples and imitators of the Lord." They buried the bishop's precious ashes at a spot where they could gather "to celebrate the anniversary day of his martyrdom, both as a memorial for those who have already fought the contest and for the training and preparation of those who will do so one day." They were sure this "conspicuous martyr" had won immortality and lived in heaven with the apostles and the deity (17).

Polycarp died on a sabbath afternoon while "Philip of Tralles was high priest and Statius Quadratus was governor—while

Jesus Christ was reigning eternally" (19). The extant texts of this bishop's story tell that his disciple Irenaeus preserved the narrative. Copyists who transmitted the story are named. Authenticated in such painstaking detail, the story gained an importance that can hardly be exaggerated. When others who knew it faced martyrdom they expected similar things to happen to them. In turn their stories came to resemble his, although narrative conventions rarely erased the particularities of each martyrdom. Thus Polycarp's story tells us what actually happened, if not to him then to those who believed the story, including later martyrs who re-enacted it. It combines the usual ingredients of early Christian martyr-stories: preternatural courage under trial and torment, visions foretelling the manner of death, hints of identity with Christ and of his dying in and with them, direct flight of the soul to heaven, and burial with veneration by fellows in the faith.

Those ingredients make up the unique story of Perpetua and her companions, which is striking for the fact that it includes more autobiography than third-person narrative. Perpetua and her friend Saturus told in their own words about their imprisonment and about their visions. The editor, possibly Tertullian, introduced the accounts by pleading that these recent and extraordinary records of the faithful deserved more consideration than classic ones. Then came the two martyrs' visions, predicting details of their death and of their entry into paradise. The editor recorded the deaths as fulfilling these visions, implying that the souls went heavenward as prophesied. Perpetua carefully identified the governor and the adjutant in charge of the jail, so that the episode can be fairly reliably dated (in 202 or 203) and placed in or near Carthage.

Vibia Perpetua, twenty-two-year-old mother of a suckling baby boy, belonged to a good pagan family from a town near Carthage. Five catechumens being trained for baptism, including Perpetua and her personal slave, Felicity, were arrested. Perpetua's father urged her to renounce her religion. She preferred to suffer. She gave her baby to her mother, then got permission to nurse him in prison. Her brother, also a catechumen, advised her to seek a vision. She received four. In the first she climbed a very high, narrow, bronze ladder, edged with knives and spikes and hooks, mounting it by stepping on the head of a fierce dragon. Saturus preceded and encouraged her. At the top she entered a large garden, kept by a gray-haired shepherd who was surrounded by people in white clothes. The shepherd welcomed her and fed her milk.

Afterward her father renewed his pleas that she recant for her son's sake, but she stood firm during the hearing and sentencing. Then her angry, distraught father refused to hand over the child, who thereupon was miraculously weaned. Perpetua miraculously stopped lactating. In the second vision she saw another brother, Dinocrates, who had died with cancer of the face at age seven. He was suffering in a hot, dry place and could not reach the high rim of a pool of water. She awakened and prayed for him. In another vision he reappeared, healed of the cancer and refreshed by water from the pool, whose rim had been lowered. The prison's adjutant recognized the spiritual power of the catechumens. Perpetua's father came a last time, tearing his hair and cursing her because she refused to recant.

In the last vision a deacon named Pomponius led Perpetua from prison to the amphitheatre to be killed. Instead of wild beasts, the devil in the form of a vicious Egyptian came to fight her. She miraculously changed into a man for the fray and vanquished the enemy. As she "began to walk in triumph towards the Gate of Life" she awakened. "I realized that it was not with wild animals that I would fight but with the Devil, but I knew that I would win the victory. So much for what I did up until the eve of the contest. About what happened at the contest itself, let him write of it who will" (119).

Saturus then beheld Perpetua and himself being borne by four angels to a beautiful garden where their martyred friends and more angels greeted them. As they talked with these fellow martyrs, the angels advised them, "First come and enter and greet the Lord" (121). An enthroned, aged man with white hair and a youthful countenance kissed and touched them. Outside the gates Perpetua met their bishop and their teacher and helped them enter.

The narrative concludes in the third person by relating the premature birth in prison of Felicity's daughter and the trials, last meal, and death of the condemned Christians. Perpetua went to her punishment cheerfully, and Felicity was "ready to wash after childbirth in a second baptism"; indeed, "they rejoiced at this that they had obtained a share in the Lord's sufferings" (127). Christian prisoners named Saturus and Revocatus (a slave) fought wild beasts, while for the women the devil chose the form of a mad heifer to match their sex. Perpetua encouraged the other trainees to remain faithful and unafraid. Saturus climbed the scaffold and "took the sword in silence" to receive his second baptism. Perpetua followed him, but the executioner's sword struck her bone. The young matron "took the trembling hand of the young gladiator and guided" his sword "to her throat. It was as though so great a woman, feared as she was by the unclean spirit, could not be dispatched unless she herself were willing." The story ends as it begins, with the editor's advice that "for the consolation of the Church these new deeds of heroism . . . are no less significant than the tales of old" (131).

Perpetua was indeed a model martyr. Though Saturus encouraged her by his precedent, she relied on no mediating persons or sacraments. On her own worth she asked for visions, healed her pagan brother's suffering soul, reconciled a bishop with his priest, wrestled directly and personally with the devil, and shared Christ's suffering.[17] Christ did all these things in and with and through her, yet he did them directly, immediately. He promised in her visions to welcome her into paradise with his own touch and kiss. Her slave-girl spoke for both of them when a prison guard asked how she, who was suffering greatly in childbirth, could endure the more awful tortures of the wild beasts. Answered Felicity, "What I am suffering now . . . I suffer by myself. But then another will be inside me who will suffer for me, just as I

shall be suffering for him" (123-25). The example of Perpetua's courage converted the adjutant of the prison and many
others. She and her friends "marched from the prison to the amphitheatre joyfully as though they were going to heaven, with
calm faces, trembling, if at all, with joy rather than fear. Perpetua went along with shining countenance and calm step, as the
beloved of God, as a wife of Christ." They turned the birthday
of Caesar, Geta, brother of Caracalla, into "The day of their victory" (125-27).

Christians in Lyons apparently were living quietly when, for
unknown reasons, perhaps some calamity, the populace suddenly
(in 177) turned the officials against them. Ten recanted. Nine
were named who suffered brutal atrocities and died faithfully.
One was a slave-girl, Blandina, whose mistress also became a
martyr. Blandina's stamina fatigued the men who, working in
shifts from dawn to dusk, tortured her. When she confessed to
being a Christian, at once her body was anaesthetized and her
spirits were reinvigorated. Hanging on a post as bait to wild animals, her body formed a cross and inspired her friends who saw
in her person "him who was crucified for them" (75). Still she
or Christ's spirit in her survived. She was brought to watch others suffer, but their pains no more than her own could shake her
faith. After all others were dispatched, "like a noble mother encouraging her children, . . . duplicating in her own body all
her children's sufferings, she hastened to rejoin them"; scourged,
attacked by animals, roasted on a hot griddle, "she was at last
tossed into a net and exposed to a bull" (79). But she rose above
all this suffering and even above dying "because of her intimacy
with Christ" (81). To prevent Christian burial the populace reduced to ashes the torn, broken, charred, bloody remains of all
these martyrs and threw them into the river. In this way they received the common burial for which Christian martyrs usually
yearned. These gory details emphasized the conviction that prejudiced people and crafty governors were unjustly, indeed without
reason and at the devil's promptings, attacking the body of
Christ and heaping sufferings upon good fellow citizens. Their

memory lived on. Their entry into bliss stirred survivors to emulate and celebrate them.

Nobody declared Christian loyalties to the empire more clearly than one Speratus, spokesman for twelve martyrs who were tried (in July 180) at Carthage. The proconsul Saturninus offered them "the pardon of our lord the emperor" if they would return to their senses. Speratus protested, "We have never done wrong; we have never lent ourselves to wickedness. Never have we uttered a curse; but when abused, we have given thanks, for we hold our own emperor in honour." (Had he read or might he have written *The Epistle to Diognetus,* cited above?) Saturninus insisted that they swear by the genius of the lord-emperor. "Speratus said: 'I do not recognize the empire of this world. Rather, I serve that God whom no man has seen, nor can see, with these eyes. I have not stolen; and on any purchase I pay the tax, for I acknowledge my lord who is emperor of kings and of all nations' " (87). The twelve were beheaded. Their account, wrote Musurillo, along with the portion on court proceedings in the account of Cyprian, "is the closest of all our extant Acts to the primitive court records" (xxii).

Cyprian's martyrdom (in 258) is told in a straightforward story of his examination and exile, arrest and trial, execution and burial. Much is known from his letters about this prominent Roman and influential Christian. Decius' edicts drove him into hiding because he thought it more important to superintend the Christian congregations around the thriving city of Carthage than to become a martyr. On returning, he asserted his episcopal authority and set the conditions under which lapsed Christians could regain full membership. When Valerian's edict (in August 257) forbade Christian assemblies, the proconsul exiled Cyprian, who cleverly avoided incriminating his priests by citing Roman laws against informing. The next year Valerian decreed punishment for all Christian ministers. The prefect recalled and arraigned Cyprian, who professed his religion and refused to perform the state rites. Sentenced to die, he thanked God, and "the crowd of his fellow Christians said, 'Let us also be beheaded

with him!' " (173). Carefully he knelt on his cloak to give his
tunic to his deacons. He asked his friends to give some money to
the executioner who cut off his head. That night the faithful carried his body in a candlelight parade to a certain cemetery and
buried it.

Here are no visions, no torments, no miracles (except that the
ailing proconsul died a few days later), no higher praise than
that of calling Cyprian "blessed" and a "holy martyr chosen by
God" (170). By then, however, this bare-boned story belonged
to an established genre. Cyprian's confidence in his heavenly destiny and the fortitude he drew from Christ's presence are all the
clearer for remaining implicit, "and the courage of his last moments was to be an inspiration for a long time to come" (xxxi).

Stories about later martyrs (after 250) commonly presupposed
rather than declaimed the heroes' loyal citizenship and underscored the presupposition by calling the magistrates at best misguided for trying and sentencing Christians. The "wicked prefect" who watched Conon die marveled at the martyr and dashed
off to other business (193). The mad, blind, bloodthirsty, wild,
and vicious prefect who condemned the men Marian and James
(in 259) wrought his frenzy on "those who were living freely
for God" and also on "those who, though earlier driven out into
exile, had become martyrs in spirit though not yet in blood"
(197). A Christian "named Aemilian, who enjoyed equestrian
rank among the pagans," faced his death sentence joyfully
(205). At Caesarea in Palestine lived a Christian "named Marinus, who had been honoured with many posts in the army and
was known for his wealth and his good family" (241). When
accused of disloyalty by a fellow soldier, jealous for the post to
which Marinus was being promoted, he "showed even greater
loyalty to the faith" and was beheaded (243). Nothing in these
records hints that Christians took themselves for dissidents or
for persons of anything less than true allegiance to the established order. They worshipped their deity who had become man
and they refused to denounce him or to worship other deities.

To be sure, the accounts of martyrs like Marinus introduced

the new phenomenon of soldier-martyrs. In Numidia (in 295) one Maximilian refused enlistment because he was a Christian. His father, who collected taxes to outfit soldiers, rejoiced "that he had sent ahead such a gift to the Lord, since he himself was soon to follow" (249). One Marcellus, a centurion first class, threw to the ground the symbols of his military oath because, in his words, "it is not fitting that a Christian, who fights for Christ the Lord, should fight for the armies of this world" (253). These military martyrs, even the veteran soldier named Julius, were refusing to serve in an army whose duties by then included trying and in many cases executing fellow Christians! A soldier named Dasius lost his head for refusing to take his turn officiating in ritual sacrifices to Saturn. But under Diocletian, it must be noted, Christian martyrs' willingness to suffer and die for their faith was converting many pagans. In another new phenomenon of those days, as noted above, Christian women suffered and even sought death to protect their chastity; their virtue also drew converts.

Even though these stories belong to hagiography, they subtly reveal the experiences and attitudes of their heroes. Furthermore, they clearly indicate the exemplary role that martyrs played in forming the ideal response of the early Christians to the tension of dual citizenship. Far from being models of dissidence or subversion, the martyrs drew a clear and simple line beyond which the faithful should not carry their allegiance to the pagan Pax Romana and its pagan emperors. Thereby they endorsed loyalty to the empire up to that boundary. They renounced neither of their citizenships, but they kept their priorities straight. Their dying when authorities misguidedly demanded the worship of deified emperors stamped approval on their fellows' living in cooperation with authorities who more reasonably represented the sacred imperium.

The martyrs' extraordinary devotion to Christ improved ordinary devotion. Their virtual re-enactments of his death certified their own salvation and vividly aroused their friends' hope of salvation. Fructuosus, the bishop of Tarragona, and two of his deacons were burnt alive (in 259), and in their simple story not only Christ but "the divine Trinity was visible also in them. For to each at his post in the flames the Father was present, the Son gave his aid, and the Holy Spirit walked in the midst of the fire" (181). The earliest reliable story of a martyr had Polycarp and his companions conversing with Christ, who was present with them in the flames burning them, "in one hour buying themselves an exemption from the eternal fire" (5). This venerable martyr gained immediate immortality in heaven and veneration on earth. So did his successors. One moment Christ accompanied them in their sufferings, the next they went with him to his glory where they could plead cases for the living. When Roman officers arrested Fructuosus, he asked permission to put on his sandals, and as he prayed "there were Christians with him, comforting him and begging him to remember them" (177). When at the amphitheatre he removed the shoes, a Christian named Felix "grasped his right hand and begged him to remember him. The holy bishop Fructuosus answered him in a loud voice so that all could hear: 'I must bear in mind the entire Catholic Church spread abroad in the world from East to West' " (181).

After terrifying tortures, a lector named Marian in Numidia (in 259) had a vision of a heavenly court at which "sat a judge of very handsome countenance"; as Marian climbed the towering scaffold who should appear but Cyprian to invite Marian to sit beside him and observe the proceedings, after which the two accompanied the judge to his palace (203). A Roman plaque (of the 300s) depicts Christ sitting on his judge's throne, surrounded by the apostles pleading the cases of their clients, who in a typical Roman tribunal scene stand behind a railing awaiting judgment.[18] Marian and Cyprian foreshadowed such a scene when martyrs became latter-day apostles who in heaven sought favors for faithful friends on earth. As Christ's dying won their salvation, their dying won them places in heaven as agents of Christ dispensing salvation to those who sought heaven after the last judgment. Meanwhile, believers on earth were celebrating the martyrs' blessedness on their heavenly birthdays and were being healed at their shrines.

This close association of the martyrs' deaths with Christ's self-offering lent emphasis to sacrifice as a motif of Christian religion. In this context the standard rite of offering bread and wine, prayer and alms, in thanksgiving or eucharist came to represent Christ's self-sacrifice. Thus the eucharist at once re-enacted the crucifixion and by association celebrated the sacrificial victory of martyrdom. Early Christians had commemorated Christ's resurrection on Sundays; now their weekly rituals rehearsed the crucifixion too. Gradually, annual festivals gained prominence. Easter became popular (after 100), although the proper date for the feast has always caused controversy. The birthdate of Jesus was long debated until, in Constantine's time, it was linked to the pagan rites rejoicing in the rebirth of the sun in late December. Long before that, annual festivals celebrated the birthdays into heaven, indeed the "crucifixions" and "resurrections" of the martyrs at their burial places. Martyr-masses, first local but soon widespread, almost certainly antedated the Christ-mass and were surely freer from pagan influences.

Yet Christians had no corner on martyrdom in ancient times. Doubtless Plato's fine account of the principled, ironic death of Socrates marked upon the classical imagination the ideal of dying for the sake of conscience. At the time of Alexander the Great there appeared collections of stories about philosophers and heroes who died for high ideals. During the Maccabean revolt (about 176-63 B.C.E.), a nameless Jewish mother and her unnamed seven sons underwent cruel tortures under King Antiochus IV Epiphanes rather than eat swine's flesh against the divine laws. Several Christian martyr-stories allude to this mother. After Domitian, the "good" emperors allowed eulogies of political figures who had been put to death by earlier despots.[19] Tertullian held up these pagans, who were killed for conscience, as examples to encourage Christian martyrs. So did Clement of Alexandria, who alone among early Christian writers warned against the cult of the martyrs. But the teacher Justin Martyr and later the preacher John Chrysostom derided the pagan martyrs, and their view prevailed among Christians until Dante reintroduced Socrates and Seneca, Zeno and Vergil, to Christians as heroes worth emulating.

Distinguishing the Christians was of course their imitation of Jesus in suffering cruel deaths unjustly for the sake of deity and the redeemed. They shared his rewards in heaven, received veneration on earth, and dispensed divine favors. In all of this Christ was a present companion who suffered with them and in effect won their rewards for them. This pattern appeared in the earliest stories and remained basic even when hagiography carried the accounts to extremes. Since martyrs after Polycarp faced their deaths well aware of this pattern, it is apparent that their experience or at least their consciousness of the experience unfolded according to the pattern.

Exaggerated hagiography kept the structure of this experience even when the conventions of religious romance added incredible repetitions and supernatural interventions. One example, perhaps the most extreme, suffices. According to a Coptic codex (assigned to the 800s), one Paēse refuses under Diocletian to sacrifice to the gods when examined by the duke of Alexandria. His naked body is scraped to the bone, but the archangel Raphael (whose Hebrew name means "God heals") heals him. Over and over again the duke devises more and more horrible ways to mutilate and incinerate Paēse. Over and over again Raphael heals him and turns hot flames into cool breezes. The saint asks to see his widowed sister, Thecla, who lives with her son in a distant city. To save time, Raphael sends an angel to summon her. To buy time for her travel he puts the hex of illness on the duke. When on docking in Alexandria the sister learns that her boat was sailed by archangels and her traveling companions were the Virgin Mary and the mother of John the Baptist, Thecla faints dead away. The Virgin revives her. Meanwhile, the duchess has been converted to Christianity and sends for Paēse to cure her husband with the sign of the cross. Being healed leaves the duke ungrateful. Now Paēse and Thecla undergo tortures so ingenious that it takes Raphael and his angelic companion Gabriel and even the Virgin Mary to assist and heal them. With each successive miracle a multitude praises Christ, further frustrating the duke. Dozens profess belief, and the duke has them beheaded. An angel gives Paēse a preview tour of heaven, where he marvels at the splendors earned by a bit of suffering on earth. More tortures bring more rescues and more conversions. At midnight who should come but Christ himself to praise the holy brother and sister; he promises to protect them and to have erected in their honor a shrine whose devotees he will reward. Driven to his wits' end, the duke persuades a ruler in southern Egypt to take Paēse and Thecla away. En route they are beheaded and their souls fly heavenward.[20]

Even this most stylized account leaves intact the standard ingredients and pattern. Martyrs were more than Christ-figures, for they re-enacted his passion and ascension. Christ did in and with them what he had once done for them. Like him, they were good citizens unfairly accused and tried, unjustly sentenced and executed. Like his body, theirs suffered torments. Like his spirit, theirs soared in confidence of victory. Like his death, theirs became the beginning of new and glorified life. Like him, they achieved another "immortality" in the memories of the faithful on earth to the end of time. As his agents, they dispensed healings and favors and encouragements and benefits. Like the places of his suffering and death, the places of theirs became holy. As his death modeled theirs, their deaths would model those of some of their fellows. And wherever death entered the pattern it signified entry into life.

A bishop of Alexandria (from 247 to 264) named Dionysius conferred Christlike status on persons who suffered for their faith short of death. After imprisonment or torture they exercised power in the church by forgiving and readmitting lapsed Christians, arguing that Christ wanted the repentance and not the death of sinners. Dionysius wrote, "Thus even the divine martyrs among us, who now sit by Christ's side as partners in

His kingdom, opened their arms to their fallen brethren who faced the charge of sacrificing."[21] The text is ambiguous enough to support the interpretation that the persons who made these decisions were later killed and became full martyrs. In any case, being a martyr established a peculiar identity with Christ. The martyrs became his special agents. Much like the officials of an imperial court, they dispensed his justice and mercy. In that sense, they gained the status of christs.

The martyrs, replaying Christ's passion and ascension, harbored no death wish; rather they rejoiced in an eternal-life wish. That wish included a desire for the empire to recognize the greater benefits available through their prayers than through supplicating the pagan gods. They rendered to Caesar everything Caesar justly claimed, but they died rather than unjustly worship (to them) false deities in the place of honor deserved by Christ alone.

MONKS

Constantine dreamed (in 312) that if he painted Christ's monogram on the soldiers' shields and banners he would conquer Rome and reign as Caesar. Suddenly the Christians' tension between earthly and heavenly citizenships, stretched to the tautest by Diocletian and his fellow rulers, went slack—then taut again in the other direction! For generations the Christians had begged for religious toleration. Suddenly, they got more than they asked for: toleration plus privilege; eventually, the favoritism of official intolerance toward other religions. Diocletian demanded that they denounce their deity to prove allegiance to the empire. Constantine enlisted their deity in support of the empire and began to make loyalty to Christ the test of loyalty to Caesar. He and his successors (except for Julian) undertook nothing less than the infusion of the Mediterranean-European world with the sacral power of Christianity, embodied in a new capital at Constantinople and in emperors who were no less absolute and no less sacred for being Christian. The effort achieved grand success in the east until the coming of the Muslims. The program took a very different course in the west, and there were in effect (by 364) a Greek-Christian empire of Constantinople and a Latin-Christian empire of Rome. The two grew more and more distinct except for their shared feature of resting social cohesion on conformity to the Christian religion in its Greek or Latin form. The monks responded with a religiousness designed to set limits on this new merging of the earthly and heavenly citizenships. A brief survey of the period (from 312 to 476) will set the stage on which monks played their roles as successors to the martyrs.

When military skill and the magic monogram enthroned Constantine in Rome, he lost no time invoking upon his authority the blessings of "whatsoever divine and heavenly powers exist" to serve the public advantage.[22] All should worship according to their tastes, so long as their deities promoted these ends. While playing the field of an open pantheon, Constantine placed heavy bets on Christ and his followers. His inseparable religious and political policies melded Christian monotheism with Constantinian monarchy into a double instrument of social renovation. At first he tolerated all religions and unofficially fostered Christianity, while consolidating his rule in the west. Then he organized the main-line church into a force for uniting the world, while conquering the other prefectures into which Diocletian had divided the empire and becoming (in 324) sole emperor. At the last he suppressed and despoiled the old religions and made himself the bishop-at-large of the new one, while reorganizing the world under his new capital city and under himself as its eponym.

Over the centuries the eastern Christian empire centered on Contantinople. Its founder knew that great cities symbolized order for the provinces and regions of the world. He soon sensed that pagan Rome stood for an old order whose vigor was waning. His renovated, Christian world needed a capital of its own, which he situated at a virtually impregnable port where his two continents met. It reflected the glories of Rome, but it refracted the new monotheistic monarchy. On seven hills sat the imperial palace, the senate house, the Hippodrome, even the marker from which distances on imperial roads were measured. Here he built great basilicas where Christian rituals were used to dedicate the city.

He changed the succession. His dying father, junior member of Diocletian's tetrarchy, had appointed him Caesar for Britain and Gaul.[23] His biographer added that Constantine became a prince and sovereign solely by God's appointment so he would be "the only one to whose elevation no mortal may boast of having contributed" (1:24). At roughly ten-year intervals God's appointee named his three sons Caesars, generating what Eusebius called a trinity of imperial persons bearing a single sovereign nature (4:40).

When fatally ill, Constantine finally submitted to baptism in the church he had long used to unify his realm but had been unable to unite. The army promoted each son to the rank of Augustus, indicating for each "the highest supremacy of imperial power" (4:68). The world mourned while Constantine's remains were buried, according to his directions, in the Church of the Apostles with its thirteen monuments reading, left to right, six apostles, Constantine, six apostles. On coins he was shown "sitting as a charioteer, drawn by four horses, with a hand stretched downward from above to receive him up to heaven" (4:73). In the Christian imagination represented by Eusebius this emperor, who ceased dispatching martyrs to heaven and began patronizing the Christians, thereby earned his own apotheosis by that religion and his soul's ascension into the martyrs' paradise.

The new religion required some new subtleties in order to divinize emperors, but it scarcely reduced their sacrality. Robert Markus described how the blend appeared in art: "One of the most continuous threads in fourth-century art is the interchangeability of Christ and emperor in the iconographic repertoire. . . . Christ becomes the heavenly emperor, his throne the replica of the emperor's; the nimbus around the emperor's head is appropriated for Christ and his saints; the emperor's arrival at a city and his reception provide the prototype for Christ's entry into Jerusalem"; indeed, "generally the superhuman figure of the emperor emerges enhanced through the blessing of the God of the Christians. . . . Christians felt no great need to modify the current image of the emperor."[24]

Hereditary succession was maintained until the reign of Constantine's nephew, Julian, who tried to displace Christianity with the old cults. Then the line was broken by successive generals, while separate emperors ruled east and west. Theodosius I, who restricted citizenship to orthodox Christians, briefly (in 394-95) brought the areas together. Then the split became permanent. The blending of monotheism and monarchy into caesaro-papism, in which the ruler headed the religion, eventually captured the day and made Constantinople the empowering symbol of the east; by then, the declining west was reclaiming Rome for its "eternal" city.

But the barbarians interrupted Rome's successions and shortened its eternity. Eastern economic recovery never spilled into the west. Greek Christianity generated bitter doctrinal controversies within an officially single religion that exiled stubborn heretics. Latin religion bore the brunt of several schisms. Taxation ate away old fortunes, and inflation prevented the amassing of new ones. Locally self-sufficient agriculture and manufacture in the west produced low quality and little variety and stilled a once vigorous commerce. Provincial government and public construction atrophied. An enervated civilization still glittered in Germanic eyes as barbarians crossed old frontiers and invaded cities. Rome itself was sacked repeatedly by Visigoths, then by Vandals, and then brutally if briefly by Huns under Attila (from 410 to 456); Gaul fell (after 406) to Franks and Burgundians.

Then came the ironic debacle. Last in a rapid succession of ineffectual Roman emperors came the boy named for Rome's founder and nicknamed "little divine ruler"—Romulus Augustulus. Far away in Noricum a crude barbarian clad in goatskin was being advised by a Christian monk-missionary named Severinus to go to Rome and become a king. That barbarian was Odoacer. He received an army command under the eastern emperor and proceeded to Rome. He "held an emperor to be superfluous for the diminished West," deposed Romulus (in 476), sent the imperial insignia back to Constantinople, and "himself ruled Italy in an undefined lieutenancy for the sole Emperor in New Rome."[25] But the emperors of new Rome could no longer maintain order in the nearly chaotic western provinces.

The world of late antiquity in its Latin and its Greek versions based cohesion on widespread if nominal conformity to the favored religion. Privileges of earthly citizenship were gained and tested by professions of heavenly citizenship. This blending of the two no less than their previous polarization created tensions. How far were they merged? What was the distinction (if any) between religion and politics in a Christian empire (if there could be such)? Did easy baptism convey salvation or only begin a hard trail to redemption? The exemplars who reminded their fellow Christians throughout the world that the heavenly loyalty came first were the monks. To do so they fled from cities to rural and desert places. They adopted abnormal and even grotesque styles of living. They set the highest spiritual goals for themselves and pursued them fanatically. They became, in a word, martyrs without bloodshed through living by dying daily to worldly passions and rising daily to spiritual purity.

They combined seven elements into this style of life. Abstaining from sex, denying bodily desires, eating and drinking frugally, and forfeiting property were their ways of affirming the spirit's supremacy over the appetites; worshipping frequently according to their own rites, battling inward and outward temptations with weapons supplied by Christ, and exercising the soul toward higher and higher holiness were their means of gaining spiritual fulfillment in this life. They innovated not so much by following these individual practices as by combining them into a popular program that defined the highest Christian religiousness. Evidences of the particular practices by Christians go back a century or more before a monastic movement itself began. When a significant portion of the populace adopted the new religion (about 200), it was willingness to die for the faith that made heroes. At that time rigorists began to test genuine discipleship also by how much ordinary living one gave up and how much extraordinary discipline one took on for Christ's sake. When the religion adjusted to the prevailing culture under the long toleration (from 260 to 300), the ideal of extra discipline led a few persons to withdraw from the cities and from their churches in favor of solitariness. When toleration reduced the opportunities for martyrdom to nearly nothing and fused earthly or ecumenic and heavenly or uranic citizenships, the monastic movement filled the vacuum and redrew the distinction. It did the first by providing ways to die daily in "white" martyrdom without the stain of blood and the second by withdrawing from the common life to practice heavenly duties. Men and women could gain spiritual perfection and the promise of heaven by using their earthly lives to conquer the vices and to cultivate the virtues.

The monks' program and goal involved them in profound contradictions. Their acts of self-effacement commanded others' admiration. Their self-abasement earned their exaltation. Successful humility engendered pride. Those who mastered the solitary life attracted students eager to learn the art. Hermits clustered in neighboring cells around teachers and formed hermitages that developed into communes. Those communes, renouncing riches for mere subsistence, gained wealth through efficient labor and spare consumption. Isolation from ordinary Christians drew men and women to the essentials of piety and morals, of creed and cult, and the essentials thus emphasized became normative ideals for run-of-the-mill Christians. The monks who identified and analyzed the cardinal human weaknesses at the same time devised exercises that strengthened the spirit to overcome those faults. Sensitivity to temptations developed the power to resist them. Paradoxes abounded in a movement dedicated to maintaining appropriate tension between loyalty to Caesar and allegiance to Christ, between this life and the life hereafter, between body and spirit—matters that were at once contrary and interdependent.

The remainder of this chapter deals with the monks in the period when their movement remained generative and varied, before it turned conservative and standardized, before it developed complex, interlocking institutions. That institutionalization came to the west when Benedict of Nursia (in the early 500s) devised his famous and soon normative rule. To the eastern communes the earlier rule of Basil commended itself increasingly, but the assimilation of monasticism into the official Greek church came (in the late 400s) when monasteries were for the first time encouraged in Constantinople. Four aspects of the earlier monastic style of life call for description: first, its attractiveness and spread; second, its hermit and communal heroes, Anthony and Pachomius; third, the comprehensive psychoanalysis and psychotherapy developed by its theoreticians, Evagrius Ponticus and John Cassian; finally, the monks' role-replacement of the martyrs through their ascetic imitation of the very Christ whom they revered as inimitably divine.

All four topics manifest elements of both denial and affirmation. Most certainly the monks were not simply negative protesters against a privileged church. They denied their human passions only as the way to affirm heaven, the spirit, and Christ. Their way of life, reflecting the classical world's concern for hierarchical values, attracted men and women because it made the lower loyalties means to the higher ones, body to spirit, vice to virtues, Caesar to Christ. They fled the cities in which their culture embodied civilization only to build in the desert regimens and societies embodying their religious civilization. They left their congregations' worship only to found a mode of living optimally given to worship. Their flight and isolation from the institutions of church and state turned them into the most jealous defenders of those institutions. Nothing marked a great monk more than for emperors and archbishops to appeal to him for benediction and concrete advice.

Monks asserted their humility by casting aspersions on ordination. Egyptian abbots taught Cassian that the desire for church office signaled vainglory. A familiar counsel warned every monk to avoid associating with women and bishops, the two kinds of persons who would distract him from his "care for the quiet of his cell."[26] One Ammonius, famous for having memorized six million lines from scriptures and holy writers, cut off his left ear to avoid the ordination that friends had arranged for Bishop Timothy of Alexandria to bestow on him. When the friends persuaded Timothy to waive the rule against ordaining maimed men, Ammonius threatened to cut out his tongue. The friends desisted, taking seriously the threat of one who, whenever tempted by carnal desire, heated an iron and seared the offending member. Timothy was bishop (from 381 to 385), when Theodosius had just established the orthodox Christian empire in which ordination conveyed civil as well as sacerdotal authority. Ammonius mutilated himself to avoid blending his earthly and heavenly loyalties, not to deny either its appropriate place.

Yet nobody fought harder than monks to hold the church to orthodox doctrine and discipline. The Alexandrian teacher named Origen (in the mid-200s) was the favorite theologian of the monks in Egypt. When the anti-Origenist named Theophilus became bishop of Alexandria, four monks called "Tall Brothers" rushed to his city from the Nitrian desert (in 399) to defend Origen's teachings. Losing there, they hurried to Constantinople where they gained the support of John Chrysostom, then at the highest power as patriarch. Holy monks with their magical influence, in league with dedicated bishops with their pastoral authority, both buttressing civil magistrates with their political power, brought Christian sacrality into the service of social order and unity. The empire "remained a 'commonwealth of cities,' " wrote Brown, in which "the Christian bishop, now ruling large congregations and backed by the violence of the monks, had come to the fore. . . . Theodosius . . . allied himself with the 'grassroots' movements of the great cities of the empire," keeping pace with "the seismic shift that had placed the Christian bishop and the holy man at the head of popular opinion in the nerve-centres of the empire."[27] Monks did not rule church and empire, but without their support nobody else could rule.

The word for "retirement" (*anachorēsis*) that described flight from Egyptian cities to escape debts also described flight to pursue spiritual perfection; perhaps in some cases the two motives were not separable.[28] But these anchorites had all the worldly goods they wanted, and the first known commune of Christians, founded (about 320) by Pachomius in upper Egypt near Thebes, quickly became a prosperous economic cooperative. Visiting the Thebaid (in 406), Palladius found forces of tailors, smiths, carpenters, camel drivers, and fullers. One group of 1300 monks formed an efficient cooperative and regularly sent a trusted member to Alexandria to sell their goods and buy their provisions. Palladius found that "they work at every kind of craft and with their surplus output they provide for the needs both of the women's convents and the prisons." Wanting not to waste even their garbage, "They keep pigs, too," he noted, much to his disgust.[29] They wove baskets, tanned leather, made shoes, forged metal, spun yarn, wove cloth, farmed fields, harvested crops. Their economic plan enabled them at once to join and to beat the system—from each his best output, to each his least intake.

Politics as well as economics concerned them. At the end of our period a monk named Daniel interrupted only once his thirty-three-year stint living atop a tall column near Constantinople. That was to chase heretics from the church and pretenders from the imperial throne. Having cleaned both houses of society, he returned to his post. From this height he counseled emperors and empresses, generals and visiting statesmen, bishops and patriarchs. He also dispensed his magical cures to the poor and the sick. He fought demons and perfected his personal holiness. He supervised construction of the shrine in which his remains, later buried beneath those of martyrs, would become the grail of pilgrims for generations to come.

So attractive and rewarding was the response to the dominant culture that it spread like wildfire. Christian hermits first appeared in the Egyptian desert not far from Alexandria; communes began in remoter Egypt near the loop of the Nile. Syria was also an early center; the first Egyptian monks used the Syrian titles of

Abba (father) and Amma (mother). All fought demons and strove for perfection. Visitors who studied their ways (in the early 400s) adapted them to Greek and Latin areas, particularly Palladius to the former and John Cassian to the latter. In Palestine individual ascetics abhorred the world from desert mountains and caves, while others in small groups ran hospices for pilgrims to the holy places. In Judaea monks joined communes to train for the higher life of solitude. In Asia Minor the movement remained close to the provincial cities, where monks lived in communes under Basil's rule (written from 358 to 364) of simple discipline and social service. The climate of Italy and Gaul made communes more attractive than hermit life and called for easier dietary restrictions. Celtic monks undertook special disciplines like missionary journeys, and their ways spread into northern Europe. The Egyptian model commended itself in North Africa, where there arose independently the Circumcellions, who led riots and rebellions in the name of social justice. All these variations coexisted with little or no competition. Despite pockets of resistance, notably in Spain, the movement proved remarkably adaptable. By the end of our period monks had become the exemplars of spiritual power and discipline for Christians in all parts of the empire.

The most famous early hermit was the sainted Anthony. At age eighteen or twenty the boy, who had never liked school, was left an orphan in charge of his much younger sister. He did like church, where he heard and took to heart a verse of Scripture about giving all to the poor in order to attain heavenly treasure. Entrusting his sister to a commune of virgin Christian women, he studied with an old near-by hermit in labor, prayer, and learning the Bible. The devil attacked with sundry seductions, with thoughts of sister, wealth, fame, food, and pleasure. When faith and prayer dispelled these cares, the devil returned in the masquerades of a woman of the night to arouse "filthy thoughts" and then "as a black boy" who called himself "a lover of fornication."[30] Thoughts about Christ and scriptural verses repulsed these meaner demons. Anthony increased his austerity with all-night vigils, a bread-water-salt diet taken once a day or during fasts every fourth day, and sleep on a rush mat or bare ground. Next he shut himself in a tomb where the devil beat him. A friend who sometimes brought bread, thinking him dead, took him to the church. Anthony came to and returned to the tomb. Awful phantoms of beasts and snakes filled it, until the roof opened and light from Christ chased them away. At age thirty-five a hardened hermit, Anthony went to live alone in a deserted fort east of the Nile, and was unresponsive to visitors. They heard noisy demons whom Anthony repulsed by singing biblical verses and making the sign of the cross. After two decades of this routine, the sanctified monk appeared in public to teach asceticism and to work miracles.

For all his austerity he was neither aged nor emaciated. His "body was unchanged" and the "temper of his soul, too, was faultless" (14). He learned and commended ten virtues, adding "understanding, charity, love of the poor, faith in Christ, gentleness, hospitality" to the classical ideas of "prudence, justice, temperance, fortitude" (17). He taught how to use religious weapons against demons, "For they are cowards, and they greatly fear the sign of the Lord's Cross" (35). From retirement Anthony learned of Maximin Daja's persecutions and rushed to Alexandria, hoping to win the crown. The more he ministered to condemned Christians the more he "longed for martyrdom" (46). "When, at length, the persecution had ceased and the blessed Bishop Peter had died a martyr," Anthony left Alexandria and retired to his cell, where "he was daily a martyr to conscience in the sufferings he endured for the faith" (47). Many sought his advice and cures. He withdrew to upper Egypt; still people came for his blessings and healings. The more he received extraordinary visions the more he respected the institutional church and supported orthodoxy. He blessed Constantine and members of the imperial family who wrote to him.

Anthony cared about his body by not caring for it. His disdain for it and its cleanliness and health at all stages of his career served to highlight the miracle by which spiritual discipline made his flesh lustrous and uncorrupted. On a premonition of death he directed that he not be mummified but buried in a secret place lest people cherish his corpse. Yet after mortifying it for eighty-five years until he died (in 356) at one hundred and five, "he remained quite healthy, for he saw well because his eyes were undimmed and sound, and not one of his teeth had fallen out; only, near the gums they had become worn because of the old man's great age" (93). He was in better shape than those who pampered their bodies. His was purified by his having conquered its passions.

The early hermits or anchorites looking to Anthony and the early commune-monks or cenobites looking to Pachomius as their founders respected one another. Each called the other's the higher way. When a group of monks brought Anthony news of Pacho-mius' death (in 346), he praised them for being like their leader. Whereupon one named Zacchaeus hailed Anthony in words appropriate to Christ, "Father, it is you who are the light of all the world. Your fame has reached kings, and on account of you they glorify God." Anthony demurred by noting that Pachomius improved the practice in which "each of the old monks pursued his training alone."[31] Anthony had longed to see Pachomius in the flesh but was content with the hope of meeting him soon in paradise.

Pachomius, born of pagan parents in upper Egypt, marveled at the Christians who befriended him when he was being impressed into the imperial army of Maximin. On discharge he went home and was baptized. That night a dream guided him to apprentice under a hermit. He liked the life of labor, prayer, hardship, temptation, fastings, vigils, and the memorizing of scriptural verses and famous monks' epigrams. In his first vision a voice told him to build a monastery and to gather many monks at Tabennisi near the loop of the Nile. Over the years thousands of monks and hundreds of nuns gathered there to live under rules drawn by Pachomius from personal experience and experimentation.

Pachomius did not invent the Christian commune, but he first

codified that kind of life on a strict regimen designed for a chain
of monasteries under one absolute ruler. His rules come down
in a Latin translation ascribed to Jerome, in Coptic and Greek
fragments, in allusions by Pachomius' biographer, in a summary
by Cassian, and in a description by Palladius—all from within
two generations of Pachomius' death. The sources vary on details
but yield a reliable composite picture. A long probation earned
the novice his monk's garb, but his street clothes were kept in
case of his dismissal. Frugal meals eaten in silence once a day
(plus, for the weak, an evening snack) strengthened one for
rounds of prayer four times a day and for monotonous labor.
Tasks ranged from keeping the guest lodge to cooking to weaving
to basket making, and they were rotated weekly among the several houses of twenty to forty monks each. Sleep, with monks
reclining in chairs but not lying in beds, was short. Humility defined and crowned the virtues. Visiting clergy held eucharist on
Saturdays and Sundays for the men and, across the river, for the
nuns. When a virgin died, her sisters prepared the body for
burial by the men in a common cemetery. The slightest carelessness called for atonement by public penance; real wrongdoing,
by stripes or expulsion. The abbot's decision stood.

Everything done or avoided by monks under the rule of Pachomius upbuilt the spirit and purified the body, disciplined the desires of individuals, and strengthened the security of the community. Rules made everything routine. Monks were not taking
delight in drudgery; their rule was bringing everything into the
realm of the expected. Thus the rule sanitized all activities against
the evils of change and chance. Moreover, it kept the monks equal
in performing the same labor, following one spare diet, sleeping
in similar cells and postures, maintaining the same silence, learning scriptures, and reciting set prayers and psalms. This leveling of
differences squelched tendencies to specialization and to special
treatment, the seeds of pride.

The one exception to the regimen of changelessness, by which
routine overcame finitude and humility nullified sin, was the case
of the abbot. Someone had to deal with emergencies, admit nov-

ices, punish offenders, expel the recalcitrant, and in general bear the burden of power. The rule had to be interpreted and administered; if all were to submerge their wills to it, someone must be willful about it. Politics, in a word, would not go away.

Pachomius solved the political problem for himself simply by being the founder who needed no warrant. He carefully appointed two successors in order. Yet on hearing he was dead, Anthony, as though by reflex, asked who was taking over, then immediately blessed the new leader, Orsisius, with a nickname ("Israelite") and commended him to the special care of "pope" Athanasius, the bishop in Alexandria. The young favorite (and protégé of Pachomius) named Theodore deferred in every matter to Orsisius to bolster his authority with the founder's approval. Orsisius justified his very strict rule by his own spiritual perfection; "The governance of souls is not for everyone except for perfect men" because "an unbaked brick placed at a foundation near a river does not last one day but a baked one endures like a stone. So, too, . . . a man with carnal inclinations who has not been fired by the word of God . . . is destroyed when he comes to a position of authority" (126).

Notwithstanding, the burden became too heavy for Orsisius to bear. Wishing to retire, he sought guidance in picking a collaborator and chose none other than "Theodore, the man who was as one soul with the great abbot Pachomius" (129). Having installed Theodore by announcing that Pachomius had dictated the choice, Orsisius went away to a remoter monastery. Theodore, left to run the show, insisted he was only Orsisius' collaborator and consulted him about major decisions. Orsisius returned to the home office and shared power just before Theodore died, thus re-establishing his own authority from Theodore as well as from Pachomius. No problem was more vexing than the political one. The monks' heavenly citizenship, though infinite, necessarily shifted as their circumstances changed. For change, inevitable yet evil, could be disinfected only by accommodating to it while appearing to deny it.

Athanasius' life of Anthony (written 356-57) and the biog-

raphy of Pachomius (about 390) belong to a large, diverse literature about early monks, from which can be reconstructed a wide
variety of thought and practice. Underlying the diversity is a
unifying insight into human weaknesses and an integrated program for parlaying them into strengths. The first master of
monastic psychoanalysis and psychotherapy was Evagrius Ponticus, and the person who elaborated this system and transmitted
it to the west was Cassian.

To them the essence of being human consisted in having been
created by and in the image of the perfect deity. This nature was
marred and twisted by the passions, forces working toward imperfection by drawing persons away from their true being. The
recovery of original nature involved denying the passions and attaining that state of apathy (*apatheia*) in which the soul at once
contemplated deity and mirrored deity to others. In a saying
ascribed to Abbot Poemon of Egypt, "We were not taught to be
body-killers, but passion-killers." Or, in Evagrius' own epigram,
"A monk is a man who is separated from all and who is in harmony with all." More schematically, Evagrius accorded to everybody, even to "those who do not yet believe in God," the faculty
of faith, "an interior good" that begat the fear of God, which in
turn produced true love (*agapē*) and restored the soul to its
divinity.[32]

Yet demons stronger than any but the purest humans roiled
the passions. One needed to understand these powerful agents of
evil and to know their antidotes. Especially the evil thoughts
(*logismoi*), both in their general operation and as they functioned for oneself, needed attention. Evagrius, drawing from
Origen's writings as well as from his own experience and from
that of monks he knew, reduced all evil thoughts to eight principal vices, then provided an average of sixty scriptural verses to
recite against each of them. The list, later refined into the seven
deadly sins, has exerted an influence on Christians' lives too vast
to estimate. The eight faults were gluttony (*gastrimargia*), lust
or fornication (*porneia*), avarice or envy (*philarguria*), sadness
or dejection (*lupē*), anger (*orgē*), acedia (*akēdia*), vainglory

(*kenodoxia*), and pride (*hyperēthania*). In these terms the faults sound deceptively antique. Actually, they refer to modern experiences like piggishness, lechery, greed, depression, hatred, inability to care, bragging, and egotism.

The monks learned to connect these impulses in a causal chain. To be beset by one of them signaled the need to put down its antecedent; to fight lust one ate less. Cassian described each sin in its causality as to whether it existed within or arose without human nature, involved a bodily or mental act, and was externally or internally excited. Avarice and acedia arose outside human nature, the others existed within. Gluttony and lust were bodily acts, the rest mental. Gluttony, avarice, and anger were externally excited, while the last four were internally excited; and lust could be aroused either way. Lust or fornication could be committed by sexual intercourse, by masturbation, or by fantasizing. Gluttony, for example, came in several shapes. In the form of desiring food before stated times it led one to dislike the monastery. In the form of wanting all kinds of food it led to luxury and lasciviousness. In the form of seeking dainty delicacies it caused covetousness. Vainglory could be used as an antidote to certain sins, helping one avoid fornication, say, by one's desire for a good reputation. Thus it was better to be troubled by vainglory than by lust. But lust was easier to escape by fasting and change of scene, while vainglory thrived on one's success in resisting sins of the flesh and itself knew no simple cure. Specific remedies for most sins included abstinence, spiritual care of the soul, mental determination, bodily chastisements, fastings, vigils, acts of regret, change of scene, meditation on scripture, and solitude. By self-examination each individual must learn his or her besetting sin and take special pains to fight it, remembering that vainglory and pride attacked everybody alike.

Evagrius dealt very subtly with these matters, which Cassian liked to outline and chart. Evagrius noted the dynamics of early identification of and angry retort to demons before they were able to "drive us out of our own state of mind." Like modern psychoanalysts, he studied dreams for indications of the soul's state. "Natural processes which occur in sleep without accompanying images of a stimulating nature are, to a certain measure, indications of a healthy soul. But images that are distinctly formed are a clear indication of sickness," he wrote. That is, "the faces one sees in dreams are, when they occur as ill-defined images, symbols of former affective experiences. Those which are seen clearly . . . indicate wounds that are still fresh."[33] The quest for *apatheia* involved leaving wounds and affective experiences behind, the further the better.

The monks' aim of serious serenity was utterly opposed to folly and mirth. A young man named Sylvan had been an actor before joining the monastery. At first earnest, Sylvan soon began "to make merry and to enjoy himself, and besides this he used to sing fearlessly among the brethren snatches of the lewd and ribald songs which he used to hear in the theatre." Pachomius commanded him to turn in his uniform and leave the monastery. Sylvan begged for another chance and won it by persuading Petronius, a chosen successor to Pachomius, to be his surety. He became the soul of sobriety and for decades continually wept, even while eating, over the thought that "a man from the theatre is ministered unto by such holy men as these."[34] Mirth was gross.

The subtlest fault was acedia, not being able to care, which Latin moralists rendered as sorrow or gloominess (*tristitia*) and which in English became sloth. This "noonday demon" made the sun stand still and the day seem fifty hours long. The afflicted monk gazed out the window, took walks, looked at the sun wondering how long before dinner, peered around for idle company, wanted to be elsewhere, felt that his brothers did not understand him, dreamed of going to another place and becoming a real success, questioned whether monastic life was all that important or really dull and futile.

Such carelessness—not of being slovenly or not taking care but of torpor or being unable to care, of being unable to get started, of being paralyzed in will—had to be met immediately and face on, for a victory over it chased away many other demons, while delay spelled defeat. Indeed, "a state of deep peace and inexpressible joy arise[s] out of this struggle." This "demon of *acedia* . . . is the most grievous of all and . . . on this account will effect the greatest purification of soul."[35]

In a real sense, this carelessness might be called the mirror-image of passionlessness. Not caring came near to not yearning; acedia was the underside of apathy. Not to be disciplined enough to be able to care about life came very close to, yet fell very short of, being so disciplined that one could care for nothing else and nothing more than the spirit's calm.

Reciting the right scriptures helped in both cases. For acedia Evagrius prescribed fifty-seven passages; for example, these from Deuteronomy: "Hear, O Israel: The Lord our God is one Lord; and you shall love the Lord your God with all your heart, and with all your soul, and with all your might . . ." (6:4ff.). "And the Lord will take away from you all sickness; and none of the evil diseases of Egypt, which you knew, will he inflict upon you, but he will lay them upon all who hate you" (7:15). "The Lord will cause your enemies who rise against you to be defeated before you; they shall come out against you one way, and flee before you seven ways" (28:7).[36] The monk under acedia fought with the help of the deity.

While fighting, he should throw himself into manual labor, like it or not. Its routineness required only habit, not fresh resolve, and its fixity of place opposed the desire to wander. Cassian drove home this point by a story about an abbot named Paul, who lived in a cave near a grove of date palms, near a flourishing garden, and near a good spring. To send baskets he might make to the nearest market would cost more than the price they could bring. Knowing the worth of work and needing it, Paul gathered enough palm leaves each day so he would fill a cave in a year's time. At the end of each year he burnt the palms and started over again.

The apprentice Pachomius and his trainer Palaemon worked, another account tells, at spinning wool and weaving bags. When in night vigils they became sleepy and careless, work was the best cure; since they could not see to spin or weave, they went to the desert and aimlessly hauled sand from one place to another.[37]

Thus to emphasize the principal faults and to examine briefly the trickiest of them illustrates the pragmatic wisdom that the monks gained about human nature and about how to master its baser impulses. It also illustrates how secure their psychology made them. Their scheme was complex enough to bring a wide variety of anxieties under diagnosis and cure. Yet it was simple enough to allow a large measure of self-understanding and self-help, backed by ready advice from experienced masters. It did not require long years of intensive analysis and therapy. If the demons that caused the monks' maladies leave moderns incredulous, think how strange, dark, inscrutable, and unbelievable our Oedipal urges and anal fixations would have been to them! At least their scheme worked. They had many examples of men and women, both living and departed and all vividly remembered, who amply demonstrated the practical benefits and the attainability of purity of heart (*apatheia*). The stories about and the sayings of these exemplars enshrined the monks' wisdom and their successful lives.

Scripture consisted of sayings too holy to ask questions about. The monks memorized many, many passages by way of storing ammunition to fire against demons and to shoot as incantations on ceremonial occasions. When in personal battle this ammunition failed, they brought out the cannon, the sign of the cross. But one did not explain sacred scripture or ask it to give meaning to life. Monks, unlike modern exegetes, neither worried about nor sought to adopt "the biblical world view." Their wisdom, their meaning, found expression in the stories and epigrams they handed down, first by word of mouth and then in written collections, from the old, successful monks to the young, aspiring monks. Their sense of reaching from lower to higher things stretched to reaching from present to future attainments, not only for individuals but also for the monastic endeavor. For the masters were to the monastic cities in the desert what the exemplary martyrs had been in the provincial capitals—men and women who struck the ideal relation and the proper balance between the two citizenships enjoyed by early Christians.

Needless to say, the monks, like the martyrs before them, constituted a minority of all Christians under the Roman Empire from Augustus to Romulus. Most adherents of the religion lived fairly normal lives in a culture that placed low value on human life and happiness—at least for ordinary people. The ordinary Christians were ministered to by priests whose religious model guided their congregations but fell far short of the exemplary spirituality of the martyrs and monks. The chief ministers were overseers, usually connected with the main congregation of a major city, from which they managed the affairs of believers in a given region.

Extant data lead to the clear inference that very few Christians were rural people. From the beginning, the religion was urban like the dominant society around it. Christians were, to be frank, contentious people, involved in controversies and debates about matters both large and small—from the dating of their festivals to the attributes of their deity. Religious conviction drove wedges, to be sure, between Christians and members of other religions and, as well, among various parties of Christians. Thus many of them who became famous in the early histories of the church were polemical writers. But these writers and the ordinary Christians united in a pervasive and virtually unchallenged reverence for martyrs as advocates in heaven and for monks as holy men and women working miracles on earth.

CHRISTS

The monastic heroes thus achieved holiness within the span of their earthly lives by acquiring the skills of dying to the passions and of refurbishing human nature's image of deity. Two aspects of that achievement, implicit in the foregoing discussion, deserve to be made explicit in brief conclusion. They are, first, how the monks won the veneration formerly given the martyrs and, second, how they took Christ at once for their trainer in apathy and for the divine person who had absorbed perfect human nature. The two aspects hang together.

By winning while still living the rewards for which the martyrs had had to die, these holy men and women added a new dimension to Christianity, indeed to the spiritual sensibilities of late antiquity. Their mastery of demons and their dispensing of divine graces, both from within the limits or perimeters of human existence, placed these persons of great spiritual power "in the centre of people's imagination," wrote Brown. "Previously, the classical world had tended to think of its religion in terms of *things,*" but now in politics as in religion the mysteriously mighty came to the fore as the mundanely effective person.[38] Common references to monks as bloodless martyrs indicate that monastics were discovering a new way to win the old crown. Clement of Alexandria equated martyrdom of the passions with the actual shedding of blood. His successor Origen held that many Christians underwent daily martyrdom of conscience by carrying their crosses behind Christ. "White martyrdom" became a common phrase in sayings and descriptions of the desert fathers. "With the ending of the persecution," Frend noted, "the substitution of ascetic for martyr as the highest of the Christian's goals became complete."[39]

The monks self-consciously and adroitly associated themselves with the martyrs. The monk whom Palladius first introduced into his history of Egyptian monasticism recited a martyr-story about Potamiaena, who, when given the choice of having sex with her pagan master or being plunged into a cauldron of hot pitch, demonstrated the endurance Christ gave her by asking to be lowered very gradually into the boiling tar.[40] Daniel the Stylite rejected the stone-and-metal tomb bought for him by the emperor and empress. He wished "to be buried deep down in the earth and have the remains of holy martyrs laid above me"; three days before dying, Daniel dreamed that "he was allowed to see at one time all those who had been well-pleasing to God," including the whole company of martyrs, and "They came down and when they had greeted him they bade him celebrate the . . . Eucharist."[41] In a blaze of 10,000 candles Daniel's corpse was brought down from the platform on which he had died. With the capital already a storehouse of relics, the archbishop laid him to rest under what were taken to be remains of the three Hebrew children burnt in the fiery furnace by Nebuchadnezzar. The souls of the master monks were transported, like those of the martyrs, by angels to paradise.[42] From the beginning the monks were "holding before their eyes day and night not only the crucified Christ but also the martyrs whom they had seen struggle so much."[43]

The incarnate Word of God presented the monks with both a mystery and a model. Christ embodied deity, in principle immutable and inimitable, yet he also perfectly embodied the passionless humanity that they worked to attain. In three respects, then, the monks fashioned their spirituality after their founder. First, he had been the entirely victorious warrior against demons, and from him they received the weapons of their own battles—scripture verses, the holy name, and the sign of the cross. Second, Christ's pure spirit soared high above all fleshly and worldly passions, and from him they received the inspiration to purify their hearts. Third, his divinity had absorbed into itself the humanity they all shared, and to him they directed their aspiration and their contemplation. In these roles they worshipped him. Common folk who went about the business of the world, wrote Cassian, beheld Jesus "still in His humility and in the flesh . . . but only those can look with purest eyes on His Godhead, who rise with Him from low and earthly works and thoughts and go apart in the lofty mountain of solitude" where "pure faith and the heights of virtue" disclose "the glory of His Face and the image of His splendour to those who are able to look on Him with pure eyes of the soul."[44]

The most influential of all writers among and about Egyptian hermits, Evagrius, modeled the monks' warfare against demons on the Gospel stories of Jesus' temptation in the wilderness (Matthew 4:1-11, Luke 4:1-13). Each of Satan's propositions had been repudiated by Jesus' citing a verse from the Bible, a practice that Evagrius codified for the monks. His student Cassian pointed out that Christ, "the very fount of inviolable sanctity, had no need of external help and the assistance of solitude . . . yet still He retired into the mountain alone to pray, thus teaching us" monks "by the example of His retirement" to flee earthly cares "if we too wish to approach God with a pure and spotless affection of heart."[45] They bound themselves to Christ by resolving to follow what they took to be apostolic lives, adjusted to their time and place and culture. In this sense they became his apostles for the church of their day.

At the same time, Christ was their symbol and agent making divine power accessible to them. Paul the Simple, failing to cleanse a demon-possessed man by invoking the name of his master Anthony, threatened the spirit: "By Jesus, if you don't go out I am going this very minute to tell Christ, and He will do you harm." Christ rewarded Paul's fasting by expelling the evil spirit and turning it into a forty-five-yard-long dragon that he drove into the Red Sea.[46] Invoking Christ enabled Evagrius to open a locked church door whose key had been lost (38:12). The virgin Silvania studied holy writings night and day to earn special grace until "she made herself a spiritual bird" and flew on wings to Christ (55:3). Philoromus in Galatia "showed such nobility in the Christlike mode of life that even those whose family record was unsurpassable revered his life and virtue"—a Christlikeness such that "I do not remember that I was ever absent in my mind from my God" (45:1,4). Esias of Scete (died 489) compared communal monastic life with bearing Christ's sufferings and cross, preparatory to mounting that cross by entering the solitude and quiet of the recluse's cell.[47]

The monks, then, became Christ's living martyrs by imitating him, by employing his spiritual power, by adoring him, by joining him spiritually while still in the flesh, and by helping others gain favors from him. Thus they epitomized heavenly citizenship while exercising earthly citizenship. They were saints like the martyrs, yet saints in the direr setting of living by dying to the lively passions instead of literally dying into passionlessness. They endorsed the human condition by showing how to turn it into a passionless recapturing of original human nature in the divine image. Anthony went public after twenty years of the most austere asceticism and became a virtual Pied Piper, enlisting men and women to become monks. From that event his biographer dated the monastic movement's beginnings in phrases appropriately summarizing the significance of the early monks and the martyrs whose mantle they inherited. Wrote Athanasius, "So from that time there have been monasteries even in the mountains, and the desert was made a city by monks who had left their own city and enrolled themselves for citizenship in heaven."[48]

III
CHAOS

Theodicy and Prelacy in the

Germanic Kingdoms

476-962

Students of the western Roman Empire have long debated its demise. When and how it fell, whether suddenly or gradually, are questions on which scholars take sides. The historian Henri Pirenne concluded that the empire barely fell and that very late (about 800), when Muslim expansion shifted the center of European rule onto Charlemagne in the North. At the other extreme Arnold Toynbee said the empire's seeds of destruction had been planted four centuries before Augustus Caesar. But "Nobody yet is prepared," judged Arnaldo Momigliano, "to deny that the Roman Empire has disappeared."[1] Nor will any deny that Europe changed in important ways by the time the barbarian king named Theodoric died (in 526), having ruled virtually all of the old Roman lands in the west save North Africa, Britain, and parts of Gaul. The empire failed to adapt to the new barbarian form of humanity and it disappeared. Christianity remained, but only by blending the old and the new, the Roman and the barbarian, into a religious culture distinct from the culture that prevailed in Byzantium and in the preceding period in the west.

The empire in the west had first tripped when Diocletian moved the seat of government from Rome to his huge palace in Nicomedia. There he devised programs to renovate society, including the eradication of the aggressive, new religion. It tripped again when Constantine invoked that new religion as a source of spiritual energy with which to generate social cohesion.[2] Its fall is marked by the replacement of the old line of Roman emperors with the new lines of Germanic kings. Of course, the emergence of a distinctly new form of humanity, which is what the empire's fall symbolizes, cannot be given a precise date. Still, with relative suddenness came new frames for living. Latin Europe shifted its economic base from the gold coins of Rome to the barter system of the Germans. Villages and farms became the prevalent human habitats in place of cities and shops. Standing armies gave way to soldiers enlisted for particular campaigns and then mustered out until the next conflict. The technology of aqueducts yielded to that of the wheeled plow. In the areas facing away from the Mediterranean, plentiful wood enabled men to build more quickly but less durably than they had built with stone. Learning became valuable for its practicality instead of for its elegance. Western civilization, in a word, lost its urban character and turned rustic.

Descriptions of all these changes fill many a book. No change portended more ominously than the displacement of the old Roman by the new German governmental styles, the one by code and the other by customary law. Out of their familiar conventions barbarian kings fashioned new laws (after 500), binding their Roman as well as their kindred subjects. Odoacer, the barbarian who (in 476) deposed the Roman boy-emperor with the double-diminutive name of Romulus Augustulus, symbolizes this displacement. So does also Theodoric, who (in 493) brutally murdered Odoacer to gain sole dominion over Italy, which he ruled from Ravenna.

This permeation of western Europe by what the Romans derided as a base and untamed culture called forth fresh Christian energies. Thought and action newly responded to chaos and calamity in ways that set the course of history in Europe for centuries. Calamity evoked theodicy, a trust that providence would bring good out of evil. Chaos evoked a new legitimation of power as coming from God and binding all godly people.

This chapter deals at length with these typical responses, the first as exemplified by Boethius and the second by Gregory the Great. But not before treating in more (if still sparse) detail the drastic cultural shifts to which they were the responses. After discussing Boethius and the role of Christ in Boethius' religion, attention turns briefly back to Constantinople, where a different Christ shaped Greek culture and religion into forms captured in achitecture by Justinian and his craftsmen. In sharp contrast with those forms was Gregory's plan for ordering western society under a ruling and rule-giving Christ. The chapter shows at the end how Charlemagne combined the ideals of theodicy and prelacy into the first distinctly western empire in Europe, an empire in which the ruler and the ruled shared one religion.

Calamity and chaos fell hard and fast on the westerners. Rome was sacked (in 410), less than a century after the Christians had come into imperial favor. They had long hoped for that prosperity. Justin Martyr so strenuously endorsed Roman civilization that he was ready to die to show how good Christianity was for it. Christians pleaded to emperors and prayed to God that the empire, under which they had all lived, convert and nourish the young religion. Origen of Alexandria, perhaps by force of logic more than of actual expectation, looked forward to an empire composed entirely of Christians, the goal that Constantine's edict brought into sight and Theodosius' decrees achieved. In terms of their loyalties to heaven and to the empire the Christians had come to understand themselves and to define their styles of living.

Who then could rejoice when the urbanized and recently Christianized world of the west splintered into rude, barbarian kingdoms? No Latin Christian wrote admiringly of the Germans until (in about 400) a priest of Marseilles named Salvianus did so. And Salvianus was hardly praising their virtues, but only preferring their way of life to the pagan-Roman vices into which he feared Latin Christians would backslide. Since he could no longer believe the western empire salvageable, he wanted to detach Christianity from ancient Roman values more than to bring it to terms with new Germanic ones.[3] Down to Salvianus' times Christians had known the barbarians mostly as enlistees and mercenaries in the imperial armies. But these armies lately did less than the bishops and the pope to ward off depredations by Germanic kings and their raiders.

No doubt some barbarian soldiers converted. We know that enough Roman Christians lived among the Visigoths to warrant the appointment of a bishop named Ulfilas (about 341) to care for them. He labored to multiply the native Gothic converts. Similarly, a bishop was appointed (in 431) for the Roman Christians taken prisoner when the Irish raided Britain.[4] Under Theodosius the orthodox version of Christianity became the empire's

official religion, repudiating the Arians who encountered Christ
as a fellow creature. Most converted barbarians by then were already Arians and therefore were more despised for being heretical than for being barbarian or pagan. Teutonic Arians sacked
Rome and posed for Augustine of Hippo the vexing problem of
how to blame the debacle on the past pagan empire and exonerate
the present Christian one—a brilliant, if one-sided, interpretation
of the times.

Then King Odoacer, while serving in the imperial army, was
proclaimed king of Italy (in 476); he forced the boy-emperor to
abdicate, and he abolished the title and office of Augustus in the
west. This cultural shock called for another explanation, differing
from Augustine's as far as being conquered differs from being
raided. It had been one thing for a vital religion emerging from
Judaism to penetrate a Roman Empire trying to build one world
on the foundation of many religions. It was something else again
for the religion finally chosen to unify that world to come to
terms so soon with the many worlds of the barbarian kings. The
church undertook to salvage whatever of the grand Roman past
could be blended into the uncertain European future and to com-
mend the mixture to the barbarians as their best hope. Out of a
furious "clash and fusion of classical, Germanic, and Celtic
tastes, traditions, and cultures," in William Bark's pungent
phrase, "the spiritual guidance of the Catholic Church" evoked
"a society in which paramount importance attached to individualism, to adjustment and adaptation, to experimentation and invention, and to a new standard of values."[5]

Had everything Roman represented civilization, had the church
nicely confined itself to the category of religion, and had the barbarians been culturally nude, then the Christian tailor might have
fashioned Roman cloth into a Germanic-Celtic suit. But things
were not so neat. The Latins of late antiquity cherished the pre-
Christian paganism still symbolized by the city of Rome. The
medieval Germans bore a profoundly familial and individualistic
ethos. The church had deep commitments to both. Somewhat
nearer the actual pattern would be the picture of a vigorous

church introducing aspects of an exhausted tradition into a culture that would win the future. But even the metaphor of broker does less than full justice to Christianity's endorsement of the empire with its own pagan heritage and, ambivalence notwithstanding, a benediction upon the Teutons with their own, differently pagan, heritage. The colliding and conjoining of the waning and the waxing cultures took from Christianity not a blueprint of what was to be built but new attitudes conducive to the enterprise of building.

The "clash and fusion" became inevitable in the south when Odoacer became king of Italy. The same thing happened in the north when (in 486) Clovis defeated the Roman governor of Gaul. In another decade Clovis received baptism as a Catholic. With support from Catholic bishops he attacked and overthrew Alaric II, the Arian king of the Visigoths, as well as the pagan Alamanni. From Clovis' founding of the Merovingian dynasty over the Franks until Charlemagne, wrote Friedrich Heer, "the social history of the Merovingian kingdom . . . is really the story of how the two civilisations, the Gallo-Roman and the Germanic, blended and fused," with the Roman element mainly transmitted under churchly auspices.[6]

Christianity sponsored the clash and the fusion. As sponsor, the church had already "attracted the most creative minds" of the empire: Ambrose, Jerome, Hilary of Poitiers, and Augustine among the Latins; and Athanasius and the Cappadocian fathers among the Greeks. In turn it attracted leading Roman nobles of the senatorial class who became administrators and bureaucrats for the Germanic kingdoms—Sidonius Apollinaris, Benedict of Nursia, Boethius, Cassiodorus, and above all Gregory the Great.[7]

So in the west Rome tripped, fell, and spilled her cultural inheritance for Christians to pick over and hand on to the barbarians. Much was left lying. Great public edifices, no longer needed, fell into disuse, disrepair, and ruin. The populace fled the cities for the country, where service to a German lord made life a little less miserable than did bondage to a Roman landowner. Natural economy succeeded money economy. Elegant, classical Latin suffered vulgarization by virtue of sparse literature and rare literacy. Indeed, the whole Roman system of public education disappeared along with other social functions of the state, from Gaul and Britain (in the 400s) and later from Italy as well. The intellectual glories of the Greeks and the literary grandeur of the Romans mostly fell, as it were, first into filing cabinets and thence into wastebaskets.

Practical learning is what the church saved, simply because it was practical and could mingle with the practical know-how that was newly developed. Boethius in Rome, following the lead of Martianus Capella, handily divided the arts of acquiring knowledge (the quadrivium of arithmetic-geometry-astronomy-music) from the arts of expressing what was already known (the trivium of grammar-rhetoric-logic). Then Cassiodorus elaborated this scheme into an educational philosophy for monks, outlining what every monk must know. Frustrated in his plan to establish a theological academy at Rome, he withdrew from public life (in 540) to establish two monasteries at Vivarium. There he saved what he could of his scheme by assigning to his monks the task of daily studying and copying both Christian and pagan classics. Thus, according to Momigliano, "a new chapter opened in the intellectual history of Europe."[8]

But the seismic shock of Rome's fall cannot be measured simply by adding up the tasks, services, and activities that had to be reassigned, revised, recommissioned, reconceived. The Roman imperium that gave way to the Germanic kingdoms had been far more, even after the capital was moved east, than one form of government among others. It carried the cultural and spiritual freight of what Eric Voegelin called the "ecumenic empire." That is to say, "In its self-interpretation, imperial rule is the mediation of divine-cosmic order to the existence of man in society and history."[9] The barbarian rulers of course maintained a certain order for their subjects, both German and Roman—an order symbolized by their arbitrary power. What dissipated the divine-cosmic order represented in the older imperium was the series of clashes among these particular, equally absolute powers—the clash of a Theodoric with an Odoacer or of a Clovis with Romano-Gallic governors and tribal kings. Each ruler possessed ambition, but none was obsessed by a destiny. The situation invited a reassertion that the divine-cosmic order remained somehow reliable even while men and women remained somehow responsible. It also called for a new legitimation and representation of that power on earth in a divinely grounded institution, the papacy. Put another way, the situation was ripe for a profounder invasion into the mysteries of providence than the two-city scheme of Augustine. When that was done, it became timely to turn the city of God on earth about which Augustine theorized and speculated into a quite real and powerful Catholic Church under one universal, visible head. Such was the spiritual magnitude of transferring stewardship of western civilization from Romans to barbarians by means of Christians.

The term "theodicy" was coined a millennium later. Asked, Why is there something, why not nothing? and, Why do things have to be as they are and not different? Leibnitz answered that the ultimate reason of things is called God. After the fall of Rome the questions had been, How could divine-cosmic order be believed to outlive the crumbling of the imperium that had embodied and mediated it? How could social and historical chaos, visible to all, be reconciled with the ordering invisible deity's management of the universe? The theodicy of Boethius lodged itself at the center of European consciousness for a thousand years. It made the ultimate reason of all these changes the God of Christianity.

By applying Augustine and his ideas to the new circumstances, Boethius went beyond him and transformed them. *The City of God,* which until Renaissance scholars became interested in the *Confessions* remained Augustine's most influential work, discerned a double embodiment of divine order and showed the unreliability of one of them. City of God and city of this earth had variously intermingled during different epochs. The appearance of Christ brought the two into the open and strained relations that signaled the last epoch of history. The church must be catholic, and those who called themselves Christian must be made to conform under threat of the sword. The sword, however, belonged to the city of this earth. Alaric's sack of Rome and, even worse, the Vandals' storming the gates of Augustine's own city of Hippo Regius in North Africa revealed a failure of this sword to protect the church.

So Augustine traced the two cities back to creation and forward again. Whatever the epochs—and Augustine used several schemes in various writings—the divine city came increasingly into historical manifestation. The coming of Christ brought it to as full and complete a reality as it could attain in time and space. Only this divine city carried meaning and significance through the changes and chances of history; it alone would enter the eschaton. Augustine insisted on the waning and the essential insignificance of the terrestrial city, whose only purpose was to protect the church. To quote Voegelin again, "Beyond the dual ecumenism" represented by the two intermingled cities "of his present, history had no meaning but the waiting for the eschatological events."[10]

Quite literally, nothing more could develop in time, only the continued, selfsame mingling of the cities so the church could dispense grace and serve as a vestibule where heaven-bound Christians awaited the end. To Augustine belongs the credit or blame, as one may choose, for the Christian theory that the present age was the last age, a time of waiting, the *saeculum senescens.* Time passed. Life went on for men and women, but the meaning of history sat still. Nothing would importantly change.

Then Rome fell to the barbarians, who, whether Arian or pagan, felt no duty to use their sword to assist the church. Odoacer and Theodoric upset the Augustinian applecart. Was this the end for which the city of God waited? Did this crumbling of the imperial institutions simply bankrupt the cosmic order those institutions embodied? When civilization fell on earth, did God fall from heaven? What would happen to the significant city when the insignificant city no longer stood guard? Whether in grand, socio-historical terms or in terms of the crisis of a single life, these questions were asked. How they were answered set the future of Europe.

THEODICY

A Roman of the senatorial class, Anicius Manlius Severinus Boethius, whose many names signify his dignity as a nobleman, explained why things were as they were and not different. He did so in dire circumstance, imprisoned and awaiting execution by the barbarian ruler he had served as master of the king's offices.

Boethius, like his father, served his year (in 510) as consul. His two sons received the same honor jointly from Emperor Justin and King Theodoric. Trained for public service and administration, Boethius learned classical philosophy and nourished an ambition to translate the writings of Plato and Aristotle into Latin. What he achieved of this project enabled medieval students to read those philosophers' briefer treatises on logic, but Boethius' untimely death left his work unfinished. A Catholic Christian, he composed tracts about the trinitarian deity and about the person of Christ.

In the fullness of Boethius' adulthood (in 522) he left his library in Rome to become chief administrator in Ravenna for Theodoric, a Christian but an Arian and therefore a heretic in the eyes of Catholic subjects. Fearing alliances between the Roman nobility and the eastern emperor, the king accused Boethius of treason and cast him into prison, charged in detail with seeking the independence of Rome, fostering the powers of the senate, and trafficking magically with evil spirits. Imprisonment, as the victim must have known, would end only when he was put to death. Some Catholics later called him a martyr, but he furnished no clue whatever of facing earthly death as his heavenly birthday.

In prison Boethius composed a dialogue between Lady Philosophy and himself, a prose work interspersed with highly symbolic poems. *The Consolation of Philosophy* depicts Lady Philosophy comforting Boethius against his despair over his predicament of innocent suffering, of being unjustly stripped of fame, honor, dignity, even life itself. This Christian Job obviously knew the Stoic writers, for the pattern of his consolation is basically theirs. When one's basis of life and meaning suddenly crumbles under calamity, one first wants to check the despair, then fasten temporarily against further fall, then find some firmer, more permanent foundation. Patiently but uncompromisingly, Philosophy teaches Boethius to face his misfortune squarely rather than indulge in self-pity. Then she leads him to endorse the rational proposition that an entirely good God must bring ultimate benefit out of apparent evil.

Although Boethius cannot foretell what good end would come of things, this knowledge becomes the foundation of his new hope. Then he gains the original, ingenious, profound insight that to suffer while thus trusting God redeems the sufferer. Hurting helps. Since God's providence overrules human fate, ill fortune is to be preferred to good fortune. Ill fortune punctures the false hopes that good fortune inflates.

But another problem arises from this solution. To subsume under the goodness of an all-wise and all-powerful God the evil that befell men and women in times of disorder and crisis, whether personal or social (and for Boethius it was both), nullified human freedom. Such an overarching providence implied predestination. Such a deity spelled determinism.

At this critical juncture Philosophy thrusts the argument away from Stoic presuppositions about fate or fortune and introduces specifically Christian ideas about providence to replace them. "Providence embraces all things equally, however diverse they are, however infinite. Fate, on the other hand, sets particular things in motion once they have been given their own forms, places, and times." But, complains Boethius, "There seems to be a hopeless conflict between divine foreknowledge of all things and freedom of the human will." No, replies Philosophy, "For there are two kinds of necessity: one is simple, as the necessity by which all men are mortals; the other is conditional, as is the case when, if you know that someone is walking, he must necessarily be walking."[11]

In a word, the God who knew everything that would happen allowed some things to happen because man freely chose to make them happen. That was possible because such a God saw all events of all time at a single glance, simultaneously, and not in a causal, determined chain. God is good. Men are free. Freely trusting the goodness of God converts apparent evil into permanent good. Boethius arrived at all these reasons to be hopeful not by generating faith, but by following the rules of logic. To be sure, there is no logic that can demonstrate *proofs* about events that are both future and conditional. Nevertheless, long-range hope pins itself to a providential, powerful, good deity more logically than to blind fate or to fickle fortune.

The *Consolation* is literally Boethius' last word on life and justice, on suffering and God. To be sure, it tells nothing about the fall of the Roman Empire. But no sooner has Lady Philosophy come on stage than Boethius eloquently describes his personal predicament, implicating the conflicts between Roman and barbarian values, standards of justice, procedures of administration, civil rights, jurisprudence, and so forth. Boethius had forfeited his favorite work of translating and interpreting Plato and Aristotle, had left home and study to head the civil service and direct the palace officers for a king who had already proved himself wise and tolerant toward his subjects, Gothic and Roman alike. In this position of power, second only to the throne, Boethius had withstood the swindling of the poor by Gothic officers, even by the steward of the king's household. With equal devotion he had prevented a Roman dignitary from selling food at pegged prices during a famine in Campania. There is no reason to suspect that Theodoric condemned him for this even-handed justice.

Nor was the condemnation simply due to Boethius' Roman standards of nobility and style of administration, for in other instances Theodoric showed himself supportive of Roman ways, at least for the Romans. Still, the king's ethos was barbarian and his behavior at times barbaric. Who can forget that he came to rule by inviting his co-regent to a banquet where Odoacer was pinned by soldiers while Theodoric with his own sword split the enemy from head to groin? Theodoric's notion of justice was that the sovereign's bidding made things just. Boethius remained at heart a moral philosopher.

Nobody knows just why the king condemned his aide. The account Boethius said he wrote is lost. Probably Theodoric feared that a recent theological rapprochement between Catholics in the west and orthodox Christians in the east would lead to alliances between Romans and Byzantines against him as an Arian. Moreover, the king at age seventy lacked a successor-son and was seeing his plans for coexistence between Goths and Romans undercut by animosities and intrigues. Boethius was but the first of several influential Romans, including Pope John I, to be charged with treason. Theodoric is reported by a somewhat fanciful source later to have regretted having charged Boethius.

Unless Boethius is reckoned a liar in what he knew to be his final confession, his circumstance and his testimony point to the conclusion that he was framed by zealous men under his authority at court, men who played on the fears of a frustrated old king. He was also betrayed by the senate. He died believing in justice, honesty, providence, and the principle that philosophers should bear political responsibility. But he was a victim of the clash between one ethos and another, between the Gothic and Roman values that both he and his king were trying in different ways to harmonize.

But the clash and the fusion had just begun, and harmonization would be the work of centuries, not decades. The ethos represented by Boethius remained ecumenic. Sovereignty embodied a universal divine reality within the entire world that it sought to order. The ethos of Theodoric knew something about sacred sovereignty but only on the smaller, essentially tribal scale, isolated from if not simply immune to world problems. Without imputing these precise views to either man, one may fairly say that the Christianized Roman ethos required the king who sat in the room of the deposed emperors to embody order at least for the whole Latin world, while the Christianized barbarian ethos found the king's will to represent order because it was the will of the sacred and powerful ruler.

And both were Christian, although of different persuasions. Boethius was Catholic. Despite the ink that has been spilled over the absence of explicitly Christian terminology in the *Consolation,* it is a Christian book, fully in tune with the author's earlier theological treatises. The book draws upon pagan Greek and Roman sources, not scriptures, popes, creeds, councils, or churches. But two points are clear. First, Boethius, a philosopher and student of philosophy, approaches his plight via reason and argument, not faith and wonder. Lady Philosophy is reason personified. The providential deity is reason glorified. Yet the solution to personal and social calamity is the one that other Christians reached by faith; namely, mercy and justice cohered in the Almighty, into whose hands Boethius commended his spirit in the hope of eternal life. Second, he was writing a spare, honest account of how he was being consoled, not recommending how a Christian ought to seek consolation.

Certainly there is no hint in the *Consolation* that Boethius disdained or opposed Christianity, and he wrote when such a stance was exceptional enough to call for assertion. The very fact that he did not claim to be Christian reflects a humility that invited people to claim him as such. Boethius ingeniously injected the Stoics' religious confidence in the essential balance and order of the universe with a new understanding of human and divine personhood. He lived a long time before every thinking Christian felt called on to reach a judgment about grace and election, man's fall and Christ's death and resurrection, priesthood and sacraments, redemption and the end of the world. Freedom from this preoccupation allowed Boethius to write single-mindedly about a vexing question: How can those who innocently suffer have a just and good deity? To Boethius that question was poignant and human, personal and urgent.

The recent debate over whether he was a Christian may tell more about Boethius' quiet confidence in his own Christian status. Certainly generation after generation of reading Christians counted the *Consolation* among the finest jewels of their literary treasure. A cautious scholar recently called it "The most popular book of the Middle Ages"—which cannot be said of very many books.[12] Friedrich Heer confidently asserted that "Boethius' great work has been published more often in succeeding centuries than any other books except the Bible and the *Imitation of Christ*" because "it contained the first satisfactory definition of the individual" as the embodiment of rational nature.[13] Down the centuries in times of social and personal trouble Christians have drawn comfort and courage from the book. It was translated into English by King Alfred, again by Geoffrey Chaucer, and yet again by Elizabeth I. It originated the Latin Christian literature of consolation and plumbed the human spirit more deeply than its Greek counterpart, Chrysostom's Letter to a Young Widow.[14]

When things have been drastically different from what Christians thought they ought to have been, when the affairs over which they believed God ruled have seemed mismanaged, Boethius' answer has commended itself: In the long run and on the long view, profit arises from misfortune, yet men and women are free to strive and they should strive to make things as good as they can be made to be. The folly that gives rise to despair lies not in striving for the good but in relying upon the fame and glory and honor the world gives to those who seem to succeed. So far, so good.

But does taking the long view solve the problem of persistent, long-range evil, or only short-range personal or social crises? If innocent suffering becomes compatible with the justice of God because the innocent one benefits from the suffering, what of innocents who suffer without discernible gain? What of the male infants slain by Herod or the dwellers of Nagasaki and Hiroshima or the millions of Jews victimized in the Holocaust?

These are modern questions, based on the assumption that humans call God to the bar and judge his justice. Not so for

Boethius, whose human long-range view was to God but the twinkling of an eye, and whose human standards of justice and benefit, simply because they were human, fell far short of the perfect or divine standards. In the crisis of crumbling civilization and in the poignancy of personal despair, Boethius found that wisdom tended to liberate and that the absolute wisdom of divine providence liberated absolutely. Such wisdom disinfected the corrupting influence of the disordering powers that crushed the best aspirations of persons and civilizations.

Personal and social liberation by wisdom from bondage to the power of misfortune is a theme that comes close to the heart of the Christian religion. The topic thus raised, predestination, occupied Christian intellectuals for many centuries, until (in the 1100s) attention turned to the basic theme of Boethius' philosophical translations and commentaries, the question of genera and species, of universals and particulars.

But more important than this agenda-setting for intellectuals, his way of framing the issues of providence and predestination gave Christians, through widespread studying, copying, and translating of the *Consolation,* a sure-win religion. Whatever happened *had* to be for the best, because God, being all-powerful, managed all that happened to his purpose and end; also being good, he must bring things to a good end. Augustine had guaranteed the eschaton for which Christians waited and had provided the church as the safest waiting room. Boethius demonstrated rationally that when to all appearances the fate of the pious soul or its society looked most hopeless, just then there was available the most hope. Underneath the chaos of human experience lay certain order, grounded in the divine rationality. Things could change, even drastically, but religious confidence was correct in holding that all would work for good in the end.

But to what authority does the book appeal, and whence arises its uncanny influence? There are five answers to that question, four of them simple and the last subtle. First, the book grapples with a perennial question as old as Job and Aristotle and Plato. Boethius reframed the question compactly and boldly: Can a good and just providence allow undeserved misfortune without robbing man of free will? Second, he answered it rationally, neither mysteriously nor miraculously. Misfortune in the long run proves profitable, and (as Howard Patch wrote) "although God never for an instant loses control of the whole universe, mankind also has a sufficient degree of free will to retain moral responsibility."[15] Third, Boethius made the question and the answer personal as well as historical, and did so in uncommonly poignant personal and historical circumstances. Fourth, the obvious debt to Plato, Aristotle, Neoplatonism, and the Stoics lent authority.

These reasons, however, do not account for the book's *Christian* authority, for its appeal to monarchs like Alfred and Elizabeth I, to poets like Dante and Chaucer, to theologians like Thomas Aquinas and Albertus Magnus, and to many more. Hauntingly absent is the figure of Christ and its authority for Christians—or is the absence only apparent? When Lady Philosophy cured her pupil of self-pity, she persuaded him to elevate his thought to the divine. He fervently prayed to God, maker of heaven and earth, who governed the world with eternal reason.

The prayer occupies the famous ninth poem of the third book. No doubt, this poem derives from the first part of Plato's *Timaeus;* the text admits as much. But no doubt also, as medieval commentators knew what Patch reiterated, "These verses seem closer to Christian hymns than to Greek poetry. Touched with Platonism they doubtless are, but with something more."[16]

The "something more" is that the prayer is implicitly framed by the trinitarian and christological belief that Christians were affirming in their creeds, a faith here veiled in allusions instead of being spelled out in traditional terms. Rather, Boethius cast the Christian myth in the metaphors of classical philosophy. Wisdom raises his spirit to the seat of the heavenly father, creator of heaven and earth and all things visible and invisible, at which seat sits the light of reason. To Boethius is given the vision of the divine beginning and end and a vision also of the divine reason who is the bearer (*vector*), the leader (*dux*), and the pathway (*semita*) of human existence amidst its perplexities.

Boethius is inspired by wisdom (spirit) to approach the divine reason (logos) who is the way, the truth, and the life, the alpha and the omega, and thus he comes to know the coinherence of mercy and justice in the creator (father) of the universe. We can be confident about this trinitarianism because an earlier, obscure writing by Boethius shows that he had studied Augustine's great work, *De Trinitate,* and analyzed it by means of Aristotelian logic. There Augustine's three-in-one that God *is* stamps its image on creation and human experience as something creatures *have.* Boethius was enough taken with this notion, which has profoundly shaped Latin Christianity and its derivatives, to ring a change on it in terms of eternity and time; God *is* eternal and His creatures may *have* perpetual life.[17]

As to the presence of Christ, the *Consolation* gives only hints of Boethius' experience. He had, however, written a brief tract refuting two already condemned views of Christ, Nestorius' doctrine of two natures (and two persons), and Eutyches' teaching that there was one nature after the union of persons. The Catholic teaching that prevailed in the west and that Boethius preferred assigned Christ two natures, divine and human, in one person. Boethius liked the same middle way in doctrine as he liked in logic and in virtue. More important, this little study brought Boethius to his definition of "person" as "The individual substance of a rational nature" (*naturae rationabilis individua substantia*), a phrase cherished by theologians down to Karl Barth: "Person is the single rational individual essence."[18]

Therefore there are enough pieces, if not all that we might like, to the puzzle of how Christ appeared to Boethius. Christ was the perfection of personhood, one, individual, rational substance; his two natures, the rational nature of deity and the rational nature of humanity, set him midway between the extremes, mediating each to the other. On this reading, then, Lady Philosophy in the *Consolation* merges into the figure of the logos,

Christ. She embodies divine rationality and human rationality. As a person uniting the two she is able to bring each to the other. The way, the truth, and the life constituted reason or logos. Boethius' Christ focused the rationality of the Greeks and the order of the Romans upon the problems of Christians facing the barbarians by revealing the rationality of God and the order of his providence. Chaos is ordered by reason, not coercive force, and the authority of that order is its rationality.

The Christ of Latin theodicy represented order and reason, whether one looks for that figure in Augustine's *City of God,* in Paulus Orosius' history, in the chronicles of Isidore of Seville and the Venerable Bede, or in the works of any other Christian orderer of worldly chaos and calamity down through those of Otto of Freising and the great scholastics. For making that Christ of theodicy speak to personal as well as social crises, the philosophy of Boethius stands unrivaled. The Christ of theodicy guaranteed that when things were not as they should be, the way they were was ultimately for the best because God turned every circumstance to his providential plan. The Christ of theodicy also guaranteed that this plan did not rule out, though it might overrule, human freedom, responsibility, and action. Men and women could and should strive to make things come to be as they should be; namely, imbued by the same reason and the same order. The Christ of theodicy was the simultaneous, perfect embodiment in one person of divine reason and human reason, divine order and human order.

BYZANTINE CHRIST

The theodicy of Boethius, invoking the figure of Christ as the union of divine and human order and reason, engendered hope and confidence throughout the period under consideration. In a word, he made the quest for order significant whether or not it was successful. When Theodoric died (in 526) much of the old western empire owed him loyalty, but there was no successor. The very next year brought to the imperial throne in Constantinople the astute and ambitious Justinian I, who reigned nearly four decades. He aspired and schemed to bring western Europe under his rule and thus to reunite what Diocletian had put asunder.

The effort proved costly to the remaining Romans and to the barbarians. Italy was again a Byzantine province (by 552) but only until the invasion (in 568) of the Lombards. The brutal wars that brought reunion under an exarch at Ravenna "ruined Italy, and especially Rome, as no German invasion had ever ruined it."[19] A plague struck the peninsula. Paul the Deacon described the scene when "the dwellings were left deserted by their inhabitants, and the dogs only kept house. The flocks remained alone in the pastures with no shepherd at hand. You might see villas or fortified places lately filled with crowds of men, and on the next day, all had departed and everything was in utter silence. Sons fled, leaving the corpses of their parents unburied; parents forgetful of their duty abandoned their children in raging fever. . . . You might see the world brought back to its ancient silence: no voice in the field; no whistling of shepherds; . . . there were no footsteps of passers by, . . . and human habitations had become places of refuge for wild beasts."[20]

Expulsion of the Ostrogoths left northern Italy ripe for the Lombards and the Roman provinces ripe for the popes. Ravenna alone exhibited the culture of Byzantium. The reconquest of North Africa, brief as it was, prepared the way for the wildfire spread of Islam in the next century, not only along that shore of the Romans' lake but into Spain and northward to its mountainous frontier with the Franks.

But if Justinian churned the waters of change in the west, much more did he freeze the river of history in the east. Byzantium's political stability is hard for westerners to conceive. From Zeno the Isaurian (in 474) through Justinian ran a continuous dynasty for nearly six centuries, barely punctuated (from 797 to 802) by the Empress Irene. Allowing for the renewal of that line by Isaac Comnenus (in 1057) and by Isaac Angelus (in 1185), and overlooking the crusaders' Latin kingdom of Constantinople (from 1204 to 1261), the continuity reaches to the capture (in 1453) of the city by Turkish Muslims.

As to Christianity in the east, Justinian helped fix a holy tradition that would endure for many more centuries in the "third Rome" (Moscow) and in the national churches of modern Eastern Orthodoxy. Justinian's ecumenical council (of 553) only affirmed the doctrines he, as head of the church, already favored. It condemned the teachers and teaching he had earlier condemned, even theologians who had received approval by name at the council in Chalcedon a hundred years before. His council is counted the fifth of the seven that Orthodox Christians regard as normative for all time, but the sixth and seventh councils settled their controversies by appeal to the tradition that Justinian's had defined.

That holy tradition centered spirituality on a Christ in whom humanness melted into and was absorbed by divinity. Justinian portrayed this spirituality in stone in the great church he built in the capital. Hagia Sophia (meaning Holy Wisdom) had been the name of Constantine's church on the same site. Thus the new building invoked political as well as religious tradition for what it newly represented. Just as the Christ who begets Orthodox spirituality is the divine, perfect person who has taken up into himself flawed, finite, human personhood and rendered it flawless and infinite, so the perfect masonry dome, representing the infinite, joins with and draws into itself the rectangular, finite, cross-shaped basilica.

The Orthodox Christ was a mystery requiring intricate and subtle theological skill to explain how his human nature was engulfed into his divine nature. Similarly it took architectural and engineering inventiveness to fasten a true dome to four columns set in a square. The Romans who built the Pantheon's true dome needed simply a perpendicular, cylindrical support. Justinian's architects solved a more intricate problem of design. First they planned a dome with a diameter equal to the diagonal of the square of columns on which it was to rest. This dome must extend far beyond the sides of the square. Slicing off these exten-

sions *vertically* made the two figures join perfectly, but the
dome was no longer complete. Rather, part of a dome rested on
arches made by the vertical slicing. Slicing it again, this time
horizontally just above the arches, created a circular base to
which a true and complete dome was perfectly joined.[21]

Now the hemisphere of the dome, representing divine perfection and infinity, joined completely with and visually drew into
itself the perpendicular, right-angled, cubical form, representing
human imperfection and finitude. The church in its design proclaimed the Byzantine Christ that its ornamentation displayed.
Although the agreed-upon formulas of doctrine were the same
for east and west, the Latin Christ was one in whom the human
nature called distinct attention to itself as much as, and distinct
from, the divine nature. Eastern Christianity always tended to
emphasize the divine logos as subsuming the humanity. The doctrine about Christ that both accepted was being interpreted with
this emphasis by Leontius of Byzantium, so that Christ's personal
humanity was included in his divine substance, just when Justinian built Hagia Sophia.

The Byzantine historian, Procopius, was another contemporary of Justinian who described many of the emperor's buildings.
He marveled at the brightness of Hagia Sophia's interior, resort-
ing to language about Christ in describing what he beheld: "it
abounds exceedingly in sunlight and in the reflection of the sun's
rays from the marble. Indeed one might say that its interior is
not illuminated from without by the sun, but that the radiance
comes into being within it, such an abundance of light bathes the
shrine."[22] This light streams from heaven through forty win-
dows around the base of the high dome, giving the impression
that the dome floats in thin air. The supporting structure seems
to ascend toward the source of light. In eastern spirituality there
was special emphasis on Christ as light of the world, the light
that shines in darkness and is not engulfed by the finitude it
illumines.

Hagia Sophia further attests the inwardness of this spirituality.
The building is massive, with multiple, half-domed apses added

to the central form. But the exterior is undistinguished, while the interior mosaics, made of bits of glass and stone applied to walls and ceiling, are dazzling. Against their ethereal blue and gold backgrounds are decorations, symbols, inscriptions to Justinian and Constantine, angelic figures, in short, the heavenly host. Into the finite world that they decorate floods the light of the world; the inner life of those whom this Christ redeemed was irradiated by him and in turn radiated his glory. Western basilicas of the time faced outward on the world and admitted one only to send one forth again into that world. Hagia Sophia drew creation within itself where the world became illumined, glorified, and redeemed, made stable against the flux of history.

Thus the architectural innovation of the true dome functioned to fasten attention on holy tradition. In five short years ingenious Greek architects and 10,000 laborers built the church, using the emperor's sponsorship and treasury to symbolize the stability and continuity of Byzantine spirituality and imperium. Holy tradition in the east embodied the only true spirituality and displayed its founder-exemplar. Whatever revised that tradition or changed that exemplar became by virtue of its novelty suspect and spurious. Thus Justinian fixed orthodox spirituality in the east by imperial decrees.

For the west he decreed (in 554) restoration of Roman rule, resuming free distribution of grain to soldiers and citizens, reviving the educational system, and organizing a bureaucracy to be manned by Greeks. But the real effects of the decree in the west were minor, for (in Peter Llewellyn's words) "Gregory the Great, at the end of the century, was still exercising through his agents a strict protection of Italian rights."[23]

PRELACY

Gregory brought to historical reality Augustine's vision of the church as the renovated Rome, giving western Christianity its own universal imperium in the institution of the Roman curia and in the persons of the popes. To this end Gregory worked out and put into operation a new justification of power and authority whereby the Christian ruler ruled in the place of Christ over Christian people according to Christ's rules. In response to the chaos attending the empire's fall Gregory turned to Christ as the source and guide of power by which to reorder the world.

Nobody knew better than Gregory how thoroughly power could corrupt those who exercised it over others or how thoroughly such corrupt power depraved those over whom it was exercised. Gregory by age twelve had seen Rome captured (in 545 or 546) by the Gothic King Totila, who (rightly) blamed the Byzantines for the Italians' troubles. Then Justinian's brilliant General Belisarius rewon the city, only to lose it again to Totila, from whom it was taken again by the Byzantine General Narses. Each time rule changed the cost of conquest was levied on those conquered. Gregory recorded that Benedict of Nursia in those days debated a priest on the fine point of whether Rome would be ruined by its conquerors or "crumble upon its foundations."[24] When Totila first took the city, only five hundred males survived and eight of these were slaughtered at St. Peter's Basilica, where they had taken refuge. Boethius' widow, Rusticiana, was seen begging in the streets. When Narses retook Rome, "Italy lay exhausted, devastated but liberated" from Gothic rule. After Justinian died (in 565), Narses abused his command so badly that Roman delegates asked the emperor Justin (in 567) to dismiss the general because they preferred Gothic slavery to his tyranny. In the next year the Lombards invaded northern Italy and their Duke Faroald I of Spoleto (in 579) "had moved to besiege Rome itself." In that year Pelagius II, himself a German, succeeded Benedict I as pope and prophetically turned his attention to the Franks whom he regarded as "the divinely appointed neighbours and helpers of this city." This pope's representative at Tiberius' imperial court in Constantinople was Gregory, the young aristocrat and former prefect of Rome now turned monk.

At the capital Gregory learned how the emperor's devious negotiations with barbarian kings were aimed at saving the empire from the Lombards; Roman hopes lay elsewhere. Pelagius (in

586) recalled Gregory to Rome, where he survived the terrible flood (in 589) of the Tiber. The ensuing plague took Pelagius. Gregory was his secretary, and naming a successor took no deliberation. As pope until his death (in 604) Gregory reorganized the ecclesiastical, civil, economic, and military administration of the city and its provinces. He also extended papal influence over all Italy, and began to spread throughout Europe a new social order built on the organizing power of the Roman church.

Gregory perforce began his ordering activities at home. Most of the old Roman senatorial families had fled to the east, giving or bequeathing their depleted estates to the church. No senate was to be found. No imperial resources could be counted on. Gregory himself guided Rome and Italy toward precarious recovery in the face of renewed Lombard sieges. He literally measured the wealth of the Roman church by what it distributed to the poor and needy. He ruled it and its lands and above all its sacred city. From that power base he made himself pope of the northern nations, extending Roman Christianity even to England. He reformed temporal and spiritual administration on his Christian theory of power, which he codified into rules for ruling. To bishops and through them to all Europe he addressed the *Pastoral Rule* (*Regula Pastoralis*). Llewellyn wisely called the work "the key to a bishop's life, and so to civilization in the succeeding centuries," thus underscoring the dictum of the French historian, Montalembert, that "this book gave form and life to the entire hierarchical body, and made the bishops who have made modern nations."[25]

The book takes its basic ideas from the monasticism that enchanted Gregory, in particular the monasticism that Benedict of Nursia had set down earlier in the century in the rule of life for his commune in Monte Cassino.[26] During the decade before Gregory became pope, Lombards sacked that monastery. Its monks moved to Rome. On their pattern Gregory governed his own monasteries, and he sent the rule with the monks who accompanied a Benedictine named Augustine to Canterbury in Britain. There the Benedictine regimen combined with the missionary principles of the older Celtic monasticism to spur the evangelization of Germany and France. Gregory set out to organize the whole church of the west into a vast monastery on Benedictine principles under the pope at Rome, with the aim of making for Europe a monastic civilization.

In converting Benedict's rule into the civilizing, ordering principle of a society of Christian nations, Gregory brought two main features of the regimen to the fore and muted another one. Drawing partly on the eastern monastic rule of Basil and very heavily on the writings of Cassian, Benedict planned for each commune's economic self-sufficiency as the basis of its life of corporate and personal meditation on scripture. The Egyptian hermitages and communes that Cassian visited and described had learned that the values of economic independence carried over into the monks' actual and psychological independence from the world and interdependence upon one another.

Second, Benedict emphasized the authority of the elected abbot, who himself must obey the rules of which he was interpreter and administrator. Third, the monks must keep residence in one place (*stabilitas loci*); this made their fellow monks into lifelong companions in seeking holiness and it turned the monastic buildings and lands into their sacred, spatial universe. Vows of obedience, of stability, and particularly of converting one's life to God provided hourly, daily, yearly agendas to sanctify the monks' time. Only implicit were the familiar but later vows of poverty and chastity, for the aim of economic self-sufficiency implied poverty and stability involved chastity.

In modeling his administration of the church on these lines Gregory expanded the first two principles. Central to his theory and practice were economic self-sufficiency and obedience by all, including the ruler, to the rule. All were to share in producing and consuming goods cooperatively, from each according to his ability and to each according to his need. The ruler's power remained absolute only so long as he fashioned his own life according to holy rules. The principle of stability took care of itself in a society that had largely bound itself to the land.

Over this planned monastic civilization Gregory held supreme power as abbot of Europe. To be sure, in letters he addressed the emperor in the east as "lord" (*dominus*). Yet he staunchly repudiated the claim (in 595) of the patriarch of Constantinople to the title, "universal patriarch." Western kings he called his sons (*filii*), for his Roman church held pre-eminence traditionally over the Christian churches and by Gregory's enlargement over the entire society of Christian republics in the west. Reaching beyond the old Roman territories still under imperial claims, as Walter Ullmann wrote, "Gregory I's *societas reipublicae christianae* over which the Roman Church exercises its *principatus* unimpeded by considerations of a constitutional nature, is the prophetic vision of medieval Europe." Again, when Gregory first took the papal title, "servant of the servants of God" (*servus servorum Dei*), he adroitly reinforced his theory of power and achieved "an inverted exaltation of his office." For as pope he mediated (in Voegelin's phrase) "divine-cosmic order to the existence of man in society and history," at least throughout western Europe.[27] He wielded Peter's authority. To Christ alone was he subordinate and to the standards of Christly ruling he held himself and his bishops.

Gregory's was a true innovation in the legitimation, indeed the sanctification, of the authority of certain persons to rule others. On the assumption that all Europeans would become Catholic Christians he was legitimating the authority and power of one person over all others. This breakthrough symbolized the emergence of a new form of human existence. The emperors after Octavian and those in the east after ·Diocletian and Constantine drew their authority, on Octavian's theory, from the rulers' *arētē*—their virtue, their nobility, their excellence, their valor, the sum of good qualities that comprise character. Particularly the military despots from Commodus through Carus in the century (from 180 to 283) after the Antonines learned that to be found mean and despicable was to erode the power base of *arētē* and to be thrown back from internal authority onto external coercion. Coercion only made one all the meaner and more despicable.

Gregory regrounded this internal authority in Christian holiness, exhibited not as personal *arētē* but as service to Christ and conformity to Christ's standards. Aware of the conflict between his theory and that of the empire, he reminded the emperor Maurice that Constantine (as reported by Rufinus) had told the bishops in council at Nicaea, "You are gods, constituted by the true God; it is not right that we sit in judgment over gods."[28] Little does it matter whether Rufinus quoted Constantine correctly when both parties assumed that he had. In the west this new derivation of power from the Christian deity commended itself to popes, bishops, abbots. It also attracted kings of the European nations, whose authority thereby received a sanction sufficient to hallow their use of force to protect and advance Christendom.

The source of this power was higher and symbolic access to it was more direct than anything the Byzantine emperors possessed. They could only stand on their brief tradition as Christian rulers and wish they controlled the west. More than a century after Gregory's death, Pope Gregory II wrote Emperor Leo the Isaurian, "We derive our power and authority from the prince of the apostles, Peter, and we could, if we wished, pronounce judgment upon you, but you have already pronounced judgment on yourself and on your counsellors: and you and they may just as well remain accursed."[29] Leo the Isaurian had first threatened to prosecute Gregory II for treason for refusing to pay taxes; he then offered to abstain if the pope would back Leo's opposition to the veneration of images, then a topic of heated debate in Byzantium. The encounter marks the epoch's most crucial confrontation between popes and eastern emperors and indicates at once the permanent emancipation of the papacy from that imperial interference and the spiritual primacy of the popes over the western kingdoms.

That is not to say every monarch of western Europe supinely

did as the pope dictated, for the relation between spiritual and temporal sovereignty was left clouded by both Gregory I and Gregory II. It is to say, however, that down through the empire of Charlemagne and to the coronation of Otto I as Holy Roman Emperor (in 962), the rooting of earthly rule, both temporal and spiritual, in the divine authority remained the effective function of popes bearing Christ's commission through Peter to oversee all Christians. The Greek Leo had answered Gregory II's rebuffs in four words that characterize caesaro-papism in the east: "I am king and priest" (*basileus kai hiereus eimi*).[30] To be sure, Charlemagne as Frankish emperor and Otto I as German king bore the title *sacerdos,* or priest, meaning that they had power to make ecclesiastical appointments and that by virtue of the anointing ceremonies of coronation they were persons bearing sacred authority. But the westerners' authority came from Christ through, not over or around, his church and its popes.

The papacy could embody and transmit divinely grounded imperium to rulers because Gregory the Great made good his claim to be not the source but the conduit of Christ's authority over God's people. The later medieval popes made less and less of the distinction between fount and channel, but they never entirely forgot that they were servants to the servants of God and vicars of Christ, sacred in office and holy in person, but not themselves divine.

Gregory's *Pastoral Rule* drew this distinction very clearly. In large part he instructed bishops to take careful note of the particular circumstances of persons they admonished and to adjust the admonition to the case: poor and rich, joyful and sad, servants and masters, wise and dull, impudent and bashful, forward and fainthearted, impatient and patient, kindly disposed and envious, simple and crafty, healthy and sick, fearful and brash, silent and talkative, slothful and hasty, meek and passionate, humble and haughty, obstinate and fickle—the list continues. All this practical advice, sensitive to the varying conditions and characteristics of the human situation, followed from the central ideal of authority and its administration on behalf of Christ over Christians, by the godly to the end of godliness.

That theme, like the entire book, is bolstered by copious scriptural citations, interpreted in a richly and sometimes mystifyingly allegorical way. To take a random example, when Psalm 67:23 says, "Let their eyes be blinded that they see not, and ever bow thou down their backs," the bald text simply asks God to curse the psalmist's enemies. Gregory leaps entirely over the literal meaning; for him, when rulers whose eyes spied out the course of affairs lost the light of sound knowledge, the ruled were bowed down by the burden of sin.[31] For medieval readers this way of mining the Bible for hidden meanings educed the most cherished gems of all, the mystical or spiritual messages that the deity had tucked into the literal words of the text. We grasp what Gregory meant not by discounting but by weighting these allegories, regardless of literal meanings. Gregory spiritualized the scriptures by way of grounding his new theory of power in the Bible's author, Christ, who called himself "the Truth."

The Pastoral Rule has enjoyed no great popularity in modern times, but for many centuries it provided the most satisfactory, the most appealing, the most Christian theory and program of politics. Power was to be held suspect, not praised; power was to be accepted as a burden by men sufficiently wise and humble to wield it responsibly, not to be sought by men ambitious for fame. Boethius had taught, and Gregory learned well, that glory and honor and praise and high position provided delusions of happiness that eventually crumbled into misery. But Boethius wrote as one frustrated and crushed by chaos. Gregory wrote as one bringing order. Both took the long view and the humble stance. Theodicy gave to medieval Europe a Christian way of coping with occasions of failure; prelacy gave them a means of coping with occasions of success.

Gregory's scheme of prelacy can be understood only by bearing in mind the vast change that took place as the citified empire of antiquity yielded to an agrarian and in some ways already feudal world. City life flourished on the acts of individual citizens in relating themselves directly and publicly to government. Those acts expressed the ideal of the city (*polis*) out of which Alexander and then Octavianus built the Mediterranean-European world. This mode of life gave way to agrarian life centered on land, which had to be owned and used, and on services, which had to be rendered and rewarded. With the money economy largely in default in the west, the ownership of vast lands fell into relatively few hands. Papal estates of enormous expanse had grown, as noted above, to the point that upon taking office Gregory automatically became the richest person in Latin Europe. The people who managed and tilled his holdings required sustenance and safety, for which they pledged labor and loyalty. Only a complex, many-storied hierarchy could articulate the system in which indirect and essentially private relations connected people with government. The underlying ideal unabashedly set some persons over others, and pre-eminence culminated in Christ's vice-regent on earth, the father (pope = *papa,* abbot = *abba*) of the world.

Pre-eminence in authority over others belonged to the few, according to Gregory, "who enjoy special gifts of virtue, and for the training of others are exalted with great endowments, who are clean by the love of chastity, powerful by the strength of temperance, filled with the richest food of doctrine, humble through the long-suffering of patience, upright with the courage of authority, gentle through the grace of kindness, strict with the severity of righteousness" (1:5). These virtues conferred no privilege, but great responsibility—indeed, the burdensome obligation to exercise power. Refusing that obligation meant forfeiting the virtues, which in combination were nurtured by the ruling that they prepared one for. Still, the role was dangerous, for whoever ruled was tempted to misrule. He who "is panting for the summit of authority, feedeth himself in the secret mediations of his thoughts on the subjection of others, rejoiceth in his own praise, lifteth up his heart to honour, and exulteth in the abundance of affluence" (1:8).

But personal virtues, however outstanding, were themselves

insufficient to sanitize the corrupting tendency of power. There must also be vocation, a calling by God to exercise authority vicariously. Gregory's example here is Moses, who "would have been proud if he had undertaken the guidance of an innumerable people without trembling; and again, he would have shewn himself proud if he had refused to obey the command of his Creator" (1:7). The summons is at once to virtue and to authority. By nature the ruler was no better than others, for "nature made all men equal." But while he was to "be a companion of well-doers by lowliness," he should also be "aroused against the sins of transgressors by the zeal of righteousness." A ruler must never put himself above his virtuous subjects in virtue but in the face of wickedness he must "acknowledge at once the power of his preeminence." Therefore, "all who are in authority should consider in themselves, not the power of their order, but the equality of their condition; and delight not to be set over men, but to be useful to them" (2:6).

What Gregory meant by "ruler" was a bishop. The bishops of his day, however, ruled in the temporal as well as in the spiritual realms. The book thus treated sacred governance (*regimen sacer*) at several levels—governance over sacred people by sacred officers, governance in the sacred office of bishop, and general governance that was sacred because power and authority derived from deity. In all three meanings Gregory spoke of the charge, the business, and the weight of governing, which issued in preeminence of office over others (*principatus officio,* and *praeesse ceteris* or *praeferri ceteris*).

Such pre-eminence made for actual inequality between ruler and ruled, even though all men were by nature equal. Therefore, the pride of wishing to be feared by natural equals was unnatural and wrong. But it was right for the ruler to be feared by subjects who had little fear of God. There was no pride involved when persons in authority elicited fear not for their own glory but for God's, not for their own welfare but for their subjects'. The most corrupting influence of authority was the pride of high station and its prerogatives, the pride of looking down on those who had no choice but to look up. "He, in truth, ordereth this power well who knoweth both how to hold it and how to fight against it: he ordereth it well who knoweth to be lifted up by it above transgressions, and knoweth with it to be settled in equality with the rest" (2:6).

Authority exercised in the place of Christ remained under Christ provided it was exercised as Christ's own authority. Authority over the godly consisted in being godly with them and for their benefit. Authority over the ungodly consisted in resisting their ungodliness with every means to the end of making them more godly.

Therefore, the ruler must do not what *pleased* the ruled but what *ought* to please them. One learned the difference by studying and meditating on scripture, the sacred rules by which all ought to live. Like Benedict's abbot, the discipliner was under the discipline by which he disciplined others. As Heer wrote, "Benedict's Rule was the first constitutional charter of Western Europe," and in the monasteries "the monks became the first Europeans."[32] But the one who spread that charter beyond the monastic enclaves to the whole church and to European society at large was Gregory, the first monk to occupy the throne of Peter and the first pope to establish that throne's pre-eminence over the Latin, Teutonic, and Celtic peoples of Europe.

The primacy extended through the hierarchical grades of monks and secular clergy into the governance of the entire church, including its lands and all who cultivated and rented them. Gregory organized the papal patrimonies in a way that began to anticipate the feudal polity and manorial economy that came to prevail two centuries later. His prelacy devolved its authority down several strata of governance. The patrimonies lay throughout the Italian peninsula and extended to the islands, prominently in Sicily, and as far afield as Dalmatia, the Gallic territories of Marseilles and Arles, and North Africa near Carthage. Some lands were cultivated, mostly for grain and olive crops. Others were leased. For each patrimony the chief governor, directly responsible to the pope, was a ruler (*rector* or *defensor*). Gregory filled these high offices with clergy who already owed him obedience. Nevertheless, rectors and defensors took special oaths before him, vowing that they would faithfully administer the lands, benefit the church, protect the poor, and serve the pope. As his agents they even checked up on the bishops in their regions. These rulers were organized into a college with its own hierarchy, as were Gregory's subdeacons and lay notaries. The rector or defensor of a patrimony ruled its managers (*actores* or *actionarii*), who leased the lands and collected the revenues and produce. They in turn ruled the "family of the church." To the family belonged the serfs (*coloni* or *rustici*), who cultivated the soil, and the slaves, who provided labor. Down low in the chain of command, serfs and slaves ruled their wives and children, who at the end of the line ruled the domestic animals.[33]

While the theory of virtuous rule over the virtuous and forcible rule against vice prevailed at each level, the degree of virtue expected and achieved diminished sharply down the grades. Such is the human condition. "For, as I remember to have said in my books of Morals, it is clear that nature made all men equal; but, through the variety in the order of their merits, guilt putteth one behind another" (2:6). Below the rectors and defensors, to judge from Gregory's letters, guilt increased by leaps and bounds down the ladder of managers. The family of the church suffered much abuse. By law even the serfs (not the slaves) could appeal decisions of their rulers all the way to the pope, but legal right did not carry ability to obtain redress. The pope's authority capped an enormous pyramid, and there could be only one pope. Gregory could hardly suffuse the whole system with his own high standards of personal virtue and official justice. He tried mightily, working so hard that he harmed his health and became enervated by a persistent, low fever.

Both in running the church proper with its patrimonies and in ruling Rome with its provinces, Gregory lived up to the standards of justice and generosity for which he was long remembered as the finest exemplar of his system of power. He supervised elections of bishops and now and again vetoed them. He consecrated at Rome the bishops of the Italian dioceses, except that the archbishops of Ravenna and Milan consecrated their assistants (suffragans). His immediate successor, Sabinian, facing a famine and losses by flood of church grains stored in Rome, sold the grain that Gregory had distributed free and became so unpopular that his funeral cortège was stoned. Gregory even appeared to Sabinian in a vision and denounced his lack of charity.[34]

The recorded generosities of Gregory would fill a book. For the bread and circuses of the pagan emperors he substituted the bread and charity of the best popes. He begged correspondents to send clothing for the three thousand nuns whom the Roman church was supporting. What the patrimonies produced through the labors of worthy and unworthy persons belonged to the deserving poor. He gave to institutions as well as to individuals. He sent money, wine, oil, and fowl to an oratory in Palermo. He sent ten mares and a stallion to a hospital in Sicily. He sent money, cloaks, blankets, and beds to monks at distant Mount Sinai. An abbot in Isauria asked fifty solidi for his monks' needs, then feared the request was excessive and reduced it to forty. Gregory responded, "Since you have been so considerate of our property, we must not be less considerate towards you. We have sent you, therefore, 50 solidi; and for fear this should not be enough, we have added 10 more; and lest even that should not suffice, we have sent you 12 more in addition. And herein we recognize your love for us, that you place full confidence in us, as you ought to do."[35] A favorite project was the ransoming of Christians taken captive by the Lombards. Gregory authorized the bishop at Fanum Fortunae (modern Fano) to sell the sacred communion vessels to pay ransoms.[36]

Charity tested the virtue of rulers. Concrete deeds of loving the neighbor, the essence of Christ's rules, sanitized authority and power. At the time of Gregory's birth, as noted, Cassiodorus had added to the duties of his monks the stewardship of learning and culture. Quite as importantly for medieval Europe, Gregory added physical and spiritual care for the needy to the duties of the entire church, secular and monastic. He charged monks with secular responsibility and he monasticized the secular church, all to increase charity and make power safe. He also constantly checked up on those thus charged. Suspicion of misfeasance among his administrators pervades his letters, just as credulity about visions and miracles pervades his *Dialogues*. He commended a young widow, so passionate that her physicians said if she did not remarry she would sprout a beard, for choosing chastity in a nunnery, for preferring the heavenly marriage that begins in grief and ends in joy over the fleshly marriage that begins in joy and ends in grief. This Galla, sister of Boethius' widow, Rusticiana, grew her beard but did not mind the deformity, and she died from cancer of the breast with a vision before her eyes of St. Peter welcoming her into heaven.[37]

But all that Gregory did and wrote was written and done to extend the society of Christian republics under the headship of the pope. His most famous missionary endeavor of sending a band of some forty monks to bring England into the papal fold should not overshadow other efforts to convert to Roman Christianity pagans and heretics in Gaul, Africa, the Italian islands, and the Lombard regions of northern Italy.

Gregory became and made the subsequent popes the grantor and the guarantor of sacred power in western Christendom. The oft-quoted summary by Homes Dudden bears repeating. "Already we find the Bishop of Rome a political power, a temporal prince. He appoints governors to cities, he issues orders to generals, he provides the munition of war, he makes a private peace, he sends ambassadors to negotiate with the Lombard king, he determines with sovereign authority what must be done in Rome, he encroaches without the slightest hesitation on the rights and privileges of the civil government."[38] And beyond Rome, he ruled Christ's people throughout Europe. He founded Latin Christendom and made himself and subsequent popes its indispensable symbolic head, if after him not always its actual governor.

What Gregory exemplified—and what was emulated throughout Europe—was nothing less than the combination of Christ's authority and charity on earth. Christ's caring for the poor and needy was implicit in the image of the Good Shepherd. Gregory's thought and piety joined to that figure one of a victorious and all-powerful ruler, the divine source of human rule. Official doctrine about Christ had been settled by his day to the satisfaction of the western church in the formula (in 451) of the council in Chalcedon. Gregory stood with this orthodoxy, adding the important feature of Christ's having won the right to rule mankind.

The devil had won that governance, as Gregory construed the myth, first by successfully tempting Adam and Eve and then by relying on God's justice to sentence them to live under Satan's sway. The evil one became ambitious and tried to capture the second representative of mankind, Christ incarnate, in his deceptively weak, human form. The ploy failed. With clear justice God then took away Satan's power to rule mankind and conferred it on the victor. In a word, "In striking Him over whom he had no rights," Satan "lost the power of striking those over whom he had rights."[39] Gregory's Christ recovered dominion not only by this battle with Satan, in which he died and rose again, but also by teaching how men and women should live and by living out what he taught. Human redemption consisted, then, in serving and in ruling for Christ instead of for Satan, in suffering with and for him who became king through suffering, and in obeying this divine-human king's commands.

In commissioning Peter, Christ had entrusted the administration of his governance to the Roman church through the popes. But Christian authority required the validation of charity. To guard against pride and ambition, which prompted the abuse of authority, Gregory would grant nobody, not even the most saintly, full assurance of personal redemption. Nobody could be sure he or she had done enough penance or enough good works to rest comfortably in the hope of salvation. "The hope [*anchora*] of the heart is the weight of fear [*timor*]." Again, "Hope [*spes*] and fear [*formido*] should be unceasingly united in a sinner's heart."[40] Ritualized as a sacrament, penance centered on attrition, the fear of punishment for sin. The discipline of charity required good works as a condition of salvation.

Of course, these visible signs of the probability of salvation certified the right to exercise governance over others. Christ both legitimated and delegated his power over Christian people to rulers who lived Christian lives and ruled by Christian rules. Thus Christ became the super-king, victorious against the devil, reigning over the universe from a heavenly throne and establishing the earthly throne of Peter from which further delegations were made to kings, bishops, and abbots.

One of several hymns attributed to Gregory, the one Luther called the best of all hymns, is addressed to King Christ, maker of all (*Rex Christe, Factor omnium*), and whether or not Gregory composed it the attribution accurately tells who Christ was for him and for the Christian style of life he exemplified.[41] So does the later mosaic that now adorns what had been Gregory's headquarters in Rome, depicting St. Peter enthroned as Christ's earthly vicar, wearing the stole that symbolized his service to the heavenly ruler, bestowing the pallium on Pope Leo III, and giving a banner to Charlemagne whom Leo would crown emperor of Christendom.

CHRISTS

To Gregory's regal Christ, the winner, bestower, and norm of rule over Christians, is to be traced the right and power of Charlemagne to unify the Germanic kingdoms under one Christain emperor. For it was Gregory's idea "of the Christian empire, in which the duties of a ruler are prescribed by religion" that "became common in Charlemagne's reign."[42] The two centuries between Gregory's death (in 604) and Charlemagne's coronation (in 800) brought to Peter's chair nobody whose influence compared with Gregory's, yet everybody in this succession enjoyed the pre-eminence and exercised the patronage he established. A succession of refugee Greeks (in the 600s) used the chair to promote learning and the copying of documents. A Syrian from Antioch named Sergius I (pope from 687 to 701) reorganized the *Schola Cantorum* traditionally credited to Gregory. This body of singers expressed the awe and solemnity of papal prestige. Similar choral groups became popular in the courts of northern Europe. Llewellyn points out that "It was from the *Schola* that the imageries of sovereignty spread in the eighth century to the the Frankish kingdoms."[43]

More than anybody since his namesake, Gregory II (pope from 715 to 731) extended the influence of Roman Christianity into the territories of Germany through the labors of the English bishop, Boniface. Gregory's theory of power guided Zacharias (pope from 741 to 752) in advising Pepin, Charlemagne's father, that because he bore responsibility for rule as major domo he deserved the title of king. Sacred authority and sacred power flowed in the holy oil with which Boniface anointed Pepin king (in 751), a procedure that Pope Stephen II repeated three years later. By this act Stephen purchased Pepin's protection of Rome from the Lombards and deflected any further moves the eastern emperors might make to draw the Franks' allegiance away from the west.

At about this time (nobody knows just when), there came into being documents purporting to record an imperial dedication to the popes of the governance of Rome and the western provinces. This "Donation of Constantine" spuriously makes him the donor and Pope Sylvester the donee. Its almost unquestioned acceptance as genuine (except by Otto III) down to the Renaissance shows the extent to which Gregory's legitimation of all power by the church had pervaded the European consciousness, even that of Charlemagne.

Welcome as it would be to know certainly whether Pope Leo III at the Christmas mass in Rome (in 800) surprised the Frankish king or had connived with him and to know also whether Charlemagne in his heart was acknowledging the pope's prelacy and primacy or merely doing what he thought would bolster his power, the fact remains that Leo did bestow the imperial crown and Charlemagne did accept it. Throughout the time of expansion and the era of dismantling the Frankish empire, the regal authority of Christ devolved through popes to bishops and abbots, to kings and emperors, to nobles and landlords, to freemen and serfs. The tables were turned only by the Saxon King Otto I, who became (in 962) the first Holy Roman Emperor—if that title means that the emperor's holy rule included the papacy.

Rule on behalf of Christ characterized Charlemagne's conception of himself, particularly when he was successful. The assurance of theodicy that God would bring good from evil comforted him in failure. After several campaigns against the Saxons, he forced their baptism (in 778 and 779) at the point of the sword, against the advice of his counselor Alcuin. He had such great trouble with the wily Widukind's encouragement of paganism among these people that the irate Charlemagne beheaded 4500 Saxons without a hearing. Then he waited for providence. Widukind was baptized (in 785) with Charlemagne his godfather.

Similarly, the king accepted his costly failure to wrest northern Spain from the Saracens, even when his efforts were frustrated in part through an attack on his supply train by Basques who were Christian. Accepting this defeat, he went on to more victories. A king suspicious or unsure of the source of his power might have turned against the pope. And when Charlemagne had so vastly consolidated his rule that he could establish at Aix-la-Chapelle a settled court instead of a peripatetic one, he constructed an octagonal cathedral at his palace in which to give thanks to the Christ whose vicar had crowned him emperor.

In this cathedral Charlemagne's throne and the benches for his court sit high above the altar, the stage on which clergy made thanksgivings and supplications. This arrangement symbolizes the tendency, which only in a later period became a full-blown program, for the emperor to consider his rule an inherent right. Eighteen months before the famous coronation in Rome, Alcuin had written that "the summit of the worldly hierarchy," which had been held at first by the "vicar of the blessed Peter" and next by the eastern emperor "who exercises secular power in the second Rome," now was Charlemagne's by "the royal dignity which our Lord Jesus Christ has reserved for you so that you might govern the Christian people." This dignity "triumphs above the other two dignities, eclipses them in wisdom and surpasses them."[44] Still the dignity came from Christ through Peter, and the person appointed to rule over "the Christian people" had to follow Christian rules, not the sovereign's arbitrary will.

At the coronation in Rome the pope first "adored" Charlemagne by three times prostrating himself and touching his forehead to the ground. Then a number of noblemen acclaimed him three times with the rehearsed greeting, "To Charles Augustus, crowned by God, great and peaceful emperor of the Romans, life and victory."[45] Yet the religion Charlemagne required his subjects to be baptized in and to practice united the society he ruled, and that was the Roman Catholic religion with the pope at its head. Monks and secular clergy, not then sharply distinguished, owed their ordinations and their spiritual marching orders to the pope. The priests by Charlemagne's direction had to learn the Paternoster, the Creed, rites for exorcising demons, the Book of Penances, the Roman church calendar, the biblical texts for Sundays and holy days, and " 'Roman singing'—the office as it was given in Rome."[46] Each subject must belong to a parish and be taught the true faith and its rules for daily living. People who lived similar lives and prayed to the same God obeyed the same emperor and his minions. Roman Catholic Christianity became the glue that fastened Charlemagne's subjects into a coherent empire.

It remained single and cohesive only as long as the great Charles himself lived. Apparently forgetting that he had wrested rule from his brother Carloman, he divided his holdings among his sons, just as his father and Charles Martel and the Merovingian kings had done. "It is probable," wrote Heer, "that Charlemagne did not regard the title of emperor as heritable in the same way as that of king, but thought that a ruler should obtain it by his own efforts, as he had done."[47] It is certain that Charlemagne's own efforts to obtain it had culminated in his receiving the blessing of the pope. His devotion to the church, to Christianity as the religion of the realm, and to the cultivation of learning under the auspices of that religion are interests that he handed down to his sons as heritable.

He and his immediate successors used their power to uplift and enlighten those subject to them, to promote godliness in accordance with Gregory's plan. They sent missionaries to instruct and to baptize, as Gregory had done. They established monasteries and reformed monastic discipline, as Gregory had done. They ordered every bishop and every monastery to instruct the clergy and would-be clergy "in the psalms, musical notation, chant, the computation of years and seasons, and in grammar; and all books used shall be carefully corrected"—if Gregory had not done so, tradition said he had. They ordered that "bishops shall set up schools where letters and the science of the Scriptures shall be taught; in these schools . . . shall be brought up those to whom the Saviour says with justice: 'Ye are the salt of the earth' "—as Gregory had no opportunity to do but predictably would have done in better times. One of their bishops ordered that "In the villages and townships the priests shall open schools. If any of the faithful entrust their children to them to learn letters, let them not refuse to instruct these children in all charity" and "let them ask no payment."[48]

The more christly the populace could be made, the more christianly power from Christ could be exercised over them. Making people christly involved education, and education involved scholarship. Alcuin sought accurate manuscript sources and had copyists double check their work. He taught the leading thinkers of the next generation, drilling them in grammar and in scripture, in Boethius and in Augustine. These pupils followed his footsteps under Charlemagne's sons.

Thus the legitimation of power that Gregory worked out came to produce a brief but luxurious flowering of Christian learning and culture. Not that the so-called Carolingian renaissance recovered the noetic glories of the Greeks and Romans. It was on the whole as pragmatically designed for holding society under one religious power as was the wheeled plow for tilling the hard soil of northern Europe. The point is that everything the Carolingians undertook was designed to church—the verb must be intensive, to *bechurch*—the people of Europe, to bechurch their behavior, their ethos, their self-consciousness, their loyalties, their institutions, their expectations, their daily lives. This program of bechurching needs to imply very little about the cultivation of warm Christian piety and profound Christian belief. Carolingian society was not so much Christendom as churchdom. Nevertheless, the power that Christ dealt down its hierarchies both temporal and spiritual (so far as the two can be distinguished) drew those who ruled and those who were ruled into a single, earthly, ecclesiastical body of Christ.

As Europe was Christianized, Christianity was Europeanized. When the Carolingian dynasty splintered, there arose Gregorian prelates like Hincmar of Reims (archbishop from 845 to 882) and Nicholas I (pope from 858 to 867), who commanded and corrected princes. By the century's end the church joined the feudal order that it had promoted and it suffered depredations by the Scandinavians from the north and the Magyars from the east whom it had tried to convert. This religious reinforcement of the political and social divisions of Europe, whose brief confederation under Charlemagne split into tribal and feudal duchies, indicates not the specific failure but the general success of Gregorian Christianity. King Christ then devolved his rule through popes not to a strong emperor nor even, in much of Europe, to strong kings, but to territorial bishops and princes and dukes and abbots. This permeation of the more localized cultures by the church became the necessary condition for bringing into being the Holy Roman Empire (in 962) by Otto of Saxony, the new kingdom of France (in 987) by Hugh Capet, and eventually the Norman kingdom of England (in 1066) by William the Conqueror.

That new unification of Europe arose from new crises as well as from the old churching. After the Carolingian federation disintegrated, learning gradually flagged. Monasteries were sacked (in the 900s) by Vikings and Slavs. Raw paganism again entered the European field of vision. Rule fractured into local lordships. Lineages of rulers were broken. There is no way to estimate the number of Latin manuscripts of Boethius' *Consolation* that literate men and women pondered in response to these troubles. But there are clear indications of a Boethian revival, for people were again turning to theodicy for assurance that Christianity was a no-loss religion regardless of historical calamity. The *Consolation* began at this time to penetrate into the vernacular languages of these more localized, less Latinized subcultures. And the translators and their readers, suffused with the values of the Christian church, added explicitly Christian matter to the theodicy that Boethius had left. There was Alfred, king of England (from 871 to 899), who struggled with the Danes and other Vikings who had invaded England (in 865), defeating them (in 878) but leaving in their hands much of his eastern territory, known as the Danelaw. Wishing to revive monasticism, he had to rebuild many ruined abbeys. He yearned to turn into English a small set of books most beneficial to the culture and religion of his subjects. One was Gregory's *Pastoral Rule,* another was Boethius' book. He personally undertook the translating of the *Consolation,* inserting references to Christ and Christian men, making Lady Philosophy over into Divine Wisdom, bending and paraphrasing passages and introducing themes that made the dialogue distinctly English as well as explicitly Christian.

At the monastery of St. Gallen in what is now Switzerland the scholar Notker Labeo (who lived from 950 to 1022) rendered the work into German. His scholarly notes explained the text. A writing appeared in the French dialect of Provence (in the 900s), hardly a translation, but the story of Boethius versified into a warning to youths that the world was becoming more evil; young people who learned Boethius' story would trust God instead of possessions. The ladder of virtues consisted of steps "made of Alms, Faith, Love, Goodness, Fidelity, Largesse, Joy, Truth, Chastity, Humility." Lady Philosophy has come "to signify something very much like the medieval idea of Wisdom, the second person of the Trinity."[49] The theodicy of Boethius, all along widely copied and read in Latin, thus entered the common tongues.

When the Gregorian scheme for ordering chaos was successful, Christianity got the credit. When chaos prevailed and the Boethian theodicy offered the counsel and consolation of trusting in providence so as to underscore human freedom and responsibility, Christianity was not to blame. The fluctuations of European history from the Roman Empire's fall to the Holy Roman Empire's rise brought to usefulness first the way of life built on theodicy, then one built on prelacy. The alternation continued with the ups and downs of society. Together they made Christianity a religion of all seasons, in times of calamity confident and in more prosperous periods efficient.

It cannot be said that they outlived their usefulness, for such options enduringly appeal to men and women. But the new cultural endeavor of unifying Christendom at once merged and changed them. An analogy holds between theodicy and the mystics' quest for intimacy with the divine; just some similarity appears between the organizing genius of prelates and the theologians' organizing all knowledge about God. But these analogies do not begin to account for the eruption of a distinct form of European humanity in the period of mystics and theologians to which the next chapter draws attention.

IV

UNITY

Mystics and Theologians

in the Holy Roman Empire

962-1556

Earnest Christians under the old Roman Empire approached heaven by the avenues of dying as martyrs and living as ascetics. The less fanatical prayed and obeyed in order to ensure good resurrections at the last judgment. Then, under the Germanic kingdoms, very different Christians awaited the demise of their tired old world, certain that God's providence would bring a good ending and confident that they could exercise Christ's authority on earth between his first and second comings. The next period (from 962 to 1556) produced its own models of Christian living, expressing the aspirations and abilities of a distinct form of humanity.

These Europeans occupied a new site in lands facing the Atlantic Ocean and the North and Baltic seas. They no longer sensed time to be running out and the world to be running down, so they looked for history to give subtle but reliable clues about the success or failure of their enterprise. Disunity and division among mankind signaled that they failed and that antichrist would come.

To forestall his arrival, they labored all the harder to unify mankind under a universal Christendom. Every mark of unity signalled success. Their desire to achieve what Paul Johnson has aptly called "the total society" involved a combination of renovating the Roman imperium and fashioning a new, ecumenic, religious empire.[1] The task of renovating while innovating enlisted effort in the causes of Christianity against paganism, of Catholicism against heresy, of cross against Muslim crescent, of the Latin church over the Greek church, of new learning against general ignorance, of subordination of pope to emperor or emperor to pope against divisive rule—in sum, of unifying a world that was simultaneously expanding and splintering. Those six efforts marked the main events that framed the awareness of Europeans during the era now under consideration.

The period opened when Otto I of Saxony, crowned Holy Roman Emperor (in 962), became the first person to depose the pope who crowned him, the first emperor to judge who was and who was not the rightful pope, and the first profane ruler to be arbiter of his rule's sacred source. Otto thus opened the medieval contest between temporal and spiritual authority over which sovereign headed the unified society. The period closed with Charles V, the last Holy Roman Emperor to be crowned (in 1530) by a pope, Clement VII. Charles signed his abdication papers (in 1555) one month to the day after the Peace of Augsburg dealt out the territories of Europe to inimical Christianities, either Protestant or Catholic by the territorial rulers' preference.

During the reign of Otto I, the practice first spread of reading events as signs about the coming of antichrist. Abbo of Fleury wrote (about 970-75) that he had "opposed with all my strength this opinion" that antichrist would soon arrive. Bishop Arnulf of Orleans told the council of Verzy (in 991) that the church was split east and west, had lost Africa and Asia to Islam, and that the papacy lacked power and honor, so "One would say that the Antichrist is ruling us."[2] There would come a time at the end of our period when the antichrist waited no longer, for he did arrive—for the Protestants in the popes, for the popes in the Protestants.

In this period the world at once enlarged and divided. European awareness about the physical world expanded in mind-boggling ways. At the beginning of the period, men and women lived in small, confined spaces. The Vikings, to be sure, had sailed far and wide, but the rest of the Europeans had long kept close to home. Pilgrims before Otto's time attended local shrines. Then the sacred magic of Rome attracted larger numbers, and soon the holy scenes around Jerusalem again attracted attention.

The fact of two European language cultures loomed increasingly large as travel touched more lives. In Otto's time the linguistic barrier zig-zagging across Europe from northern France to the Austrian Alps went virtually unnoticed.[3] In Charles's day many people spoke more than one vernacular tongue and scholars were learning Greek and Hebrew in addition to Latin.

Asia and Africa had been no more than quaint place-names in

Pliny's ancient writings. Suddenly, the crusaders began exploring farther afield. Before long (by the 1500s) Europeans had touched the coast of every continent, had traveled through China and India, and had penetrated into the Americas.

The world of medieval Christians kept expanding outward. It also kept splitting inward. The westerly countries developed strong and eventually competing monarchies. The progress of the Holy Roman Empire from Otto I to Charles V ran toward more and more independent territories, eventually more than three hundred, federated into a less and less authoritative diet, or parliament. Many forces—pagan conquests and settlements, stubbornly heretical movements, the encroaching Muslims, a weakening eastern orthodoxy, the revival of classical learning, and the jealousies between lords temporal and lords spiritual—dislodged old securities and aroused energies for various interests and new tasks.

The expanding and dividing world invited a daring spiritual exploration to test how far deity could unify and humanity could be unified. There was an exploration and renovation of the past. The European tradition provided rich symbols to energize the oneness that human society strove to embody. These historic emblems needed to be recovered and put to new uses. The ancient Roman imperium could not be forgotten any more than Charlemagne's brief decades of hegemony in the west. The Holy Roman Emperors identified with Charlemagne by being crowned and holding court at Aix-la-Chapelle, a center of political unification.

The symbols of spiritual energy still radiated over western Europe from Rome, domiciling the most vivid western reminders of the founding of Christianity. The tomb of Peter, keeper of heaven's keys, and the bones of Paul, planter of the worldwide church, were Rome's own holy objects. Relics of other saints and martyrs had been exported all over Europe to a network of shrines that competed in potency with wonder-working remains of local, holy heroes.

Moreover, Rome continued to haunt Europeans with reminders that it had achieved the grandest ecumenic empire ever. Otto III as emperor and Gerbert of Aurillac as Pope Sylvester II were claiming (by 1000) that they together re-embodied the imperium of Octavianus, the Augustus chosen by God to make last-minute preparations on earth for Christ's incarnation. During one crucial century (from 1123 to 1215), no fewer than four ecumenical councils met at the Roman palace that Constantine had given to the church, and those councils dealt extensively with political as well as ecclesiastical affairs. In Rome, Pope Innocent III demanded political fealty from the crowns of Europe.

Such retrospective renovation was matched by forward-looking innovation. Such were the unprecedented probings into the nature of deity exemplified by the mystics who attained absolute acquaintance with God and the theologians who acquired universal knowledge about God. The mystics provided assurance that the unifying religion did not mistake the inner nature of the divine reality it embodied, while theologians explained that reality so cogently that every well-instructed conscience must consent. But these probings brought their own problems.

The mystics labored mightily to attain moments of rapture, only to find God's inner being receding and their experience of it nearly ineffable. They invaded ever more deeply, stretching ordinary language and thought in their effort to explain experiences that by definition words could not capture.

The theologians, objecting to the notion that only a few could approach the divine ground of all, made knowledge about God a condition of acquaintance with God. Since men and women by nature were rational, notwithstanding the many who behaved unreasonably, they explained the divine so that no reasonable question or objection could bar one from understanding and accepting Christianity. Yet intellectual coinage changed. New thought forms appeared. Previously unconsidered arguments and objections arose. Some sources came newly to light. The base of metaphysics shifted. The constants that the theologians found reliable were their precise Latin and their immutable object of study.

Bernard of Clairvaux stands out as an exemplary mystic. Not

every contemplative climbed the precise spiritual ladder he recommended, but nobody rivaled his adroitness in making personal unity with God the basis for personal management of the church's affairs. Analogously, by cogently demonstrating God's existence and the necessity of Christ's redemption, Anselm of Canterbury became a model theologian, placing reason in the service of God and religion. His theology in its own way unified church and culture, faith and reason, creator and creatures. Both responded early to the period's typical cultural crises, and both were the precursors of many imitators.

DISUNITY

Pagans created the earliest of these crises. Norsemen had ravaged (by 900) the coastal and river settlements of western Europe. People feared their piracy perhaps even more than their paganism. But Normandy became a Christian kingdom (by 950); then the Normans conquered an England already accustomed to Danish Christian kings. Southern Italy also became a Norman-Christian kingdom.

Norsemen had to adjust, not reject, their nature-paganism. Their mythic eschatological battle, called Ragnorok, took the Christian name Armageddon. Shrines, crosses, and relics replaced sacred glens, trees, and stones. Christianizing medieval pagans meant mingling two sources of spiritual power into a single but grander magic under Christian terms and symbols. To the east Otto I drove the Magyars (in 955) from Augsburg into Hungary, where they thrived under Christian kings. The Wends, whom Otto then defeated, were the only pagans to resist membership in Latin Christendom. Otto's comrade-in-arms at the Battle of Lech, Ulrich the bishop-king of Augsburg, joined with his clergy and people in pagan ceremonies.[4]

Medieval paganism provided the substance and Christianity the form of religion. The mixture proved to be a potent unifying power. As Thomas Aquinas would formulate the principle of combination, grace did not destroy nature but presupposed and perfected it.

Grace also perfected the sophisticated, long-forgotten pagan learning of Greece and Rome that Europeans recovered in ever stronger waves throughout the period. This injection of pre-Christian thought forms demanded rethinking the faith and re-shaping the world view to account for the fact that Plato's and especially Aristotle's logic opened a vaster universe to the intellect than any Christian in the west since Boethius had imagined. Greek Christians had never lost what the Latin Christians were recouping, yet the Latins learned it not from the Greeks but via a circuitous and ironic route. Heretics exiled by the Greek church transmitted the philosophy and ethics of antiquity to their Muslim hosts, who passed it on to Jewish scholars, who with Arab scholars turned it into the Latin of western Christians. Eventually, Renaissance scholars began to seek original Greek and Latin sources, but for a long time (until the 1300s) it was the sons of Abraham who conveyed the intellectual substance of ancient pagans to the Europeans who gave it Christian form.

Grace could not perfect but only try to destroy the heretics whose stubborn refusal to be unified made them literally the disgrace of medieval Christendom. From the appearance of the Cathars in southern France (in the late 1000s) down to the Reformation and Counter-Reformation, the church enforced conformity as the price of taking and keeping the name Christian. Entrance into the fold was made easy; conversion, however superficial, pointed toward unification. Deviance, however peaceable, meant deformity. The Cathars knit together various strands of Manichean dualism that survived from late antiquity. This radical separation of good from evil fit well the earlier attitude of awaiting the end of the earthly city from a comfortable seat within the city of God on earth. The church shifted its organized efforts, even that of monasticism as reformed under the abbots at Cluny, to prolonging history and keeping antichrist at bay. No room was left for those still awaiting the end, and the Cathars were definitely awaiters.

There were also heretical renovators who recaptured early Christian ideals and thus embarrassed the medieval church. Peter Waldo, a moneylender in Lyons, became guilt ridden (in about 1170) over his ill-gained luxury and read Christ's teachings about property. He proclaimed wealth evil and poverty good. He formed bands of beggars who wandered about urging that true Christians must imitate the apostles. By joining this movement, common folk stood to gain security, adventure, and a taste of the spiritual dignity that most clergy were denying to laymen. In Germany, Spain, France, and Italy the movement flourished, anticipating those of the Wycliffites or Lollards in England and the Hussites in Bohemia.

Waldenses became confused with Cathars in the popular mind. The church answered them all with a single message: conform or die. Innocent III launched a crusade (in 1208) against the Cathars. Atrocities in the massacre at Bézier the next year were as vicious as only divine sanction could make them. The Fourth Lateran Council (in 1215) forbade clergy to take part in the trials by ordeal that the church had learned from the pagans. Then Innocent IV (in 1252) officially condoned torture to force heretics to confess and abjure their dissent—a crueler trial by ordeal.

Absolute acquaintance with and universal knowledge of God justified imposing uniformity in Christian belief as the condition of being allowed to live. In this view, to persist in heresy prolonged a soul's punishment in the hereafter because religious dissent disobeyed a good conscience. To cut short the earthly life of a soul thus in league with the devil might increase its chances in purgatory. Teachings and practices about the souls of the dead expanded to make purgatory a grand unifier of the departed with the living and of sinners with saints, indeed of the church with heaven and of time with eternity. Unified Christendom consigned heretics and sinners alike to work out their salvation in this afterlife church.

If heretics were the greatest internal embarrassment, "The existence of Islam was the most far-reaching problem in medieval

Christendom," according to Richard Southern; indeed, it was "a problem at every level of experience."[5] While Muslims were sweeping over Mediterranean lands from Palestine and Egypt through North Africa and Spain, Europeans realized that Christianity's territories were shrinking. But they saw these foreigners only as Saracens (*Sarra geniti*), people who claimed descent from Abraham's first wife Sarah. That they bore a powerful, monotheistic faith rooted in the Hebrew Bible and articulated in the revealed Koran was an insight late in coming (in the 1100s) to Latin Christians. The destruction of the Holy Sepulchre in Jerusalem by Caliph al-Hakim (in 1009) seemed like antichrist's attack on an increasingly popular object of pilgrimage. But Islam's high religion, advanced science, and flourishing culture dawned on the Europeans' awareness only when the first crusaders conquered Antioch (in 1099) and established the kingdom of Jerusalem.

Crusaders gained booty, fresh supplies of relics, and papal indulgences from sins—altogether-scant reward for the huge human and material resources spent (from 1096 to about 1300) in repeated, costly, clumsy campaigns. But throw into the balance an awareness of several new worlds—of ancient learning, of Muslim science and medicine, of technology, of new foodstuffs and games and goods, indeed, of Asia and Egypt as places with histories and cultures—and the investment paid handsomely. For the first time all the kingdoms of Europe joined in a common endeavor. The encounter with Islam gave western Europe a sense of being a distinct culture with its own religion, making it all the more urgent for Christians to gain intimate acquaintance with and knowledge about their distinct deity.

This self-consciousness of the Europeans developed also from their breach with the eastern orthodox religion and the Byzantine empire. The textbooks date the break (at 1054), when the papal legate and the orthodox patriarch declared blanket, mutual excommunications by Latin and Greek Christians. In fact, the mistrust and enmity had passed the limits of reconciliation nearly a century earlier. A bishop of Cremona named Liutprand, the last westerner to be trained in the art of diplomacy with the Greeks, failed (in 968) to negotiate a Byzantine bride for young Otto II and accused the Byzantines of being indecent, lying, heretical fleshpots and infidels.

So they remained in the Latin mentality; indeed, it is doubtful that their reputation is much improved in the modern western mind. Their legendary wealth and their abundant treasure of holy relics attracted pillaging crusaders who established (from 1204 to 1261) a Latin kingdom of Constantinople. From this conquest the Byzantines never recovered. A century later their empire had shrunk to the areas adjacent to the capital, and in another century (in 1453) Constantinople itself fell to the Ottoman Turks. Thereafter, Eastern Orthodoxy centered in Moscow, which came to be regarded as a third Rome.

By doing in the Byzantines the Latin Christians rid themselves of the embarrassing image of two Christianities. In the process the religion lost the city and empire of the Latin Constantine who had admitted Christians into the mainstream of western civilization. Indirectly, to be sure, the Greek church's writers fed insights to Latin scholastic theologians and mystics, who nevertheless studied and contemplated a thoroughly European deity.

The theology they wrote rendered this God understandable to reasonable men and women who understood things in the European way. The mystics designed techniques of meditation that joined their souls into the very being of this deity. This medieval quest for absolute and universal unification is mirrored in the period's power struggle between the institutional bearers of secular and sacred authority. Of course, in the European mind of the time these were not separate spheres. But if grace was to perfect nature, one had to identify the agent of grace and the locus of nature. The marriage vow, for example, remained a natural contract between partners even as it was hallowed into a sacrament of the church. The peculiar medieval institution of knighthood arose from what moderns would call secular origins, yet the knights became horseback warriors defending religious virtue and dedicating their swords on the altars of Christ.

While such profane institutions were being partly sacralized, the exercise of godly rule that Gregory the Great had sanctified was being differentiated into spiritual and temporal embodiments, especially after the reign (from 983 to 1002) of the young Emperor Otto III. Like his grandfather, he chose popes according to his liking, first his chaplain and cousin, Brun (Bruno of Carinthia), and then his brilliant tutor, Gerbert of Aurillac. Friedrich Heer wrote, "As Gregory [V], Brun should reincarnate Gregory I . . . ; as the second Sylvester, Gerbert should with Otto III, his new Constantine, restore the sacred unity of Empire by reconciling Rome (both Romes), Church and Christendom."[6] In this brief but grand moment of renovation Otto nullified temporal rule by the papacy, dismissing the "Donation of Constantine" as a forged memordandum and only out of personal affection for Gerbert naming the pope administrator of lands around Rome. Emperor Otto took the title "servant of the apostles" (Henry II signed himself "servant of the servants of Christ"), borrowing a version of the papal designation initiated by Pope Gregory I.[7] In a contemporary depiction Christ on the cross wears no crown of thorns but a crown of thrones, the identical imperial crown that Otto III wore. The savior's countenance is that of an emperor.[8]

By unifying papal and imperial power in himself and his popes, Otto was not reducing but rather extending the universal sway of Peter's successor to undergird his own absolute rule over the four provinces of his empire, Germania, Roma, Gallia, and Sclavinia. Gerbert as pope spiritually governed this empire and the rest of Christendom, meddling in French affairs of state and encouraging national churches in Bohemia, Poland, and Hungary. In his pontificate, he lived out his pledge to Queen Adelaide, widow of the Hugh Capet whom Gerbert had made king of France: "if so decreed I will defend the unity of the church against all schisms by my death."[9] Otto died unmarried (early in 1002); Gerbert, the next year. What they had joined together their successors soon put asunder.

For half a millennium to come, the distinction grew ever

sharper between absolute temporal rulers, drawing power from the inherent nature of their offices, and universal spiritual rulers, the chief dispensers of grace. The "process of limiting the scope of the appeal to the supernatural in human affairs had," wrote Southern, "as its counterpart, a process of limiting the interferences of secular persons in spiritual affairs."[10]

A succession of strong popes (after 1050) began insisting on a celibate clergy in order to keep the laity, who lived in the natural estate of matrimony, under the priests, who were custodians of the supernatural. Celibacy also kept the clergy from bequeathing church lands to legitimate sons. It concentrated this ownership in episcopal, later archiepiscopal and papal offices.

By renouncing the natural order of sexuality—at least of marriage—the clergy symbolized their allegiance to a universal, earthly, Christian society that knew no territorial boundaries. The impertinence of the more ambitious medieval popes consisted in their particularizing this society when they strove for sacred absoluteness by means of coercive power. Emperors and kings, indeed the entire secular hierarchy, ruled in clearly bounded territories over particular peoples with their definite customs. The impertinence of Otto III consisted in his aspiring to secular universality by means of an apostolic commission.

When the spiritual and temporal officers collided head-on, neither could prevail. Gregory VII, bent on freeing the church and its clergy from familial and feudal entanglements, took his case to the people and encouraged boycotts against priests who either kept concubines or bargained with secular rulers for their preferments. In this ploy the pope fought fire with fire, playing on popular anticlericalism to remove the causes of anticlericalism. When he extended the same reforms to powerful bishops and archbishops, he drove these conservatives who dealt in mundane affairs to endorse (in 1076) Henry IV's deposition of Gregory.

The pope retaliated in kind, adding the sting of excommunication and releasing Henry's subjects from all their oaths to him. The king dramatized his repentance by standing barefoot for three days in snow outside the castle Gregory occupied in Canossa and forced the pope to the mercy of absolution. Seven years later (in 1084), Henry marched on Rome and deposed Gregory; the Normans that the pope enlisted to defend the city sacked it instead. Gregory died in exile. But his successors again excommunicated Henry, leaving him rightless as a condemned Christian and powerless to hold his throne against jealous men, including his own son. Henry, too, died in exile. When they collided, the twin powers simply canceled each other.

When they cooperated, popes and kings soon united Europe in the most stupendous of its common endeavors, the crusades. Universal popes convoked and absolute kings executed those campaigns. More usual than collision or cooperation was compromise, as seen in the struggle between popes and kings over the right to install bishops in their offices. Bishops bore universal authority of the church in dioceses whose boundaries limited their administration to territories ruled by kings. Bishops ordained clergy and they also administered church lands. Their authority came from popes, yet many voted in imperial diets; German and Italian bishops had concurred in Henry's deposition of Gregory. From whom should bishops receive the symbols and authority of their offices? Popes and kings disagreed. Precarious compromises (in the 1100s) allowed investiture by both. But tension remained unrelaxed between the absolute and the universal ideals. Social order depended on their cooperating while social dynamism depended on their competing.

Compromises proved costly to kings and emperors contending against the mightiest popes and to popes held captive by the strongest temporal lords. Innocent III (pope from 1198 to 1216) arrogated the right to veto elections of emperors and claimed fealty from every kingdom, including England. But King John's barons and bishops forced him to preserve their liberties in the Magna Carta. And when the later Capetian and the earlier Valois kings of France made popes their puppets at Avignon (from 1309 to 1377), denying them residence in holy Rome, bishops and archbishops continued to embody the authority of universal

Christendom. When two popes, one at Avignon and one at Rome, each claimed to be Christ's only vicar on earth, unity was imperiled, as it was again when reforming councils (from 1414 to 1439) debated the limits of papal supremacy.

Still, Roman catholicism exercised its magic as the spiritual bond of Europe. Even the Renaissance kings who asserted their divine right to autocracy were not simply recapturing the anointed priesthood-kingship that had empowered earlier monarchs like Charlemagne. Absolute temporal authority and universal spiritual authority remained mutually dependent throughout these crises. Only the Reformation (both Protestant and Catholic— Martin Luther's and Ignatius Loyola's) effectively broke the tension by erecting territorial churches under regional monarchs and synodical ministries.

To summarize, several crises prompted medieval Christians to find mystical union with and theological explanations of the divine being. The new appearances of paganism and heresy within Latin Christendom, its rude awakening to Islam and to the extent of planet earth, its expulsion of the eastern church, and its admission of classical learning—all posed challenges for the unification of a total society. The complex rivalry between temporal and spiritual authority spurred on the quest for the twin ideals of the absolute and the universal.

MYSTICS

The mystics and the theologians responded to these crises with twin religious expressions. A basic change in the practice of penance turned the confession of sin into a launching pad for the soul's ascent toward union with its maker. A basic change in the procedures of study made human reason an agent for understanding the inner nature and attributes of its maker. The mystics' desire for union with God has been seen as a protest against the aridity of the theologians' dogmas. It is important also to see the medieval theologians' desire to make God knowable by all reasonable persons as a protest against the mystics' elitism. In turn, the mystics' spiritual discipline challenged the theologians' egalitarianism.

In the inherited world view the deity was perfect, eternal, transcendent, and utterly good, while the human soul was marred, finite, earth-bound, and utterly sinful. Movement toward such a deity by such a soul on its own merit was unthinkable. Only the miracle of reconciliation by the god-man ransomed the captive soul from its bondage to evil. When Irenaeus long ago had dramatized this transaction in a schematic myth, the duty of the reconciled soul was never again to sin gravely. Soon forgiveness for sins less notorious than those of murder, apostasy, and adultery became available through an arduous procedure of public confession. The sinner, expelled from the congregation, would kneel outside the church-house or house-church during worship for a long period, perhaps even a year or more. Performing this penalty and avoiding further sin earned a restored membership. Repetition of grave sin meant decisive, final expulsion. Bishops, then priests as well, came to judge the gravity of sins and their appropriate penalties.

By Charlemagne's time Celtic and Latin penitential practices were being fused in standard manuals listing all sorts of crimes, particularly sexual offenses committed by clergy and laity, and prescribing the degree and duration of punishment that fit each crime. A short but quite severe penalty might substitute for a much longer and less arduous one. An old Irish table of such commutations allowed a year of very hard penance to be paid off by three days and nights of rigorous fasting and psalm singing with "intent meditation of the passion of Christ and with contrition of heart and earnest repentance to God with remembrance of the sins, every one of them that he remembers."[11]

When commutations emerged, private·penance was beginning to take care of the minor sins. Then public penance fell to near disuse, since it was regarded as available only once and then only for scandalous sins. Sins confessed privately to a priest were "sealed," not to be made public in any way. By implication, performing public penance revealed the degree, if not the precise nature, of the sin thus expiated. Urgent measures were taken (after 1050) to popularize private confession and penance.

Privacy in turn drew attention to the inward attitude of the penitent as deserving or not deserving forgiveness. Regret for sin out of fear of punishment (attrition) was far less deserving than regret for sin out of love for the deity one had offended (contrition). Attention focused on contrition (in the 1100s and 1200s), although degrees of penance to be done as satisfaction were still discussed. A Franciscan scholastic named Alexander of Hales, who accepted attrition as a lower form of contrition, regarded the higher kind of regret as a "total conversion of the reason and will to God, so that God is loved above all things and sin detested beyond all things."[12]

Such "conversion," however complete, lay beyond the soul's own reach and thus required grace that implanted the love of God. An abbot in Paris named Richard of St. Victor described this grace as God's softening the sinner's heart. Contrition remained, however, a condition of worthy confession rather than the product of absolution. The psychological and religious intricacies of these moves resist neat simplification. Their main effects were to privatize sin, to separate the two kinds of regret springing, respectively, from fear and love, to probe a person's psychological state for signs to determine which kind of regret dominated, and to heighten social and personal pressures for exhibiting signs of the higher regret.

Altogether, these moves signal a religious breakthrough of tremendous importance, because they made the deity partner to one's ability to show proper sorrow in confessing sins. Changing the preferred motive for confession from fear to love turned a curse into a blessing, turned self-accusation of unworthiness before deity and society into self-readiness to honor God and to be charitable toward others—with God's help. Sinning (and then regretting of having sinned) became the first step in loving God. The first rung of every medieval mystical ladder became contrition for sins, already in itself an ascent toward the top rung of union with God. If temptation remained at every level, so did the means for overcoming it.[13]

At his Burgundian monastery Bernard of Clairvaux erected mystical stairs leading from the soul's carnal self-love and sin to its conjugal union with the heavenly bridegroom, Christ. Bernard wrote *On the Steps of Humility and Pride* (in 1125), outlining his quest for God up twelve steps and analyzing the grades by which pride could tempt monks to descend corresponding treads. In penance, grace stirred the sinner's heart to contrition; here the selfish desire for deity prompted the soul to rise beyond itself and the carnality that all men shared. At the top this carnality was purified, but in earthly life one never escaped it. One made three basic moves in mounting the twelve steps. Humility began in the awareness of one's carnal existence, grew as charity checked self-love with concern for one's neighbor, and rose to purity of heart in desiring God. Deity entered into partnership at each stage. The Son humbled human reason by conjoining to it the divine reason. The Spirit purged the human will with charity toward the neighbor.

Then "this blessed soul the Father binds to himself as his own glorious bride. Now the reason is no longer preoccupied with itself and the will is no longer concerned with other men." In the divine king's chamber "for a short time, just one half-hour, while there is silence in heaven, she sleeps in that desired embrace. She sleeps but her heart watches and is fed with the secrets of truth on which later, when she comes to herself, her memory can dwell. There she sees things invisible and hears things unspeakable which it is not given man to utter."[14] In a brief metaphor Bernard thus epitomized the medieval mystical experience. Creaturely unworthiness is humbled, the soul rigorously prepares itself through disciplines of charity, only a few souls attain to rapture, the union with deity becomes complete for only a brief time, the bridal soul experiences the ecstasy of being outside herself, and the experience is memorable but ineffable. Of course, Bernard took great pains to describe his vision of these "things invisible" and to teach his knowledge of these "things unspeakable."

So that monks might know the direction of their souls' movement, he also invented a stairway of pride and named the twelve descending steps: curiosity about one's attainment, levity of mind, laughter, boasting, singularity, self-conceit, presumption, self-justification, hypocritical confession, revolt, freedom to sin, then habitual sinning.[15] Monastic spirituality could plunge as well as soar.

But only the monks' discipline prepared the soul for the blissful moment of absolute acquaintance with God. Chastity, continence, spiritual studies, frequent prayer, obedience to the superior, peaceful living among the brethren, poverty—in a word, the strict life of a Cistercian monk over many years were necessary to prepare Bernard's soul to dare ask for the divine kiss; even then, only in certain moments came this extraordinarily ardent and affective love for God.[16] Bernard praised the monastic profession. "It makes those who live it and love it stand out from other men as rivals of the angels and as hardly men at all." Since that life "restores the divine image in the human soul and makes us Christlike, much as baptism does," it deserves to be called a second baptism (read: martyrdom!).[17]

Monastic discipline constantly renewed humility, the *sine qua non* of loving God, who by nature eminently deserved to be loved beyond measure by all humans. Christians bore this obligation emphatically. Monks vowed to subordinate everything else to it and strove constantly to excel in loving God. That they carnally loved themselves reflected their sin, but that they loved at all reflected their creation in the image of the God who was love and existed to be loved.

All creatures loved themselves for their own sakes. Restrained by the duty to love their neighbor, they could begin to love God for their own sakes. Tasting the sweetness of loving the one who alone deserved all love, they could purify carnal love and love God for his own sake, and then it became a joy to love their neighbor. The highest attainment would be to love themselves for God's sake. This last level could be reached only when the heart and soul were freed for pure spirituality in the general resurrection—a reservation Bernard made quite explicit in his book, *On the Love of God.*

But the book goes on to tell, quite affectively, even sensually, of the soul's delight, its becoming drunk with the spiritual drink of truth. Bernard claimed at least enough experience of the highest level of love to be able to describe loving the self for God's sake. And when late in life (from 1135 to 1138) he wrote a long series of sermons on the Song of Songs (*Sermones super Cantica Canticorum*), he was autobiographically specific, if not about eternal union with God, at least about the experience of his own, ardent, passionate soul-bride's being kissed with the kiss of the mouth of the trinitarian deity.

Although the Song of Songs taken literally is a very erotic Hebrew poem, Bernard shared the medieval consensus that made the idealized male lover in the poem signify Christ; the woman who passionately wanted to be ravished by him stood for the church and for the souls of its members. The soul or bride, as Bernard elaborated this allegory, yearned for the divine kiss with which humanity had been kissed by Christ's incarnation. Seeking the kiss of the triune deity, the bride approached the Son for the favor (8:5). This "carnal love is good, through which carnal living is excluded" and "the world is condemned and conquered. It is improved when it is rational; it is perfected when it is also made spiritual" (20:9).

First the bride must be humbled, her carnal love purged, by kissing the bridegroom's feet and sprinkling her tears upon them to cleanse herself. Even then she did not leap to his mouth but next kissed Christ's hands to beg his pardon and to honor him. These kisses were granted to those who were making progress (7:1, 4:1). The chaste bride, undeserving of these first and second favors, was falling in love so passionately by this time that she yearned to be kissed with the kiss of the divine mouth.

Bernard made much of the point that he did not speak of the divine lips but of the kiss that united the Father and the Son with the kiss that was the Holy Spirit. When the bride received this kiss she was enveloped briefly in the deity's own being.

The language of medieval sexual love carried a great tonnage of allegorical freight, before Bernard in the early literature of courtly love and from Bernard onwards in the literature of mysticism, especially among the Cistercian monks who followed in his footsteps. Whether these two streams of erotic writing ran separate or confluent courses, they show striking parallels. The courtly lovers as well as the mystics belonged to elites and were themselves elitist. For both groups sexual lore covered layers of meaning. Both employed carnal passions in the pursuit of virtue and purity.

Bernard found additional sources of allegory. Medical and culinary terms worked their spell: for example, in progress toward salvation one must amputate the tumor of bad habits, pour out the ointment of devotion, apply the medicine of penance, feed on the food of good works, drink the beverage of prayer, enjoy the quiet of contemplation, dream of divine things, and love God (18:5-6).

But all is the language of affect, of the feelings whose highest emotion was sensual love. The ladder of salvation could also be made with the rungs of yearning: "compunction, . . . devotion, . . . the labor of penance, . . . the work of piety, . . . zeal for prayer, . . . the leisure of contemplation, . . . a plenitude of love" (18:6). Allegories were needed to say what in principle could not be said directly in plain language. For "the experience of the kiss tells more than any words" (9:3).

Nor can the allegories be deciphered as direct analogies. The bridegroom's breasts have nourished the suckling bride, imparting to her the love that prompts her to ask for the kiss, and the kiss has enlarged the bride's own breasts with the milk of grace (9:7)! Absolute union of the dependent soul with the independent deity pushed even allegory to the breaking point. Although

Bernard knew more about conjugal love and kissing than one might expect of a chaste ascetic, the metaphor served to convey the bridal intimacy of this amorous mystic's experience.

Simpler language described the lower levels of spiritual mounting. And the first level was contrition, regretting sin for its dishonor to the offended deity. "The ointment of contrition of course is good, made up . . . from the recollection of past sins and poured on the Lord's feet. . . . But far better is the ointment of devotion, distilled from the memory of God's beneficences and worthy to be poured upon Christ's head" (12:10).

All Christians could and should be contrite, and all should strive for higher rungs of spirituality. But "The ability to glory in God alone can come solely from God . . . ; it is as true as the truth which is its object, and is a truth so rare, that only an exceptional few even of the perfect can glory in perfectly possessing it" (13:6, *et in veritate tam rara, ut vix vel paucitas perfectorum perfecte glorietur in ea*). Among these very few of the perfect Bernard placed himself. Christ the Word had blended the mystic's person into divinity briefly but very often (*pluries*), usually without warning or presentiment, suddenly, always an intangible yet overwhelming presence that inflamed Bernard's heart and soul. Just as suddenly, the Word withdrew. Small wonder, he declared, that a person chosen for such experiences should elect the language of the bride (*vocem sponsae*) to recall—both to remember and to plead for the return of—his soul's lover (74:5, 7).

This heavenly Christ was still the human Jesus who established on earth his united and unifying body, the church. One body could have only one head, invisible in the person of the ascended Christ and visible in the person of his proxy on earth, the pope. Zeal for that body and its head made Bernard the monastic and mystic also the most influential man of affairs in all Europe. Some five hundred of his extant letters "constitute, with possibly the exception of the semi-official chronicles, our most reliable source for constructing the history of the second quarter of the twelfth century."[18] Eighty-eight of these letters gave directions for settling matters under consideration by sitting popes. Others summoned kings and peoples of whole nations to the second crusade. Still others laid down policy to Cistercian abbots, including the policy of forbidding monks to crusade. From London to Jerusalem cousins and uncles, kings and queens, bishops and archbishops, monks and nuns, nobles and commoners, dukes and countesses received Bernard's advice, pleas, arguments, cajolings, and orders—all aimed at unifying Christendom and improving piety.

For all his self-confidence, a patent selflessness undergirded the man's authority to order everybody about. Intimacy with the church's founder issued in the insistence that the popes regard themselves and be regarded as higher than mere vicars of St. Peter. They were the very vice-regents on earth of Christ in heaven, officers bearing an unequaled imperium. Bernard made the pope a universal lord, who "disposes of kingdoms and empires and presides over the princes, nations and peoples."[19] All other rulers, high or low, existed solely to serve the welfare of Christendom as defined by the popes, with Bernard's ready advice and instructions. To the extent that the popes (of the 1100s and 1200s) commanded respect as Christs on earth, it was Bernard who promoted them to that status.

But he was no mere broker of ecclesiastical might. For an unquestioning piety and devotion suffused his person and career. A novel Christ appeared to Bernard, who popularized the figure of the savior with whom he grew familiar. For both cultural and religious reasons the Christ of these times and places became a vividly human and winsomely humbled person, lowly but pure, defeated in suffering and death but victorious in resurrection and ascension. In his earthly scenes he appeared to the pious. "The sacred image of the God-man being born or sucking milk or teaching or dying or rising again or ascending is present to the one praying" (20:6). The helpless baby and the dying man evinced the compassion, the carnal love, and the sympathy that was latent in every person. Jesus the teacher then demanded the disciplined uprightness, the life of charity toward the neighbor, the restraint that was needed by every person.

In Bernard's words, "the human heart has affection for the fleshly Christ and what he did and commanded" (20:6). Because the lowly, beloved Jesus was the lofty, loving son of God, the carnal love that one expressed toward him underwent transformations and purifications into rational and then into spiritual love. By the most refined spiritual love, made of the material of carnal love, the most perfect lovers could receive the divine kiss from the ascended and glorified Christ. "For when I name Jesus I set before me a man who is meek and humble of heart, kind, prudent, chaste, merciful, flawlessly upright and holy in the eyes of all; and this same man is the all-powerful God whose way of life heals me, whose support is my strength. . . . Because he is man I strive to imitate him; because of his divine power I lean upon him. The examples of his human life I gather like medicinal herbs; with the aid of his power I blend them, and the result is a compound like no pharmacist can produce" (15:6).

Whether Bernard's quest for absolute union with God evoked or simply responded to this newly human Christ can hardly be decided. In medieval art before Bernard, the humanized savior appeared here and there. Bernard and his Cistercian followers helped the figure pervade Europe. If historians must assign plausible causes to phenomena that are improbable to their critical minds, then it must be said that these mystics' piety produced this Christ. But if historians are to take religious phenomena on their own terms, critically interpreted, then it must be said that this newly personal Jesus Christ presented himself and produced the mystics' piety.

The crusades focused attention upon the known scenes of Jesus' earthly career, in particular those of his birth and of his crucifixion and its aftermath. The crusaders' contact with Muslims who stressed the humanness of their founder as the prophet of Allah very likely promoted parallel attention to Jesus as the human agent of deity. Those who reached Palestine could hardly have avoided sensing that he had been there long ago. Certainly they brought home relics of these scenes, relics more potent even than those of the old Roman saints and apostles. They brought straw from the manger crib, pieces of cloth from the empty tomb, vials of the Virgin's milk, and other matter connected with the earthly Jesus. The baby who lay in that straw and sucked that milk, the dead man who lay in that tomb and left there his garment, sparked Bernardine mysticism. But the accessible infant or dying man was the one who arose to open the way to heaven where the mystic had access through him to rapturous union with God. So it was not, strictly speaking, the humanness of Christ that commanded Bernard's devotion. The Christ to whom Bernard had access became accessible in order to lead from initial carnal compassion for his human weakness and suffering to devotion for his benefactions and then, in the cases of the spiritually elite, on to a pure nuptial embrace by his ascended divinity.

Bernard had no interest in a historical man named Jesus. Nor did he dote upon purging the mystic's soul of its human limitations and imperfections. Other mystics after Bernard shared his interest in an accessible Christ but developed a more inward, inactive contemplation that began with negating all affirmations about the world and even about God. This negative way (*via negativa*) had remote roots in a body of writings known as the pseudo-Dionysius, to which Bernard seems to have been oblivious.

An unknown person, writing in Greek (about 500) and drawing heavily on the Neoplatonism of Proclus, divided all supernatural beings into heavenly hierarchies. The church and its sacraments and orders of ministers formed corresponding hierarchies on earth. Christianity adopted the Neoplatonic ladder of ascent to spiritual union with God, the rungs of the ladder being purgation, illumination, and union. Christianity also adopted the Neoplatonic deity, absolutely pure spirit without attributes. Then the traditional divine names and traditional attributes (e.g., omnipotence) functioned not as descriptions but as anagogues, as earthly terms for heavenly beings. Theological language referred, that is, to familiar things on earth, but by also referring to deity this language prompted the human mind to rise from familiar things to mystical, spiritual transcendence. Once the spiritual ascent began, one had to deny the language and the things named in order to approach the desired deity. A book by the author of this new basis for Christian religiousness bore the name, *Mystical Theology;* it detailed the soul's ascent by anagogue from involvement in earthly finitude to union with infinite deity.

The compatibility of this metaphysical and mystical scheme with the Greeks' Christ, a divine being who took human nature up into himself, made the pseudo-Dionysian writings immediately and pervasively influential in the east. Since the writings bore a name found in the Bible as belonging to the one Athenian philosopher whom Paul converted, they quickly gained near-scriptural status. They were long unknown to the westerners, who learned little Greek. Western synods (in the early 600s) and Gregory the Great himself regarded the works as authoritative but did not study them. The emperor named Michael of Byzantium made a gift (in 827) of the Greek texts to King Louis the Pious, who commissioned a translation. It was unreadable, so King Charles the Bald reassigned the task to a court scholar named Johannes Eriugena.

Eriugena's writings and translations had almost negligible impact before our period. Then the theologian Anselm of Laon and the mystic Hugh of St. Victor studied them. Hugh, a contemporary of Bernard, joined the Augustinian canons of St. Victor in Paris (in 1115) and wrote a commentary on the *Celestial Hierarchy* of pseudo-Dionysius. He belonged to the rapidly increasing number of religious persons who had attained enough confidence in the unified Christendom that was their identifying community to dare turn attention to the minute details of their own and others' religious experiences and personalities. Always asserting their own humility and always calling their successes gifts rather than achievements, these people, during half a millennium after Bernard, wrote an outpouring of autobiographies, analyses, letters, guides, handbooks, instructions, and speculations about the inner workings of individual persons who contemplated the holy and became holy in the contemplating. The vast majority were monks and nuns.

The variety and richness of these experiences and reflections frustrate all attempts to classify Christian mysticism into neat types with precise patterns of sources and influences. All who entered the divine presence this way claimed that the episode defied description, yet many almost compulsively tried to describe both the stages of preparation for ecstasy and also what took place in the actual moments of union. A broad consensus began to develop around the pseudo-Dionysian outline of the main stages of purgation, illumination, and union, but these phases bore a variety of names.

Mystics of Bernard's style stressed feelings, emotions, carnal love, spontaneity, the composing of visual and other sensory impressions, affective descriptions of the heart as cold or warm, and continuity between the stages of ascent. The opposite emphasis fell on the intellect, reason, quiet contemplation, disciplined meditation, the negation of images and impressions, analytic descriptions of the mind as in darkness or light, and discontinuity from one phase of practice to the next.

Hugh and his student Richard, who succeeded him (in 1162) as prior of St. Victor, exemplified this second emphasis. Hugh developed three ways of bringing spiritual things under intellectual consideration. By thinking about them he received the ideas that they presented to the senses or to the memory, and he likened this perception to a green log that begins to catch fire, crackling and smoking. By meditating on them his mind lingered on and sought to discover what lay hidden in the ideas with which he toyed; the log dried out and burned with a bright flame. Advancing to contemplation, he abandoned analysis and thought altogether to let himself passively be grasped by the wholeness of the sacred idea; the glowing log became one with the fire and burnt without flame or smoke or sound as log and fire merged into one another. The stages were quite distinct.

Hugh's progress started with the self and the world it knew by perception. He jumped to analysis of the vanity of this external world and to meditation upon the superior inner world of the spirit. He then leaped from this wisdom to intellectual love in a rarefied, purified state of the soul, still intellectual in quality but at last passive and utterly receptive in aspect. The preliminary stages, also intellectual, were active, although their mental labor served not to affirm or attain so much as to negate and erase. Nor did the stages flow calmly from one to the next. It is as though Hugh changed planes twice in his flight to receive a touch or taste of the divine. The fleeting experience of the highest love made him forget everything else except the wound of desire to love even more deeply, and finally that feeling also lapsed into the experience of absolute stillness.

The quest for God via negation preoccupied Richard of St. Victor, a Scot who assigned thinking (cogitation) to the faculty of imagination, meditation to that of reason, and contemplation to the intellect. For a metaphor of ascent he preferred the mountain, urging that all could and should climb. Very few did, and even fewer lingered at the top. The very fewest rested there, and that only "by detaching the mind from everything whatsoever."[20] The first step, cogitation, involved dilating the mind to its wider capacities. Meditation meant elevating the mind in prayer to things above. Contemplation brought an alienating of the mind from its own reality to a wholly different reality. In this last stage the soul flew about freely wherever the divine spirit blew it. Yet contemplation had its own inner dynamic. In its preparatory stages love infused the will, then filled both the will and the understanding. The third stage or ecstasy made the soul forget everything except its utter desire for the love to which it completely surrendered itself in stillness, peace, stasis, quietude, union. The whole process, however, was painful, a progress of suffering to let loose all interests save the desire for union. Finally, that desire too had to be forfeited for the ultimate peace of soul.

In this intellectual mysticism Christ remained the symbol and embodiment of love. Cognitive study (*lectio divina*) dealt with scriptural themes. The object of meditation was the wounded

Christ. Hugh wrote, characteristically, "The wounds of Christ Jesus are full of mercy, full of piety, full of sweetness and charity."[21] But the stillness at the top of Hugh's ladder and of Richard's mountain could have no object of thought, of meditation, or even of contemplation—not Jesus' wounds and not even Christ's ascended glory. The soul had to detach its mind from everything, including all objectifications of the divine.

Richard and the Latin mystics of his sort after him discovered a distinctive presence of Christ in their lives as the result or aftermath of ecstasy. At this third stage the soul figuratively died. Then it was raised again into a spiritual identity with Christ. Then it descended again into its earthly existence as he had once done. These mystics became, it is not too much to say, christs, veritable reincarnations of his spirit, as he lived in and through their lives and did their deeds of humility and charity. Intellectual drowning of their souls in the being of God prepared them for doing Christ's business among their fellow men. The medieval mystical experience of the more passionate, emotional sort issued in a quite similar quality of life.

Both types shaped the lives of countless medieval religious women and men. An intelligent survey of the lives of the major Christian mystics through history found worth mentioning only Augustine and Gregory the Great in the west down to Bernard. Then (through the 1500s) there are no less than twenty-three outstanding mystics, more than a third of them women; any student of the subject could add substantially to this list.[22]

The proliferation of manuals and lessons instructing even simple religious folk in the cultivation of contemplative skills, together with the vast number of communes dedicated primarily to mystical practice, testify to the pervasiveness and popularity of this religious style throughout Europe. An unidentifiable English country parson of Chaucer's time (about 1370) addressed instructions in contemplation to a young disciple twenty-four years of age, warning him to let only the most pious read the letter; *The Cloud of Unknowing* became a classic. A comparable work, *The Imitation of Christ,* is said to have been reprinted in more editions than any work except the Bible. Throughout our period new schemes were devised. New intensities of impression by the divine presence were attained.

Teresa of Ávila (born Teresa de Cepeda y Ahumada) brought passionate mysticism to its culmination when she became the ever-obedient bride of Christ. He began (in 1555) to appear to her in visions and as her divine husband he directed all she did or thought. Her younger associate, John of the Cross (born Juan de Yepis), attained the heights of the intellectual, abnegative spirituality, organizing it around "the dark night of the soul." The trances, visions, locutions, miracles, and levitations that occurred to Teresa contrast starkly with John's detachment from all sensory experience, his negation of all desire, his renunciation of all extraordinary spiritual phenomena. Teresa found rapture in the moments when Christ ravished her soul. John annihilated himself with long disciplines of spiritual darkness to attain divinization that could last several years. Both taught and both wrote so that others might practice their ways, and both supervised the affairs of their barefoot brothers and sisters in the strict Order of Mount Carmel.

For all their negations of and ascents from the humdrum world, the medieval mystics were guided by an impulse to refine that world. The human Jesus whom they cherished symbolized first and foremost the divine commiseration with fallen mankind. Their form of sinful humanity retained the divine image. Contrition turned their native endowments of carnal love or natural reason into the means and vehicles of intimacy with God. Their divinization or rapture provided no lasting escape from the world, but rather enabled them to reenter and improve it. In a word, absolute acquaintance with God refined the power of Christianity to maintain a unified Europe. The generation of mystics that raised this way of living to its acme of intensity and achievement, of popularity and variety, also saw the shattering of Christendom. Among both the Catholics and the Protestants mysticism eventually generated dissent and protest.[23] So many mystical ways had been found to probe the divine being that different deities were discovered to be centering different religious universes.

THEOLOGIANS

From the tenth through the sixteenth centuries Christian theology in Europe underwent elaborate definition and development. The explaining of God's existence and Christ's incarnation that Anselm adduced, the analyzing by Aristotelian logic that Gerbert began and Thomas Aquinas culminated, the devising of a standard list of theological topics by Peter the Lombard and his arranging of key sentences from old authorities in his new filing system, the audacious reconciling of opposite principles by Abelard, the stressing by John Duns Scotus and William of Ockham of God's freedom to will whatever he pleased, the clash of detailed theories about how sinners were justified after Luther made that the topic of central concern—there were all these and many more crucial developments. The continuities and changes in Christian teachings during this golden age of theology are the stuff of many church histories, and indeed they must be understood for Christian faith to survive the dubieties raised by thoughtful modern believers.

Thoughtful modern students of religion, however, may take the doctrines that medieval teachers exfoliated to be quaint, intramural concerns of the churches. Far more important for understanding Christianity as Europe's favorite religion is the fact that men were religiously devoting enormous spiritual energies to reasoning out divine things, from the grandest affirmations down to the tiniest minutiae.

The most profound and pervasive aspiration of thinking Christians from Anselm through John Calvin was to devise convincing answers to all the serious questions that reasonable persons could ask about living and dying, good and evil. This yearning for authoritative knowledge of God, accessible to all thinking people, was in itself a religious enterprise. Theologians, to be sure, were courtiers to the queen of the sciences. More important, they modeled a distinctly medieval spirituality, that of loving God with their reasoning powers. In a different way from the mystics they responded creatively to the awareness of Europeans that medieval Christendom was in theory universal and unified, but in actual fact particular and varied—at once inclusive and divisive.

The main events that drummed this fact into the Europeans' sensibility have been discussed and need here only to be recounted. Temporal and spiritual rulers maintained a constant tug of war over the embodiment of absolute and universal rule. The size of the known world expanded enormously. Paganism reappeared and persisted. In Islam loomed a rival (but, to Christians, misguided) monotheistic religion. In the Greek church loomed a rival (but, to Latins, schismatic) Christianity. Revived ancient learning jolted neat but narrow intellectual certainties and opened broad scientific vistas. Each crisis spurred new efforts to make intellectually clear the mysteries of deity and doctrine, duty and devotion.

In the preceding age of awaiting the world's end men had been content to copy over and over again the revered writings of old. It was quite another duty to explicate everything these writings contained, to reconcile their discrepancies, and to synthesize these revealed truths with new-found philosophies. Men (there were many women mystics, but Thomas More's daughter was the earliest known medieval woman trained in theology) undertook that duty as a divine calling and discharged it as an act of religious devotion. The mystics loved God primarily with heart and soul, the theologians primarily with mind and reason, which they exercised in the pious task of explaining the divine.

At the beginning of our period human reason took a new lease on life when Gerbert learned and taught the rules of reasoning found in all Boethius' translations and treatises on logic. Gerbert and those he influenced began to take seriously Boethius' definition of a person as the individual substance or instance of a universal rational nature. Concern for this self-definition led to extending the rules of reasoning and to applying them to all areas of religious affairs. The expanding corpus of Aristotle's writings available in Latin opened (in the 1100s and 1200s) an even greater power and range for reasoning. Next, attention turned to the recovered writings of Plato and later to all the Greek and Latin literature that could be found. After the Reformation, however, religious reasoning became the polemical weapon of rival faiths.

The rules of reason helped one recognize and avoid fallacies, of course, and in that sense medieval logic restrained the mind from predictably unfruitful pursuits. Far more than restraining, however, the rules liberated the mind to make many previously unheard-of moves, to speculate on new principles, adopt new procedures, make new deductions, reconcile new discrepancies, admit new contradictions, devise new combinations, and construct new syntheses. Logic gave medieval humanity a noetic versatility that the preceding age had never dreamed of. New answers begat whole litters of new questions. Topics for inquiry multiplied as new generations of questions called for rethinking the old generations of answers. Reason glorified God by coordinating all these topics under the inclusive truth of Christianity into a universal system, called a totality (*summa*) of theology. The previous age had read scripture, the church fathers, creeds from councils, and decrees of popes; the men of that period were learners of the given. But reason enabled medieval men to study, compare, sort, classify, question, rearrange, refine these authorities; men became scholars of the unknown.

To be a theological scholar meant to dedicate to God one's ever-enlarging faculty of reason and to explain God convincingly to all who possessed that faculty—in principle, everybody. Such a theologian was Anselm, who was born (about 1033) in the mountain town of Aosta in Lombardy. In the Norman monastery of Bec he understudied the learned Lanfranc, succeeding him first as prior of Bec and then as archbishop of Canterbury. His friend and biographer, Edmer, tersely described Anselm's ambition. "Hence he applied his whole mind to this end, that according to his faith" in the entire truth of the Bible "he might be found worthy to see with the eye of reason those things in the Holy Scriptures which, as he felt, lay hidden in a deep obscurity." He developed the ability "to see into and unravel many most obscure and previously insoluble questions about the divinity of God and about our faith, and to prove by plain arguments that what he said was firm and catholic truth."[24]

Of course, Anselm studied the traditional writings that lent authority to medieval Christian faith. Much of Augustine's thought held strong appeal, although he dismissed the traditional and Augustinian notion that Christ redeemed mankind by being paid as ransom to Satan. Anselm saw no force in that notion.[25] Augustine had commanded people to do as he had done, to believe in order to understand. He had arbitrarily placed his intellect under the authority of the catholic faith in order to make sense of the universe and to overcome the uncertainties and the gaps he found in the several systems of thought he had tried out. Each system that he tested had its own rules for reasoning and its own standards of what was reasonable. Nor did Christian teachings ever displace his fundamentally Neoplatonic philosophy. But Christian faith and a single, if new and expanding, version of rationality framed Anselm's universe throughout his life. He determined not to accede to faith's authority, but to demonstrate on rational grounds the cogency of what was held by faith, without appeal to scriptures or to other validating standards save that of reason.

Anselm and Augustine shared certain formulations about the relation of faith to reason and therefore they have been closely linked in the histories of Christian doctrine. It is, to be sure, the task of those histories to find dependencies and connections wherever possible. For the history of religiousness, however, the actual styles of life that the two men represent differ greatly. Granted, both were intellectual giants who explicated the meaning of Christian faith. Augustine was a zealous convert; Anselm a lifelong believer. Augustine was the last great pagan Latin thinker in antiquity to accept Christianity. Anselm was the leading medieval Christian Latin thinker to reason independently of scriptural and ecclesiastical authority. For Augustine, believing made rationality possible. For Anselm, believing made rationality necessary.

What was later called the *Monologion* Anselm had named "An Example on Meditating about the Rational Basis of Faith." The *Proslogion* was first entitled "Faith Seeking Understanding" (*Fides quaerens intellectum*). He developed Augustine's program into the far more daring one of making fully reasonable what faith taught. He addressed Augustine's slogan not to other persons as an intellectual procedure, but to his God as a prayer, "For I do not seek to understand that I may believe, but I believe in order to understand. For this also I believe,—that unless I believed, I should not understand."[26] He could, however, dismiss the authority that undergirded belief and see the truth of what he believed entirely by the eye of reason. His faith needed no proof. He delighted in seeking its affirmations by reason.

Anselm's earlier monologue about God's existence had avoided all appeals to empirical facts and the Bible, instead considering the being of God in terms of the concepts of truth and goodness. "Afterwards it came into his mind," wrote his biographer, "to try to prove by one single and short argument the things which are believed and preached about God, that he is eternal, unchangeable . . . and so on; and to show how all these qualities are united in him."[27] The task obsessed him until he lost all desire for food and drink and could not sleep. During worship, his attention strayed to this question. Suddenly the answer dawned. The brief discourse that he wrote, taken with his book on Christ's becoming god-man, articulated a universal, rational system of Christianity.

God, according to the *Proslogion,* is that than which no greater can be conceived. But that which *cannot* be conceived not to exist is greater than that which *can* be conceived not to exist. This conception of God then exists in the understanding. Some things exist in the understanding but not in reality, but the greater being must exist in both. If "that than which no greater can be conceived" exists in the understanding, God exists also in reality.

Moreover, we can conceive of God as existing *contingently* in reality and we can conceive of God as existing *necessarily* in reality. But since necessary existence is greater than contingent existence, God must necessarily exist in reality.

This argument is of one piece with that found in Anselm's book called *Why a God-Man?* (*Cur Deus Homo*). Here it is argued that if under this God there is to be religious salvation it must come about in certain ways. Then it is shown that only salvation by Christ meets these criteria. Every reasonable creature owes perfect honor to this God who necessarily exists in reality.

Through disobedience, neglect, and perversity, all men fail to show perfect honor to their creator and thereby dishonor God. Justice demands that dishonor be punished. To dishonor the infinite deity brings infinite punishment. Only infinite satisfaction based on contrition could restore perfect honor. This satisfaction *must* be paid by man, but it *can* be paid only by God. Only the god-man, sinless and exempt from punishment, is capable of voluntarily paying infinite honor from within finite creation. Jesus Christ as god-man willingly made contrition and satisfaction for all mankind by dying to honor God. Every reasonable man will accept this redemption and honor Christ and God by doing the good works Christ made it possible for him to do.

These brief summaries of *Proslogion* and *Cur Deus Homo* are not designed to draw attention to the content of Anselm's theology or to the continuities and the changes he made in Christian doctrine. They are meant to point to Anselm's distinctive religious aspiration and achievement in his reasoning about the faith without the buttresses of scriptural or creedal or other traditional authority. The recovery and development of logic were gaining enormous scope for reason, and persons were accepting themselves as individual substances of natural reason. Anselm advanced these changes by showing how the unifying power of medieval Christianity made room for rational personhood to express itself religiously and how that personhood could rationally be Christian. So far as he succeeded, his achievement dispelled fear of new knowledge as a threat to cultural unity and provided the means for Christians to occupy the widening arenas of the intellect.

Anselm's persuasive arguments arose out of the foundational assumption that universal essences corresponded to right-minded human conceptions of them. More technically, his "realism" correlated being, truth, and goodness as absolutes providing a unified basis of metaphysics. He referred all the questions his richly dialectical mind could think of to this manner of understanding the universe.

Anselm's success prejudiced the great debate undertaken by the following generation of theologians over which metaphysical base yielded the most widely acceptable explanations of the divine. Did fundamental reality inhere in things taken one by one and classified under general categories? Or were the primary realities universal ideas, only partly manifested by individual things? Peter Abelard's brilliant synthesis, to the effect that universals were metaphysically at once before, in, and after things, seems to have been too subtle for many to understand. The party favoring the reality of things, led by Roscellinus, lost out to the party favoring the priority of universals, led by William of Champeaux.

The leading theologians (of the 1100s and 1200s) preferred the priority of universals. This position underscored the importance of their subject matter and the religious dimension of their dealing with ideas and topics grounded in the divine reality. No less important, realism allowed them to absorb the recovered thought of Aristotle into the system of Christian topics that Peter Lombard devised. The agenda he set for theology started with the triune God and proceeded through creation and sin, incarnation and the virtues, sacraments and the end of the world. Into this framework they fit the sayings of the Latin church fathers, among whom Augustine held pre-eminence.

The novelty of their work was not lost on the men who blended Hellenic and early Christian knowledge into grand syntheses under the first principle of the medieval, European deity. One of them wrote (before 1130), "We are like dwarfs sitting on the shoulders of giants; we see more things, and things that are further off, than they did—not because our sight is better, or because we are taller than they were, but because they raise us up and add to our stature by their gigantic height."[28]

These investigators probed further and further into the nature of their living deity and they expressed what they learned in living systems designed to answer all the objections they could conceive. New generations advanced new ideas and called for altered or expanded systems. Between the dwarfs-on-giants'-shoulders in the generation after Anselm and the Dominican and Franciscan giants-in-their-own-right (of the 1200s) the sense of changing times became acute. Joachim of Floris, a Cistercian abbot who founded his own local monastic order in Italy, led many to the conviction that the third, last epoch of history would soon dawn. The ancient era of law had yielded with the coming of Christ to the era of grace, itself then to give way to an age when the fullness of Christ's teachings would flourish in a reformed and truly spiritual church and society.

This notion, influential through the Reformation, expressed starkly the general sense of time and history that made the medieval theologians think of themselves as participating in the novel task of unifying present culture by renovating and synthesizing past cultures. Thomas Aquinas built this task into the structure of his great *Summa Theologica* (written 1265-74). In its day the center of stormy controversy, this work in substance became the official teaching of Roman Catholics. Thomas, a Dominican monk who studied at Cologne and taught at Paris, substituted for the rather static framework under which everybody since Peter Lombard had been filing sentences from the church fathers an ingenious, dynamic plan of theology. To be sure, Peter's scheme held sway over formal instruction in theology, and indeed it underpins some systematic theologies down to this day.

But the *Summa Theologica* moved grandly from God in his own nature, to God the creator, to God as the goal of human striving, to humanity's Godward return, to Christ the way of humanity's return. In a word, the high scholastics strove by reason to embody divine reality in the symbolic form of a unified human history.

The medieval theologians developed three distinct programs for bringing the diverse streams of history into unified systems of thought aimed at praising God and persuading mankind. To their minds Augustine epitomized the entire tradition of Hebrew and early Christian history, and Aristotle summarized the Hellenic tradition. Those who adopted for their basic metaphysic Aristotle's natural rationalism as expounded by the Muslim philosopher Averroës struggled to relate it to faith with the inconclusive assistance of Augustine's thought. Franciscans like Alexander of Hales and Bonaventura used Aristotelian logic to adduce a thoroughly Augustinian philosophy and theology. The great Dominican schoolmen, Albert the Great and his pupil, Aquinas, kept their minds open equally to Greek and Christian sources as they sought to erect a transcending synthesis of the widest possible sort.

Aquinas came closest to succeeding. But for all the variety of these three approaches, and for all the massive detail of their arguments and conclusions, medieval theologians lived a single religious career of using reason to order "the unity of truth" into a "hierarchy of truths," thus to express a unified Christian world view at once pleasing to their transcendent God and convincing to their reasonable fellow humans.[29]

John Duns Scotus moderately and William of Ockham more emphatically (in the 1300s) stressed God's transcendence and the world's contingency. For them, the divine will could ordain many things that seemed to contradict the consistency of the divine intellect. Although God created fire, for instance, with the characteristic function of burning, that function could be suspended in the historical circumstance, say, of the martyrs, Polycarp at the stake or Paēse in a flaming furnace. They also emphasized the freedom of human wills, within finite limits, making the voluntary relations between deity and creatures reciprocal. This shift of emphasis from intellect to will took into account a far wider range of historical possibilities and contingencies, of peculiarities and accidents, than Anselm's logic of necessity had allowed.

But the later theologians held a steady aim on unifying the activities and structures of the world under a God who allowed creatures to know about its own inner nature. They still dealt with a deity whose ways could be set forth persuasively to men and women. They continued to love God with the mind and they sought to make their knowledge about the deity widely accessible.

As the period we are considering drew to a close, the great reformers of the church filled the stage and wrought the new forms of Christianity represented by the Lutheran, the Reformed, the Anglican, the radical, and the post-medieval Catholic churches. For church histories this reshaping of ecclesiastical institutions and reformulating of religious doctrine represent one or another kind of new start, accompanied by various defections. All parties, of course, claimed to be preserving or recapturing or elaborating the original and pure Christianity of earliest times and to be renewing doctrine according to rigorist standards. More important for the history of religiousness, these reformers represent a merging of the mystical with the theological impulses.

Young Martin Luther in his Saxon monastery took ascetic disciplines with utter seriousness in his effort to "find a merciful God." He strove to be so good a Christian that he would deserve harmony with Christ. The answer to his quest, however, was not this achievement, but rather a new insight into the character of God. The righteousness of deity, Luther learned, was not a righteousness that Christ demanded of Luther, but rather a righteousness that Christ freely and mercifully bestowed upon Luther. Justification by grace through faith is, of course, a theological insight. A new kind of knowledge about God fulfilled Luther's yearning for union with God.

This is not the place to retell the complex and interesting story of the Reformation, although the frictions among ecclesiastical loyalties that this movement introduced will make up a main part of the cultural setting for the story told by the next chapter.

Each territory adopted or developed a church suited to its own extent and form of government. By and large the major monarchies remained Catholic, except for England where a national church blending catholic and protestant elements under the monarch came into being. Protestants made little headway south of the Alps and Pyrenees; they lost the struggle for France. But they throve in the Swiss Cantons and in many German duchies as well as the city-republics.

John Calvin in Geneva, like Luther in Saxony, discovered a theological answer to the mystical question. Let those who would contemplate the future life study the scripture to learn about God as sovereign. This program commended itself widely to city people along the Rhine River. John Knox adapted it to the small kingdom of Scotland.

The more radical reformers remained closer to the mystics' style of religiousness and showed somewhat less interest in theological systems than did the reformers who maintained a union of church and state. Those who kept the spiritual realm independent of magistrates included Conrad Grebel and Balthasar Hubmaier. Both doubted the validity of baptizing infants who lacked the capacity to discern and narrate their own experience of redemption. Actually these men were not far from the religious views of Huldreich Zwingli, who emphasized inner, spiritual grace to the point of denying that finite things could convey infinite values. But Zwingli worked for the magistrates of Zurich as he purged church practices in accordance with biblical standards.

The man who became (in 1555) Pope Paul IV was named Giovanni Pietro Caraffa, a native of Naples who was one of the main organizers in Rome (about 1517) of the "Oratory of Divine Love." This association of devout persons, both clerical and lay, clung to traditional catholic doctrine while infusing their own lives and eventually the life of the church with evangelical spirituality. Their wish for cleansing of the old church came true, slowly but surely, through the decrees of the Council of Trent (from 1545 to 1563) and with the rapid rise to international influence of the Society of Jesus. In this outburst of spiritual energy is to be seen again a mingling of mystical with theological styles of religiousness, in the sense that right thinking about the character of God became the equivalent of genuine union with the divine.

Thus the theologians' distinct way of being Christian persisted, indeed, into the second generation of reformers, when Philipp Melanchthon centered knowledge of God on justifying faith, Calvin on scriptures as Christ's law, and the fathers of the Council of Trent on ecclesiastical authority. It was their immediate successors who turned the business of the theologian into making claims for one's own church and attacks against all others. A mode of life dedicating the mind to explore divine reality and to instruct universal human reason prevailed for more than five centuries before giving way to intellectual sectarianism.

CHRISTS

The medieval theologians, no less than the medieval mystics, concentrated on the human, incarnate Christ, but for different reasons. To the mystics he made deity accessible by inviting a few diligent souls to ascend with him to spiritual colloquy or union with the divine being. To the theologians he made deity accessible by issuing a proclamation to all reasonable persons about the nature of God. To mystics he came as a son who introduced a few people to his father. To the theologians he was a son who told everybody about his father.

Both, of course, paid central attention to his death. Surely the crucified Christ ranks as the most frequent and widespread of any single depiction of the founder by and to medieval Christians. In a vivid way they sensed him as dying for them in their times and in their places. The earlier figures of Christ on the cross tended to be formal and stylized, alive, weightless, often regnant, recognizably victorious by all but Satan, who was fooled by the human form of this divine being. We have seen that a crucifix made in the time of Otto III shows Christ as living emperor of the world. Western crucifixes had already begun (in the 900s) to portray a distinctly human person, dying or already dead. The head bends (usually to its right) in pain or in death. The arms stretch to support the body's dead weight. Later this realism is accented by activities of the crucifiers, now recognizable as medieval men and women driving nails into the hands and feet and lancing the breast of the savior; their sin caused him to suffer. These wounds and others made by the thorny crown drip or even spurt blood. The crowd of soldiers, disciples, and onlookers becomes a throng of contemporary nobles and serfs, fine ladies and servants, and knights in armor on horseback. As the period draws to an end, the representational and contemporizing urge rules such masters as the elder Lucas Cranach and Mathias Grünewald, whose crucifixion scenes ask the beholder to participate in a current event. Just as our period closed, Michelangelo Buonarroti made (between 1550 and 1556) a statue of himself assisting the women in removing Christ's cadaver from the cross.

Medieval men and women ate the body of Christ, for the mass became the supreme occasion of his presence and of their devotion. It was the leading belief (by the mid-900s) that the eucharistic bread and wine changed materially into his flesh and blood. For denying that change Bérenger of Tours paid the penalty of excommunication (in 1050), then denied his own teaching so he might eat the sacrament. The Fourth Lateran Council (in 1215) made transubstantiation *de fide* so that to doubt the doctrine was heresy. And the period ended precisely when various groups' varied experiences of Christ's presence with them in their eucharists became sharp. The impossibility (in the mid-1500s) of keeping Christendom united turned most decisively on this point, which split Protestants from Catholics and the several kinds of Protestants from one another.

The medieval theologians' quest for knowledge about God drove them to a concern for Christ as teacher. Again, this period held no monopoly on this depiction. These were the times of the first frescoes of the Sermon on the Mount, but the theme hardly became typical.[30] What is interesting is that the teacher-Christ suddenly became a medieval teacher, a contemporary in appearance, dress, and setting. He had long been pictured teaching the apostles. Now he addressed medieval scholars. From the time of Otto II comes the codex of Egbert, archbishop of Trier, with a conventional Christ, book under left arm and right hand raised in pedagogical gesture, teaching Peter and another man labeled simply, "apostle." Except for the presence of the two apostles, the figure of Christ differs little from that in Gottschalk's Gospel-book from Carolingian times.[31] From the middle of our period, however, comes Fra Angelico da Fiesole's fresco over the refectory door of the monastery of San Marco in Florence. Here Christ is a medieval pilgrim being detained by two Dominican friars, in obvious parallel to Christ's meeting two men on the road to Emmaus and teaching them the meaning of the scriptures. Late in the period Fra Bartolommeo made a strikingly similar fresco for the pilgrim hospice of the same monastery, in which the pilgrim Christ instructs two medieval monks who also touch his body. The teacher-Christ of Cima da Conegliano (from 1489 to 1508) stands, a colossal figure in cinctured garb, with a large book and the teaching gesture. This figure rises out of and completely dominates the landscape of mountains, a medieval village, a road, two men, and a donkey.[32] Before our period, representations of the teaching Christ are plentiful, but the conventional audiences are the apostles or the doctors in the temple. In the medieval representations Christ is teaching the medieval men and women who populate the crucifixion scenes.

A crucifixion scene illustrating a medieval manuscript shows an identifiably human Jesus, feet nailed to the cross, body leaning forward, arms freely outstretched toward a kneeling Bernard of Clairvaux, face uplifted, arms outstretched toward Christ. The two figures are ready for their mystical embrace. Six Cistercian monks look on. A painting of Thomas Aquinas shows the doctor seated, holding his books in his lap, surrounded above by heavenly figures who direct their knowledge to him. At the top is Christ, speaking at once to Thomas and to the Gospel-writers and to Peter and Paul, who in turn direct wisdom to Thomas. On his right is Aristotle, on his left Plato, making their inputs. Below reclines Averroës, whose book Thomas corrects. Lines radiate from the schoolman to crowds of contemporary admirers who receive enlightenment from his teachings.[33] Bernard the mystic finds absolute union with the deity, Thomas the theologian gains universal knowledge about the deity. Each in his own way exemplifies the typical religious aspirations of medieval men and women to unify culture under the Christendom that Christ founded and headed.

V
ALLEGIANCE

Moralists and Pietists

in the Territorial Monarchies

1556-1806

Holy Roman Emperor Charles V formally abdicated (in 1556) to spend his last two years living in semi-monastic seclusion and gazing piously at Titian's painting of the Last Judgment. More than sixty regal and princely titles recorded his rule over areas vaster than those of any previous European emperor. As supreme head of the German empire, he presided over hundreds of federated entities, ranging from city-republics to kingdoms. Charles was king of Castile and Aragon, sole ruler of an empire stretching from Naples and Sicily in the Mediterranean to the Pacific coast of South America and on to southeast Asia. Charles was archduke of Austria, duke of Burgundy and the Netherlands, and king of Hungary. And Charles was Catholic.

But the church on which hopes for a unified Europe had been pinned for centuries lay riven as never before. Enmity between Catholics and Lutherans was not the worst of it. Giovanni Caraffa, enthroned (in 1555) as Pope Paul IV, suspected the Lutherans, but he harbored deeper suspicions of things Spanish, including Spanish Catholicism. The Lutherans in turn viewed the radical Protestants, especially the Anabaptists, as worse than Catholics. Thus Lutherans and Catholics, albeit enemies, struck a live-and-let-live compromise (in 1555) at the imperial diet at Augsburg.

The people of each territory in the empire were to practice the religion of the ruler, whether Catholic or Lutheran. In the free cities both religions were to be tolerated. Other churches got nothing. Temporary and gross as the compromise proved to be, it augured a new day in which the source of social solidarity, for centuries a universal church for all areas, was transformed to the particular monarch of each area. There it remained for two and one-half centuries.

Napoleon Bonaparte ended the period (1556 to 1806) with the stroke of a pen, dissolving the Holy Roman Empire and dismissing the last formalities of a sacred European imperium. Having ordered the pope to crown him (in 1804) emperor of France at Notre Dame, Napoleon snatched the crown from the pontiff's hands and placed it on his own head. In a decade Napoleon ruled or by alliance controlled an even vaster European empire than had Charles V. He also initiated the modern era of autonomous nations.

The era bracketed by Charles and Napoleon was one of religious extremes: of extreme ecclesiastical formalism on the one hand and of extreme individual devotion on the other. Publicly, the issue of ecclesiastical allegiance erupted into wars. Neither before nor since that century (1560 to 1660) of intolerance have Christians in greater numbers pillaged, exiled, and slain one another for the faith. Privately, the aspiration for personal expertise in devoutness stimulated piety and morality. Neither before nor since that epoch have Christians in greater numbers or with more care cultivated higher mastery in personal religion.

The two extremes, however, were closely related in that the very cultural crises that produced ecclesiastical formalism also evoked religious virtuosity. This paradox will be resolved, and the emergence of moralism and pietism as exemplary forms of spirituality will be explained, by paying brief attention to these major crises: contests over ecclesiastical allegiance, flickering attempts at the restoration of Latin Christendom, compromises pointing toward religious toleration, tensions between royal absolutism and aristocratic constitutionalism, eruptions in scientific understandings of the universe, and conscious employment of the fine arts in the service of the human emotions.

TENSIONS

After the Reformation and the Council of Trent (from 1545 to 1563), every political territory of Europe defended or extended its boundaries in the interest of the ecclesiastical allegiance that the boundaries defined. The so-called wars of religion, notorious in the first half of the period, raged under banners of churchly loyalties. Through them absolutist rulers enlarged or lost territories, and constitutionalists tried to contain absolutism. Southern or Romance Europe on the whole remained Catholic and absolutist, save the perimeter provinces of France where the elite Huguenots flourished. The leaders of those French Protestants, just like Catholic leaders, believed their religion could prevail in all of France. But the battles that blazed also vented smoldering rivalries between the noble families of Guise and Bourbon and between those families and the ruling house of Valois. Philip II of Spain intervened, hoping to claim France, and delayed religious conciliation by nearly a decade. The Bourbon Henry IV, a Huguenot, vacillated before deciding that Paris was worth attending mass; Richard Dunn judged that his "politically motivated conversion scandalized the ultra-Catholics even more than the Huguenots."[1] When he made peace (in 1598) with Philip he granted the Huguenots freedom of public worship in designated towns and freedom of private worship in any nobleman's household.

Calvinists found religious sanctions for revolt against ungodly princes. Jesuits justified the assassination of Protestant rulers. Lutherans conformed their churches to the duchies and kingdoms where they prevailed. Everybody attempted to defend or extend his preferred church by arranging dynastic marriages. Thus the northern provinces of the Netherlands, bequeathed by Charles V to his Spanish successor, revolted against Philip; even in this instance it is impossible to isolate the conflict of Calvinists and Catholics from the revolt of constitutional republicans against an absolute monarchy.

Within the empire of Germany the Bohemian Protestants also rebelled against a fanatically Catholic heir to the Hapsburg throne, Ferdinand II, beginning the Thirty Years' War. This initial revolt was soon put down (by 1622), but the compromise of Augsburg had come unstuck through three generations of shifts from one religion to another as one prince succeeded another. This war, which cost Germany between a third and two-fifths of its population, was thereafter waged by non-Germans.

Soldiers of fortune caring little or nothing for religion, like Count Peter Ernst von Mansfeld II and Prince Albrecht Eusebius Wenzel von Wallenstein, exploited the unrest always for personal gain and sometimes for mere tricks. King Gustavus Adolphus of Sweden, on the other hand, cared much for the Lutherans of the north when he declared himself their military protector and then used his subsidies from the Catholic king of France to extend the territories of Protestant Sweden. It cost Gustavus his life in battle to turn the tide against Hapsburg imperialism. In the end Germany reverted to the compromise of ecclesiastical territorialism.

The earliest English Puritans antedated Calvin and Calvinism. Although they pledged obedience to all rulers, even tyrants, they also predicted rebellion against any monarch who failed to rule according to biblical precepts.[2] Eventually it became evident that Charles I would rule England by self-declared divine right even if he must suspend parliament. But when the Scots invaded the north (in 1640), he needed funds that only parliament could provide. In revenge the Long Parliament suspended the monarchy. The Puritan Revolution certainly centered on religious zeal more powerfully than had the French wars and the drawn-out conflicts in Germany. The fifty-nine men on the High Court of Justice who sentenced the king to death for treason (in 1649) were carrying to logical conclusion the biblical and moral premises of Puritanism: cut down the unbiblical and therefore immoral king.

Then the New Model Army's leader, Oliver Cromwell, presided over a Puritan republic for only a few years before disbanding parliament and installing himself as Lord Protector. Although he refused (in 1657) the title of king, Cromwell's own religious principles made him play the absolute monarch. The revolutionary Puritans conducted a religious war in the political interest of replacing territorial monarchy with a constitutional parliament in an England whose size and complexity doomed the new system to failure.

The English restored to their throne Stuart kings who were more absolutist and more favorable to Catholicism than the king who was killed for his milder royalism and his national "catholic" church of England. Only with the rigged coup (in 1688) by William III of Orange and his wife, Mary II, against Mary's father, James II, did England and then Great Britain find the blend of royal and republican government that produced (in the 1700s) the most powerful nation in Europe.

Attempts by three nostalgic geniuses to reunify Christendom under their own absolute sway clearly indicate the newness of the new age. Not accidentally, all three were Catholic. But their religion was more national than papal, and they tried, respectively, to recenter Europe not on Rome but on Madrid, Paris, and Vienna. The attempt by Philip II of Spain at the beginning of the period was genuine; militarily it failed. The last one, by Louis XIV of France, glittered with pomp and bristled with intrigue; it never had a chance. Ferdinand II of Austria made the last serious effort; it floundered.

Philip poured riches mined from his South American colonies into pan-European negotiations and campaigns. He personally managed a vast imperial administration extending to the Asian islands that bore his name. He demolished the navy of the Ottoman Turks in the Battle of Lepanto (in 1571) and in nine years he made Portugal and Brazil his own. Coveting the throne in Paris, he prolonged French wars of ecclesiastical allegiance. With designs on the German empire he sought to marry his daughter to the emperor, Rudolf II. "Philip felt personally responsible for all his subjects, past, present and future," noted Heer, "indeed for all Europeans, the Bohemians not excepted."[3] He pledged to the pope that he would never allow his subjects to be heretics (i.e. Protestants). In attempting to bring the English and to keep the Dutch under his rule he overextended himself, and English sailors (in 1588) sank his Mediterranean navy in northern waters. No successor to the Spanish throne would ever recover the power Philip had exercised at his zenith before the Armada sank. Not even his splendid efforts could put Humpty Dumpty together again.

Philip's great-grandson, Louis XIV of France, inherited the vision of restoring European unity. Acceding to the throne at the age of five, Louis reigned (from 1643 to 1715) longer than any other European monarch. After Cardinal Mazarin died (in 1661), Louis personally managed the affairs of state by drawing efficient ministers into the service, and the nobility into the subservience, of the court.

In France he was thus divine-right king incarnate, earning the reputation of having proclaimed, "The state, it is I." He held slaving stations in Africa and trading stations in India. In North America he owned but barely exploited New France, stretching from the mouth of the St. Lawrence to Hudson's Bay and from the Great Lakes to the mouth of the Mississippi. Louis probably would have conquered the Dutch had not William of Orange in desperation opened the dikes and forced him to withdraw. When William became (in 1689) king of England, his anti-French alliance gained the might it needed to hold Louis's expansionism in check. Nevertheless, Louis continued to scheme for rule over Austria and through it over the empire. But he could not even find all of Humpty's parts.

For by Louis' time the churches' influence was waning, especially in regions where monarchs insisted on ecclesiastical conformity. He dreamed of unifying Europe more around himself and his heirs than around a common religion, more in Bourbondom than Christendom. Thus the last flickering hope of restoring a religiously ecumenic Europe had been the one nourished by Ferdinand II of Austria, who during the first half of the Thirty Years' War seemed to be renovating the Holy Roman Empire. But in fact his efforts had the effect of consolidating an extensive Austrian Catholic kingdom under the Hapsburg dynasty, hardly that of restoring an imperial Europe. Ferdinand's greatest campaign quelled the rebellion of the Bohemians and drove them back into the Catholic fold. Dunn called them "the only thoroughly Protestantized community to be reconverted to Rome during the wars of religion."[4]

The Treaty of Westphalia ended the Thirty Years' War (in 1648) and showed the Holy Roman Empire to be indeed the hollow eggshell it had seemed since Charles V's abdication. It lacked every necessary condition of an actual imperium save a person claiming to be emperor. No central administration, no standing army, no system of taxation, no consensus in law, no common calendar unified it. The imperial diet, to which France and Sweden (after 1648) sent delegates, convened delegates of three hundred territorial governments ranging from mighty monarchies to independent cities. Voltaire's apothegm, "neither Holy nor Roman nor an empire," was no current *mot* for his day but rendered solid historical judgment. The Treaty of Westphalia renewed and extended the religious territorialism initiated in the Peace of Augsburg; European unity, cracked a century earlier, was now permanently shattered.

"Territorialism" more accurately than "toleration" describes most attempts during our period to disinfect religion's divisive virulence. The nobility of Poland at the Warsaw Confederation had prematurely (in 1573) tolerated and harmonized different religions. This irenic approach soon yielded to the narrow, Tridentine view that Roman Catholicism was the only Christianity and that Poland belonged to it. By the Edict of Nantes Henry IV (in 1598) let French Huguenots worship openly in specified places, none within a day's journey of Paris. The French kingdom remained officially Catholic. In Germany the Treaty of Westphalia granted territorial religious rights to Calvinists as well as Catholics and Lutherans, but in effect southern Germany was Catholic, northern Germany Lutheran, and the Rhineland cities Reformed. Even the English Act of Toleration, actually designed to unite the realm behind William and Mary, maintained (since 1689) the Church of England's official establishment. Dissenters had to swear (Quakers might affirm) loyalty to the Anglican king and queen, and ministers had to subscribe to the Thirty-Nine Articles of Religion excepting the two in favor of baptizing babies. Roman Catholics and Unitarians were proscribed. Emperor Joseph II, whose church reforms prepared Catholicism for the modern world, eventually issued (in 1781) an Edict of Toleration allowing private worship by non-Catholics.

Only in the Dutch republic did widespread toleration prevail.

That Calvinist state granted (in 1577) freedom of worship to Anabaptists and later tolerated Catholics, Jews, and nonbelievers. Mainly the business interests fought religious bigotry or uniformity. The first western nation to place governmental restraints and constraints on religion out of bounds did so near the end of our period when the United States of America adopted the Bill of Rights; even so, two state governments long retained official churches. In Europe territorial monarchs preserved territorial religion.

Very broadly speaking, the absolutist monarchs in preferring Catholicism had to contend with their Jesuit confessors, whose loyalty to Rome called into question the theory of divine-right kingship. Moreover, James I and Charles I of England found ways to make the officially "protestant" Church of England buttress absolutism, while Lutheran states generated few constitutional checks on princes—witness the rise of Brandenburg under Frederick William (died in 1688) and of Prussia under its *Junkers* and its Hohenzollern kings. Moderate constitutionalism had a long career limiting monarchy in England before the Puritans stretched it to the breaking point. Otherwise, constitutional government was the political expression of the Calvinist territories, all of them small.

Absolutist monarchs who espoused the same religion fought one another for territorial integrity and expansion. So drastic a threat to Europe as the Ottoman Turks' siege (in 1683) of Vienna not even momentarily united the great Catholic rulers. Louis XIV's agents were aiding the Turks all along. Ironically, volunteer soldiers from Germany and Poland saved Vienna. A volunteer officer, Prince Eugene of Savoy, deserted Louis' court and broke Turkish power as he extended Hapsburg rule over Hungary.

Nowhere did religion decisively determine the contest between absolutism and constitutionalism. Everywhere ecclesiastical allegiance became instrumental to politics. Puritan England came close to being the exception, but the Tudors who thrived on constitutionalism had been objects of Puritan protest. When the

Puritans took government from the absolutist Stuarts they could not keep it constitutional. And the Puritans were disappearing from England (not from English America) when the great constitutional instruments were drawn (from 1688 to 1707), first of the Glorious Revolution, then of the Act of Settlement, and then of the Act of Union, joining England, Scotland, and Ireland into Great Britain.

The century of Puritan ascendancy confused religion and politics, but failed to fuse them. Imagine yourself a law-abiding Londoner born in 1615 and destined to live seventy-five years. You are baptized an Anglican and raised to tolerate mild Puritans in your church. As a teenager you turn very high-church, and when you are married you are ready to force Anglo-Catholicism on the unwilling Scots. You raise your young children Presbyterians, but as they grow up you turn Congregationalist. In middle age you revert to moderate Anglicanism, then ripen into a crypto-Roman Catholic like your king. Before you die you are a generous, if somewhat bored, Anglican again, having been told it would not much matter if you turned Baptist. In your lifetime you have paid taxes to support Protestant kings against parliament and parliament against the same kings, to finance civil war and regicide, then to restore the lineage of the king who was executed, and finally to arrange a *coup d'état* against that lineage.

The instance is extreme, for you were living in an age of extremes. And if you had a strong bent toward religion, your concern for political and ecclesiastical allegiance paled before the consistent advice of most of your pastors. Cultivate your personal religious faculties, they counseled, by constant private practice, with the emphasis either on pious feelings or on moral behavior. Such would have been the real stuff of your religion. If you also had a healthy intellectual curiosity, you would have repudiated your inherited Christian world view in favor of one shaped by the new science.

The old view had blended Aristotle's physics, Ptolemy's astronomy, and Galen's physiology. The three elements coalesced in the early years of Christianity, which over the centuries hallowed the outlook with theological benedictions. The earth, with hell at its core, was a blob of nasty matter around which revolved concentric spheres, each purer and more ethereal than those it encompassed, the final and finest being God's heaven. All creatures stood in a hierarchy. Man fell uncomfortably in the middle, enmeshed in matter and animal brutality yet stamped in spirit with the image of the creator. Below were inanimate matter, vegetables, and animals. Above were immaterial and rational angels, archangels, cherubim, etc., and, finally, pure divinity. The chemical elements of earth, fire, water, and air constituted terrestrial existence. The human body consisted of fluids, or humors (blood, phlegm, yellow bile, and black bile), whose balance regulated health. It was all so because God made it so.

To be sure, medieval theologians had asked new questions in order to elaborate their knowledge of God and to enfold new thought forms into the unity of Christendom. The scientific revolution arose from the far more radical question of whether nature could be understood as in itself a perfect system, governed by laws discoverable through repeated observation and controlled experimentation. To understand those laws would bring nature, no longer needing grace to perfect it, into the service of humankind.

Science underwent no overnight revolution, yet the fundamental changes during the period of territorial monarchies transformed western civilization. Two investigations based on observation challenged the traditional views of the human body and the stars. A Belgian anatomist, Andreas Vesalius, published *On the Structure of the Human Body,* and a Polish astronomer, Nicolaus Copernicus, published *On the Revolutions of the Heavenly Bodies* (both in 1543); Vesalius corrected many of Galen's errors but retained his assumptions. When an English physiologist, William Harvey, demonstrated (in 1628) the circulation of blood from heart through arteries through veins through lungs and back to heart, he exploded those assumptions. Copernicus' work was advanced by Kepler. Then four men produced studies whose implications Alfred North Whitehead called "the greatest single intellectual success which mankind has achieved."[5] He referred to Galileo's research into the acceleration and deceleration of moving bodies, to Descartes' mathematical models of scientific concepts, to Huygens' powerful telescopes and wave theory of light, and to Newton's unified theories of the forces at work in the universe.

The inherited Christian world view was rendered dubious as a set of semantic instruments for understanding the universe of nature—and of man so far as he participated in nature. It remained useful as a set of spiritual symbols whose power one might or might not choose to utilize. This is not to read back into our period the antagonism between science and religion, nor even the full optionality of being religious that characterized the subsequent period. Without enmity, the earlier science quietly displaced Christian bases for interpreting the essence and the function of matter, motion, mass, the solar system, the organic dimension of being human, and human thought. Observation, investigation, mathematical models, and experimentation supplanted belief, deduction, theological models, and revelation as the means for knowing the palpable world and man's place in it. Nevertheless, the Christian myth of creation and redemption was hardly questioned.

The province of religion steadily shrank as sense impressions, thought processes, memory, and other distinctly human functions came under analysis by associational psychologists. Like empirical science, the new psychology found no ready welcome in the universities. Both were pursued by like-minded individuals who joined voluntarily into societies devoted to expertness in describing and utilizing the world of nature and man. These new understandings were achieved by the cultivation of personal ingenuity. Precisely the same quest for personal virtuosity patterned religious exercises. Religion too came to be pursued by like-minded individuals who joined voluntarily into societies devoted to expertness in describing and utilizing the world of spirit and man.

Religion shared that universe with the fine arts, the making and performing of which provided additional outlets for virtuosi and, in part, further means of cultivating devotion. Nowhere more markedly than in drama did this age of genius flourish and produce national or territorial styles. *Commedia del'arte* in Italy, historical tragedy in England (before the Puritans closed the theaters) and the comedy of manners and heroic drama after the Restoration, religious-philosophical plays and *autos sacramentales* in Spain, and neoclassical drama in France were the achievements of playrights and actors who studied, practiced, and experimented to be virtuosi in their crafts.

The other art forms lent themselves more than drama to promoting virtuosity in religious devotion. Composers and performers of music—vocal, instrumental, and mixed—systematized polyphony, developed sacred oratorios and secular operas, and exploited contrapuntal and fugal patterns. Italians excelled at the Baroque opera, Germans at classical variations on the sonata form, French at ballet. Baroque painters and sculptors and architects, working in an international movement more to the liking of Catholics than Protestants, developed remarkable inventiveness in mixing the plastic arts of painting, stucco, gilt, statuary, and building design into works that impressed the viewer with the ethereal sublimity of sacred places and themes. The less profuse Protestant art drew beholders into emotionally more-than-real biblical scenes, and the simpler Protestant architecture used the steeple to point human attention heavenward.

All these arts reflected ecclesiastical and political territorialism and they all served to some degree to instruct Europeans about their religion. More important, all opened new avenues of feeling, particularly the emotions involving a sense of dutifulness to the deity. Thus there is a spiritual kinship among such otherwise diverse works as Milton's *Paradise Lost* and Zinzendorf's voluptuous hymns, El Greco's *Burial of Count Orgaz* and Rembrandt's *Prodigal Son,* Palestrina's *Mass of Pope Marcellus II* and Bach's *Passion According to St. Matthew,* the simple spires of Christopher Wren's churches, and the overpoweringly affective rococo temples of Balthasar Neumann. The kinship is double. Each work exhibited the individual artist's distinct genius, his virtuosity in creating his own unique artifact, and also the religious artifacts created a characteristic religious mood in the hearts and souls of the people who read or viewed or sang or heard them.

By means of these religious moods men and women internalized their ecclesiastical allegiances, which externally tended to formalities, intrigues, and wars. The moods helped people test how far they had made their particular religion their own personal frame of mind and temperament. Moments of heightened religious moods became the occasions for this self-examination and self-measurement, particularly of two kinds.

One way was to take stock of one's dutifulness to the deity by the warmth of one's personal blessedness and devotion. To assist this endeavor, there appeared a flood of handbooks on how to estimate and advance one's progress in piety. These were not mystical ladders for a few souls to climb toward unity with God but charts guiding everybody to the haven of heartfelt devotion. A crude English tinker told how his life was changed when his bride brought into their house two such guides, *The Plain Man's Pathway to Heaven* by Arthur Dent and *The Practice of Piety Directing a Christian How To Walk that He May Please God* by Lewis Bayly. The titles and the incident were typical of pietists.

The other way was to measure one's dutifulness to God by the cleanness of one's conscience. For Catholics this desire centered in the confessional, where priests used a welter of manuals on how to help people justify their deeds when they did not follow the traditional rules of behavior. From Protestants this urge called forth books of maxims and case histories covering not only religious behavior itself but also everyday affairs such as relations between husbands and wives, parents and children, employers and laborers, patients and doctors, citizens and magistrates, teachers and pupils, and the rest.

Among the most famous books in England were two by Jeremy Taylor; their titles show the scope of Christian moralism. *The Rule and Exercises of Holy Living, in which are described the means and instruments of obtaining every virtue, and the rem-*

edies against every vice, and considerations serving to the resisting of every temptation, together with prayers containing the whole duty of a Christian, and the parts of devotion fitted to all occasions, and furnished for all necessities (published 1650) uses six adjectives to say the topic will be exhausted! In a year Taylor was ready with the companion volume on holy dying, on "preparing ourselves and others respectively for a blessed death," on "the remedies against the evils and temptations proper to the state of sickness, with prayers and virtuous acts for sick and dying persons and those who attended them." Such concerns typified the moralists.

A brief introduction to the Christian quest for a clean conscience in the period of territorial monarchies sets the stage for a more detailed examination of both Puritan and Thomistic moralism and then of Jeremy Taylor as a representative moralist who drew on both these sources. Then an introduction to the concurrent Christian quest for a warm heart will set the stage for paying closer attention to some representative pietists, first the Jansenists and John Bunyan, then a German, Nikolaus Ludwig von Zinzendorf, who exhibited *par excellence* the affective religious impulse. The latter survey can be briefer because the pietists expressed their heart-religion more uniformly from one territory to another than the moralists expressed their versions of conscience-religion.

But here must be entered the reminder that the two styles of being Christian existed side by side, always two sides to the coin of religious virtuosity and sometimes in the same person. The two were fully united in John Wesley, a Protestant of warm heart and high moralism, and in Alphonsus Liguori, to Catholics at once the prince of moral theologians and the epitome of affective, self-cultivated devotion to Christ and the Virgin Mary.

Both styles were ways in which devotees sought personal, religious mastery by practicing spiritual exercises. Adepts at moralism and pietism shared the sense that individual persons possessed capacities to train themselves into greater and greater excellence in exercising their religious faculties. These athletic Christians differed over whether the conscience or the heart was the primary seat of those faculties, although the moralists' good consciences led to affectionate devotion just as the pietists' heart-religion issued in works of charity. Both were egalitarian, for both kept their agenda open to participation by any earnestly religious person. Only extreme quietists cultivated inwardness for its own sake; only extreme legalists made good works the whole of religion. Representative moralists and pietists alike measured their progress experimentally, the one by testing the conscience for its cleanness, the other by testing the affections for their warmth. Both sought nothing less than perfection in practice, moralists as Jesus' obedient pupils and servants, pietists as Jesus' friends and followers. Thus both styles personalized the ideal of ecclesiastical allegiance that marked the period. Both enabled people to verify their loyalties by living up to their respective goals of Christian spirituality.

MORALISTS

Christian moralism pervaded both Catholic and Protestant territories. The public stir over ecclesiastical allegiance revived European Catholics' interest in the most thorough statement their traditional faith had ever found, the *Summa Theologica* of Thomas Aquinas. During the Reformation, this work appealed especially to German, Italian, and French scholars. Its comprehensive moral theology combines Christian and Aristotelian ethics.

Dominican scholars at Salamanca made this feature of the work speak to the concern for a clear conscience, particularly after the Jesuits spread Bartolomeo Medina's theory of probabilism. Medina wondered how to guide moral choices when he could justify more than one course of action and found none entirely commendable. To the question of whether traditional moral law always excluded human choice, he answered (in 1577) that "It seems to me that if there is a probable opinion, it is lawful to follow it, even though the opposite is more probable."[6]

Others, particularly Jesuits, greatly extended this claim of individual liberty and evaded the letter of moral law. Intricate debates ensued for two centuries. At one extreme, rigorists held that law prevailed over liberty unless the rightness of the other course was so probable as to be morally certain. At the other extreme, laxists could justify acting upon any probable moral opinion, however more probable its opposite. In between fell subtle gradations. Near the end of our period Liguori, a virtuoso in both pietistic and moralistic exercises, settled the question for Catholics. His theory of "equiprobabilism" said that only when the opinion of law and the opinion of liberty were equally probable might one opt with a clear conscience.

The ins and outs of the Catholic debate over morality hold considerable doctrinal interest for a church historian. For religious history they show this period's preoccupation with the confessional as the means of examining and improving Catholics' consciences. The elaborate moral theology produced by this preoccupation indicates how eagerly Catholics searched out religious sanctions for the total range of human behavior. Priestly authority continued to lodge, of course, in ordination, but priestly power shifted from the base of symbolizing the unity of Christendom to that of effectively supervising individual consciences and daily lives.

Confessors needed to know both moral principles and typical cases drawn from actual experience in order to teach penitents whether or not there was a sin to be confessed; if so, how grave a penance should be levied; also, how to avoid repeating the sin. Only then would the sacramental authority to apply forgiveness to the particular case come effectively into play.

Throughout our period this lore was accumulated and refined. In more recent times concern to prevent a confessor's revealing by word or gesture the nature of any penitent's confession has made such lore highly abstract and formalized. For upper-class Europeans this "priestly" power has finally passed to psychotherapists, who have developed ways of swapping records of actual cases without breaching confidentiality. In the period under consideration Catholics attained a high degree of subtlety in their moralism, centered on the confessional and derived from natural and revealed law.

A similar quest for divine sanction upon every aspect of living (and dying) led the growing number of Christians under the influence of Calvinism to a similar casuistry. Their moralism was based more strictly in the Bible as the charter of allowable human activity. Those Reformed Christians, to be sure, developed (from 1559 to 1566) confessions of faith for their various territories. The Huguenots agreed to a French confession drawn by Calvin, and there followed in quick succession the Scottish Confession, the Belgic Confession, the Heidelberg Catechism, and the Second Helvetic Confession. Common to Calvinists of every territory was regard for scripture as comprehensive positive, divine law.

All Christians, of course, looked somehow to scriptures as the norm of true religion. Calvinists went further and used the Bible as a sufficient guide, explicitly or implicitly detailing whatever Christ allowed or outlawed for his people. Nicholas Bound, an English Calvinist, published (in 1595) an exhaustive book regulating Sabbath behavior. He forbade "honest recreations" and "lawful pleasures"—even the discussion of them or of any other secular matter. All his morality focused on keeping holy the Sabbath day, and every day tended to be a little sabbath of its own. Calvinists in Cromwell's parliament introduced a bill to prohibit "idle sitting, openly, at gates or doors or elsewhere" and even "walking in churchyards" on the Sabbath.[7]

In England the Puritans, Separatists, and high and low Anglicans fought for a century (from 1580s to 1680s), over the right form of ministry, worship, and doctrine. Despite their battles they remained birds of a feather in their common concern for guiding consciences by religious principles. Where the Calvinists looked solely to scriptures, the Anglicans also searched early Christian tradition and applied right reason in lining out the norms of moral theology. Both avoided the Catholic practice of channeling moral guidance solely through private confession to a priest, although high Anglicans kept this practice optional.

Members of every party addressed vernacular books to everybody who could read them. At the extremes, somewhat ironically, the Protestants' recourse to the open scriptural norm prompted more public discussion of personal cases of conscience than was tolerated by the Catholics, whose sacramentalism tended to emphasize privacy.

For private confession, however, Protestant moralists found surrogates. After Richard Baxter had preached to his congregation in Kidderminster, "Every Thursday evening my neighbors that were most desirous and had opportunity met at my house, and there one of them repeated the sermon, and afterwards they proposed what doubts any of them had about the sermon, or any case of conscience, and I resolved their doubts."[8] Baxter, like his Puritan predecessors William Perkins and William Ames, compiled manuals on how to attain private morality and public justice. Their books depended as heavily on the case method and the complete coverage of behavior as did those of Anglicans like Robert Sanderson, John Sharp, Joseph Hall, and Jeremy Taylor. Works of all those writers, spanning the first half of our period, commanded high regard through the second half. The fact that, as the era wore on, English moralists became more rationalistic does not alter the underlying fact that conscience remained their steady concern. Jeremy Bentham's baldly utilitarian ethics were still being countered at the end of the period in terms of duty and conscience and divine law by his elder contemporary, William Paley.

Only the Lutherans failed to produce a rich casuistic literature; they deeply suspected the slightest suggestion that doing good works helped one to be saved. Their early battle cries, justification by grace through faith and scripture's sole authority, no longer united them after Luther died (in 1546); thereafter, his followers fell into theological wrangling and creedal formalism. Philipp Melanchthon insisted that faith must produce good works, but Nikolaus von Amsdorf countered that good works did downright spiritual harm. The issue polarized German Lutherans. Various parties finally agreed (in 1580) on the precisianist Formula of Concord, signed by fifty-one princes, thirty-five cities, and more than eight thousand ministers. Then the controversy grew serious over how to interpret the Formula. Lutherans did not lack desire for good consciences; they simply measured cleanliness by right belief rather than by right behavior. Rigid insistence on orthodox doctrine characterized much Lutheran religiousness through the period. The accompanying pietism engendered a distinct morality that was tested more by inner feelings of love than by codes of conduct toward the neighbor.

The moralists wanted nothing less than complete rules, drawn from Christian principles and applied to every cranny of living. The breakup of Christendom spurred them to refine principles, elaborate codes, and specify cases. Each ecclesiastical allegiance worked out its own particular yet also general systems. All these moralists shared the starting point of Aquinas' thorough enumeration of the basic issues of moral theology. But where Aquinas worked toward unifying Christendom, the new task was to give each distinct church its distinct yet coherent system of ethical decisions. Each claimed superiority over all the others by the criteria, first, the simplicity of moral principles and second, the coherent generality of rules applying to church and home, neighborhood and marketplace, legislature and courtroom, etc.

For example, since it was (and is) neither possible nor prudent in all human circumstances to tell the truth, the whole truth, and nothing but the truth, the question of lying provides a nice example of an issue that all moralists had to resolve. They resolved it differently. Telling a white lie might be entirely moral for a Spanish Catholic confessing to a Jesuit, given the reasonable probability that the lie would benefit somebody other than its author. A Dutch Calvinist could find very few (if any) occasions when telling a white lie did not soil his conscience. An Anglican following Taylor might excuse a white lie, but only as an isolated instance not conducive to habitual lying.

The infinite complexities of the question dealt with keeping secrets, withholding truth for another's welfare, lying under oath, adjusting to children's mentalities what one said, telling what one believed to be true but was untrue (or vice versa), dissembling, lying for the state in time of war, jesting, storytelling, lying under duress, affirming or denying with mental reservations, equivocating, etc. A favorite puzzler—may an adulteress deny her deed when queried by her husband if her confession would prompt him to kill her lover?—yielded a multitude of contingencies as well as a variety of solutions. Indeed, this "problem of lying," as Thomas Wood noted, was "one of the most intricate in the whole realm of morals."[9]

Each problem had to be resolved according to the principles of one's church and at the same time congruently with the way one solved a host of other problems. Posit, for example, a war: Spain against what to Catholics were heretical English and Dutch Christian states. Then pose the question of whether one should tell a lie to benefit one's country. A devout Spanish Catholic lies to aid his absolutist monarchy, and his Jesuit confessor absolves him from sin because his testimony enacts justice for the church by extending true religion and works charity for the heretics by leading them from error. A devout Anglican does the same for his parliamentary monarchy, and his confessor, say Taylor, finds it a sin because the lie contravened a (hypothetical) treaty between England and Spain; treaty breaking is unreasonable, yet had there been no treaty there would have been no lie. A devout Dutch Calvinist does the same for his republic yet by Amesian casuistry has inexcusably sinned by bearing false witness against his remote neighbor; but a Calvinist soldier in battle might have lied innocently in a stratagem of war, relying on the precedent of Joshua's ambushing the men of Ai. When three do the same thing, it is not the same thing after all!

Or, to take a less grave example, say that a foreign traveler, seeking to collect from your friend a payment of debt that would bankrupt the friend, asks you for directions to the friend's house. You give them, with the parting shot, "You can't miss it." The Catholic out of love for his friend might give misleading directions and add to the parting shot a mental reservation such as, "If you inquire further of your debtor's enemy." The Anglican might perform reasonable duty by giving sketchy but correct directions and adding mentally what common sense would assume, "If you follow very carefully what I have told you." The Calvinist must obey the commandments and give detailed directions, making explicit any reservation in his mind—say, "If you be sure to cross the third bridge over the second canal." In this case, different rules governed the avoidance of lying by mental reservation.

Such complications drove persons who religiously yearned for clear consciences into deep frustration whenever cases arose requiring subtle judgments and engendering conscientious doubt. Black-and-white decisions between palpable good and palpable evil were solved by clear rules, even if rules for a given case varied from one church or confessor to another. But was a course of action right, people worried, if one was uncertain of its rightness? Moral virtuosi needed inward assurance that their motives as well as their deeds were virtuous. And there were vexing decisions where the moral problem was not to choose right or wrong but rather to choose the lesser of two evils.

Early in our period, as noted above, the Dominicans at Salamanca puzzled over cases where an opinion based on law conflicted with an opinion based on liberty. Medina's suggestion that one could rightly choose a probable course against its more probable alternative appealed to Gabriel Vásquez, a Jesuit (since 1569) who advocated and elaborated this notion so vigorously that he threw the Dominicans on the defensive against his thoroughgoing probabilism and made it the hallmark of Jesuit moral theology. Vásquez also took part in the doctrinal struggle between Dominicans and Jesuits over the question of how to reconcile human free will with divine prescience. Luis de Molina, also a Jesuit, focused this issue (in 1588) by giving a large place to freedom and by assigning men and women cooperant roles with the agent of divine grace.

The religious importance of this controversy lies not in who was right or wrong for Catholic faith but in the fact that Molina blended the agency of freedom with the agency of grace so as to make men and women morally able to avoid *all* mortal sins. Practice makes perfect; since religious practice was at issue, God's help was needed, but since it was distinctly human religious practice, the standard of perfection was human. Francisco Suárez, a fellow Jesuit who defended Molina and became the most prolific of modern Catholic theologians, held that since it was fallen humans who strove to observe the moral law, the rules of observance must be tempered to their limited abilities.

Spanish Jesuits attained exemplary adroitness in solving conscientious problems with moral realism. They above all developed Thomist moral theology into a casuistry by which consciences could be eased in cases of doubt as well as instructed in cases of certainty. These men turned the confessional booth into the shrine of Catholic moralism.

Reformed and Anglican casuists drew from the same well of Thomism, using different buckets. First, their principles and examples needed scriptural or scriptural-rational or scriptural-rational-traditional sanctions. Second, they wrote as much to help earnest men and women work through their own moral doubts as to help ministers instruct and preserve their flocks' good consciences; the Anglicans made private confession optional and the Calvinists threw it out. Third, both groups tried to resolve moral doubts by consistently commending the course of higher rectitude instead of by justifying the course of probable ambiguity. Naturally, both condemned the Jesuits for laxity in what they took to be salving instead of scrubbing consciences or, worse, for downright lying about good and evil.

Such charges came easily to Richard Baxter, who based them explicitly on the Jansenist *Provincial Letters,* published anonymously (in 1656-57) by Blaise Pascal. Baxter set forth (in 1659) *A Key for Catholics to open the juggling of the Jesuits,* claiming to have proved it "utterly inexcusable" for a conscientious reader to become or remain a papist. Taylor had by that time finished his main casuistical works and he merely cited Pascal to confirm his castigation of the Jesuits.[10] What bothered these and other Protestant moralists was not the mere principle of the Jesuits' probabilism but the specific application of it to infiltrators, sub-versives, and even assassins intent upon forcing Catholic allegiance on Protestant territories. Just as suspect to the Jesuits was the Calvinists' justification of rebellion against an ungodly or tyrannical (i.e. Catholic) prince.

Even earlier the Calvinist Ames had condemned a Jesuit in his four-volume polemic (of 1628) called *Bellarmine Disarmed.* Nevertheless, Ames forged his main casuistical work out of metals admittedly mined from Peter Lombard, Bonaventura, Duns Scotus, Guillaume de Paris, Cajetan, and the contemporary Jesuit, Suárez—most of all, from Aquinas. Ames accused these Catholics of recommending dead works in contrast to his teaching of lively works springing from faith and conversion. He took "living to God" as the entire subject and purpose of theology. In his stress on testing true religious belief by one's aim and ability to live it out Ames spoke for the Christianity of his age.

If it is right to distinguish the pietists' practice of living blessedly from the moralists' practice of living rightly, then Ames was decidedly a master moralist, although he has often been called a pioneer pietist. Blessedness or happiness could be selfish goals. In the best of all worlds one might combine living happily with living well. But in the real world, "What chiefly and finally ought to be striven for," he emphasized, "is not happiness which has to do with our own pleasure, but goodness which looks to God's glory. For this reason, theology is better defined as that good life whereby we live to God than as that happy life whereby we live to ourselves."[11] A standard commentary on Ames put it, "The first concern is not to become happy, or even holy, but to live according to God's will and for God's glory. The will of man is the subject of theology." That is, since for Ames theology had to do entirely with practice, in contrast to speculation, its subject was the human will's conformity to the revealed divine will. Another interpreter quoted Ames's definition of theology to be the art of systematically delineating right practice in universal rules.[12]

Theology for this paragon of Reformed Christianity consisted of two parts, faith and observance, "always joined together in use and exercise, but . . . distinguished in their nature and in the rules which govern them." Penetrating through flesh and bones straight to the marrow of theology, Ames adumbrated more than thirteen hundred rules of faith-practice and more than a thousand others governing observance-practice. They cover everything. "This practice of life is so perfectly reflected in theology that there is no precept of universal truth relevant to living well in domestic economy, morality, political life, or lawmaking which does not rightly pertain to theology."[13]

In considering Jeremy Taylor as an exemplary moralist it is hardly necessary to pause for details of his life, since the way of life he epitomized appeared all over Europe during the period at hand, adjusted only for the language and ecclesiastical allegiance of the territory. Taylor was born near Cambridge, where he studied, then held a fellowship at Oxford. After a chaplaincy in the royal army early in the Puritan Revolution, he retired (in 1645) to Wales, where he wrote voluminously during the interregnum. Then he taught briefly in Ireland, where he became lifelong bishop of Down and Connor and vice-chancellor of Dublin University.

Taylor matched the best Calvinists at drawing rules for right living and rivaled the best Jesuits at considering particular circumstances when it came to applying those rules. Always eager for principles to guide particulars, he anticipated John Locke by reducing Christianity to the two fundamentals of believing that Jesus Christ was son of God and of living after his example and teaching. Whatever could be deduced from the Apostles' Creed should be believed and whatever could be drawn from the teaching and example of Christ should be done, but the deducer must demonstrate the deduction before insisting that others agree.

This reductionist in doctrine was an expansionist in morals. Should he not live long enough "to write a particular explication of all the precepts of christian religion," he hoped God would "excite some other" to write out "a full design of all special cases and questions of conscience."[14] His vast and influential writings did indeed provide rules for every conceivable condition, public and private, that might befall a Christian of his era.

All these rules came from Christ as exemplar and legislator. All were practicable. Anybody genuinely concerned to live a Christian life *could,* although not everybody professing Christianity *did,* follow the rules. For practice made perfect not in the instrumental sense that performing proper duties produced flawless persons, but in the self-fulfilling sense that the practices were designed so one could become a perfect practitioner. Dutifulness contained its own spiritual reward. The satisfaction came in doing the good deed well.

In enduringly popular manuals for everyman, *Holy Living* and *Holy Dying,* Taylor reduced the principles of Christian morality to specific exercises, remedies, applications, acts, recitations, resolutions—in his favorite word, "practices." Each chapter of the former book concluded with set prayers, ejaculations, devotions, hymns, adorations, oblations, and confessions, the earnest recitation of which achieved the desired virtue.

For example, the virtue of chastity[15] and its corresponding temptation of lust required at first seven general exercises: resist unchaste thoughts and recollections; purge sexual fantasies and imaginings that out of shame or inability could not be performed; guard against lust in the eye or heart as well as in other parts of the body; practice detesting everything unclean; use clean and decent speech; after "all involuntary and natural pollutions," voluntarily disapprove of them (*3,* 61). Then realize how easy it has become to abstain from exterior acts of uncleanness.

A married practitioner then skipped the acts designed for virgins and widows, to take these six exercises: love the spouse, but not more dearly than God; subordinate the pleasures of coitus to a higher end, like begetting a child or avoiding fornication or easing "the cares and sadnesses of household affairs" (*3,* 63); keep the sexual act itself simple and modest; regulate its frequency in proportion to good health, other duties, and temperate affection; abstain from conjugal "entertainments at solemn times of devotion," e.g. when preparing to receive holy communion (*3*, 64); pray to be forgiven any unintended indecency or immoderate passion.

Then came nine ways to repress temptations to lust: flee them instead of fighting them; keep busy in useful pursuits; sublimate sexual desire by physical exertion, diet, and ascetic postures; keep company and conversation clean; tame pride and anger, which inflame lust; whenever tempted, seek the company of reverent and modest persons; pray for mental and spiritual strength to control sexual urges; meditate on Christ and the Virgin Mary as chaste and holy persons; if by now temperate and sober but still needful of sex, then proceed honorably. Four more exercises in chastity required praying against sensuality, for temperance, for the specific inner strengths needed by unmarried persons, virgins, widows, and married couples seeking chastity; finally, general petitions for virtues and general repentances for vices.

To outline these exercises even so briefly risks violating Taylor's plea that this part of his book be read only by persons who already were, or devoutly wished to be, chaste. However, Taylor devised exercises in sobriety against voluptuousness, in temperance against gluttony and drunkenness, in humility against pride, in modesty against boldness and indecency, in contentedness against all sorts of adversities. In the public realm similar acts regulated obedience to superiors, making restitution for offenses, and the exercise of authority by kings, magistrates, husbands, fathers, guardians, tutors. Strict rules applied to the ecclesiastical duties of believing, hoping, showing charity, going to church, fasting, keeping the Sabbath and holy days, praying, almsgiving, repenting, and preparing for holy communion. An abundance of forms of devotion guided each particular duty at hand.

The self-chastener who did these exercises would never doubt the worth of working against sins and toward purity. But the whole range of cases where no such moral certainty could be had about good and evil presented problems of a different magnitude. Taylor addressed these cases in his most mature and representative work, a directory for troubled consciences published (in

1660) under the title *Ductor Dubitantium* (*Guide for the Doubting*). The long book was intended "to offer to the world a general instrument of moral theology, by the rules and measures of which the guides of souls may determine the particulars that shall be brought before them," and in addition to enable "men that are wise" and "love to inquire" to "guide themselves in all their proportions of conscience." Taylor knew that problems of conscience changed in complexity with new circumstances and he predicted that "Men will for ever need a living guide" (a confessor) as well as books to resolve their doubts and scruples (*9*, xix-xx).

Concrete examples best illustrate the comprehensiveness of Taylor's moral virtuosity. On the question of lying, already noted as a preoccupation of moralists, he began with a basic principle and raised against it the most plausible exceptions he could think of. God is truth, and man, made in his image, was bound to tell the truth, "but the question is, whether truth can be practiced at all times" when human affairs "are full of intrigues, and their persons of infirmity, and their understandings of deception" (*10*, 101). There were times when just, good, and necessary ends were served not by truth but by giving erroneous or deceptive testimonies. The doubting conscience would be paralyzed unless these exceptions were fully enumerated and exemplified.

In principle, lying violated reason as well as God. The very use of human language implied a contract to tell the truth. Thus "lying is to be understood to be something said or written to the hurt of our neighbor, which cannot be understood otherwise than to differ from the mind of him that speaks" (*10*, 102). But the truth-telling contract could be supervened by a superior right, say a direct command from God. It could be forfeited, say by a madman who deserved to be deceived because he could not judge or by a hypochondriac who deserved to be cozened by his physician. It could be suspended, say by mutual consent between enemies at war. It could be superseded, say if a lie to a neighbor did him or her great good and did nobody harm or if truth did him or her great harm and did nobody good. In rare instances the contract could even be evaded, say if a lie to an unjust persecutor would charitably save him from committing murder and would justly preserve the intended victim's life.

Lying to save one's reputation, however, lacked any saving grace, despite the fact that ancient and contemporary Christian moralists justified it. Fame was valuable, but duty more so; "although our fame is necessary for others, yet a good conscience is necessary to ourselves." Here there was neither option nor compromise, "for we must rather suffer shame than do things worthy of shame, . . . rather be disgraced than damned: for nothing needs a lie but a sin to hide it, and by a lie a sin is made two" (*10,* 114). Lest any case be left undetermined or vague, all shades of mental reservations, equivocations, false signs, deceptive or ambiguous acts, pretences, fictions, and shams were settled by the principle that to deceive indirectly differed little or not at all from deceiving directly. Poets could make fictions to edify but not to deceive. An actor might dye his hair to play an instructive role, but a hostess might not dye her hair to gain admirers. To counterfeit a coin caused harmful deceit, but to veneer a rough façade with polished marble increased beauty.

Finally, the subtleties of borderline cases presented grave dangers. It took a very canny person to remain innocent. The safer course was always to err on the side of veracity. The white lie that might be justifiable, helping its hearer and harming nobody, lured the teller into trying the next gradation, then the off-white lie led to the gray lie, each darkening of the shade being a flirtation with the double sin of harmfully deceiving the neighbor and harmfully deceiving oneself about one's innocence with the black lie.

Taylor found natural reason, uninstructed by Christian revelation, an unreliable fountain of morality, "such a box of quicksilver that it abides no where" (*9,* 293). Christ, fundamentally a lawgiver, laid down the divine will in the religion he founded, itself "a perfect system of all the laws of nature, and of all the will of God, that is, of all the obligatory will, of all the commandments" (*9,* 307). Implications of Christ's law covered everything he did not leave to human choice. Scripture was thus the charter of the conscience, but one did not need to find in it a warrant for every action. Tradition and reason interpreted scripture. Sinful habits were more heinous than sinful acts, although habits were formed by repeating acts. To counter both kinds of sin one did virtuous acts and cultivated virtuous habits. Given complete rules and the guidance of a skilled pastor, the moral Christian could surely have a good conscience, edified and careful but not scrupulous, alert and obedient but not suspicious.

Taylor's justification of adultery, paraphrased and abbreviated in the following case, may show moderns how they must strain to appreciate the fine tuning of Christian moralism. John, married to Joan, and Mary, married to Mark, are in love with each other. John determines to kill Joan and take Mary away from Mark. John confides in Charles, who diverts him from present murder and subsequent adultery by advising immediate adultery with Mary. This course is charitable, for Joan's life is saved and John avoids a great crime by committing now a lesser crime he would anyhow have committed later. But there is a subtle condition. If Charles has reason to believe that John's adultery with Mary would enrage Joan and drive her to adultery in revenge or to kill John or Mary (or enrage Mark and drive him to adultery in revenge or to kill Mary or John), then the course is immoral because it leads to another sin (*9, 249*).

The art of moral virtuosity was to set the aim high enough to make practice strenuous but not so high as to put perfection of practice out of reach. But Jesus Christ, as both the teacher to be obeyed and the model to be imitated, had taught certain unobeyable precepts and, as god-man, had done inimitable things. According to Jesus, to be angry with another made one liable to judgment, to insult another was worse, and to call another a fool meant hell; if another holds something against one, one must find reconciliation before performing a religious duty. Who could obey such teachings, which equated mere anger with murder? First, Taylor tempered the injunction by saying that it applied only to anger without due cause. Then he excused the initial impulses of anger, "the twinklings of an eye . . . , the propassions [emotions preliminary to passions] and sudden and irresistible alterations; for it is impossible to prevent them, unless we could give ourselves a new nature" (2, 434).

Christ's legislation consisted, then, of his *obeyable* commands. Taylor saw that this concession was dangerous and he guarded against indulging the "propassions" unless they were genuinely unpreventable. Duty included "frequent and habitual mortification" of the impulses toward anger (2, 435).

This way of moderating moral demands to human ability was familiar, as already noted, to the Jesuit Suárez. Sinful men and women were trying to avoid sin and to acquire righteousness. They were limited by their own nature (aided by grace) and personalities (reformed by religion). The satisfaction came from practicing well, from becoming a virtuoso in virtue. The practice of obeying Christ achieved perfection when one tried as hard as one should.

Each particular effort that one expended in imitating Christ paid its own reward. Indeed, "the nature of all holy exercises," of "every work of grace," was to be "full of pleasure in the execution, and . . . abundantly rewarded, besides the stipend of a glorious eternity" (2, 40). Acts of religious duty produced "a facility to the action," in a way causing themselves to be done; "so does every exercise of the life of Christ kindle its own fires . . . , and makes an univocal production of itself in a different subject" (2, 43). Like good King Wenceslas of legend, Jesus walked through the snow of life ahead of his servants, making footprints to ease the way for those who followed him.

But followers must not presume to walk everyhere he walked. He exercised the prerogative of divinity. They must imitate his human nature and only so far as their imperfect human nature allowed. Christians were not to go walking on lakes. The superhuman Jesus never laughed and only once rejoiced; such gravity was beyond his followers' ability. By Taylor's rule, "whatsoever He commanded, and whatsoever He did, of precise morality, or in the pursuance of the laws of nature, in that we are to trace

His footsteps" (*2, 45*). Nor did he model everything to be done by Christians. They sinned, not he. They were to repent, not he. They lived as husbands, wives, parents, merchants, lawyers, schoolchildren, not he. His sensibilities, being those of "a delicate and virgin body of curious temper, and strict, equal composition," were such that his crucifixion "was naturally more full of tor-ment" than were those of "the ruder thieves, whose proportions were coarser and uneven" (*3, 311*).

The whole life of Christians imitated the large themes of Christ's life on earth. His suffering and affliction modeled their lives of discipline, self-denial, rigor. Where he exhorted particu-lar imitation it was binding, but he also commended as excellent many optional acts. Men and women *could not* imitate his human perfection. They *should not* imitate his exercise of godly wrath. His teachings instructed and his example encouraged his follow-ers. In trivial matters, however, like having communion after supper instead of before breakfast or using Judaean wine, imita-tion became "mimical and theatrical, trifling and superstitious, a snare to consciences, and a contempt of religion" (*9, 490*).

Christ the preceptor and model of morality appeared in Tay-lor's long book, *The Great Exemplar* (published in 1649), which Charles Stranks called "the first life of Christ ever to be written in English."[16] Bare narratives told of the annunciation, of Christ's fetal life in Mary's womb, of his birth and its wit-nesses, of his circumcision and presentation in the Temple, of the slaughter of the innocents, of the flight into Egypt, of his dis-putation with the doctors, of his baptism and temptation, then of each year of his public ministry. Long moral lessons were drawn from many of these events. The Sermon on the Mount prompted a discourse on the Ten Commandments and on Jesus' additional injunctions to charity, prayer, and fasting. His baptism occasioned a long argument for the legitimacy of baptizing infants.

The lesson drawn from the scene of the Virgin and child was that mothers should suckle their babies until their breasts dried up instead of hiring other women to wet-nurse them and should affectionately rear their own children as Mary did Jesus instead of putting them in the care of foster mothers. The Virgin's "paps were as surely blessed for giving Him suck as her womb for bearing him" (*2,* 80). Other deductions instructed Englishmen to avoid dueling and to confine lawsuits to cases of reparation.

The human Jesus taught Christians their proper duties that the divine Christ enabled them to perform. "Christ took upon Him our nature that He might learn us obedience, and in that also make us become like unto God" (*8,* 341). Taylor found his great exemplar more imitable than saints whose lives were full of long fasts, "prodigious penances," visions, and ecstasies. Jesus purposely modeled an attainable religiousness, holy but ordinary. The lives of "certain beatified persons" were recounted "to amaze us and to create scruples." The life of Jesus was told "to lead us in the evenness and serenity of a holy conscience" (*2,* 41). This human exemplar was also the Christ whose most poignant epiphanies came to Taylor in the Lord's Supper. The boy Jesus had upbraided his parents for searching him out in highways and villages, when they should have known "that I ought to be in My Father's house," which is exactly where the worthy communicant would find him, for there Christ "loves to dwell, where He communicates His blessing and holy influences, there and there only are we sure to meet our dearest Lord" (*8,* 5).

Taylor knew and approved the pietists' experience of Jesus' presence in the heart, but he subordinated it to morality. In sum, "we lead Jesus into the recesses of our heart by holy meditations," but "we enter into His heart, when we express" or imitate "Him in our actions" (*2,* 46).

PIETISTS

The complementary mode by which Christians in the time of the territorial monarchies became religious virtuosi was the practice of piety or affective spirituality. As noted above, this mode of living commended itself to Europeans belonging to every kind of church and to persons of every station in life. Its origins can be traced to the beginning of our period (the late 1500s) and it continues to appeal to moderns. Affective Christians sought an intimacy with Christ that is reminiscent of the medieval mystics' quest, but the resemblance is superficial in that the pietists took the human, suffering Jesus for their deity and they rejected the mystics' elitism.

Peter Canisius, a German of Jesuit persuasion, was instrumental in transforming traditionally elite Catholic spirituality into a popular program for everybody. Shortly before his death (in 1556), Ignatius Loyola had revised the *Spiritual Exercises* by which he had initiated and trained the members of his Society of Jesus. This astute book showed a spiritual master how to put his trainee through a full-time, month-long meditation, first on sin and hell, then on the kingdom of Christ, then on Jesus' sufferings, and finally on the risen and glorified Christ. All five senses were brought into the act as one's eyes pictured, say, the souls of the damned writhing in hell, one's ears heard their moans, one's nose smelled their burning flesh, one's touch felt the heat, and one's lips tasted the salt of their tears. The senses, the imagination, and the understanding in combination spurred the will toward spiritual purity and toward absolute obedience to the Society and the church.

Canisius redesigned this scheme (in 1588) into one for popular use, condensing the long, individual exercises into briefer retreats for groups wanting to develop more personal, more cordial religious sensibilities. Soon the Jesuits were reserving accommodations and even building their own houses for retreats by larger and larger groups over shorter and shorter periods, down to three days—one-tenth the time planned by Ignatius. Then these programs for groups withdrawing to special places for their pious exercises were found useful also in missions to groups remaining in their familiar surroundings. By the end of our period, missions, novenas, retreats, and visitations had elicited a powerful and widespread interest throughout the Catholic territories, an interest that nobody did more to promote than Liguori in Italy.

While the Jesuits were making their popular piety into an international movement, each European territory was witnessing a distinct emphasis in heart-religion. In central Germany the Lutheran pastor Johann Arndt protested the regnant religious formalism by helping people accept Christ as the beloved leader of their lives. Against the highly forensic Lutheran doctrine of salvation Arndt put forward a more cordial scheme, calling for heartfelt repentance as the way to invite Christ to dwell in the believer's heart and to make holy the believer's day-to-day life as well as his explicitly religious life. Arndt wrote the first popular devotional books for Germans, beginning (in 1606) with a work on *True Christianity,* to which he later added five more parts. The sudden popularity of this call for vibrant Christian experience through pious practices prompted Arndt to write *Paradiesgärtlein aller christlichen Tugenden* (1612), once quaintly rendered as "Heavenly Flowerbed of Christian Graces" (English translations are called *Garden of Paradise*).

Arndt was adapting to the yearnings of his own time and place a long-popular literary genre known as gardens of the soul. And next to the *Imitation of Christ* his became the most widely used devotional books in Germany. Like the moralists, Arndt wanted people to live righteous, upright lives, but he insisted that only the holy heart could perform truly good works. Upon this foundation the famous leaders of German pietism, August Hermann Francke and Philipp Jacob Spener, built a movement that permeated much of Lutheranism.

Shortly after Arndt wrote his books, two French Catholics devised a plan to undercut the Jesuits' dominance of their church and to develop a piety so trenchant and a discipline so rigorous that the Protestants would rush back to a reformed Catholicism. Neither end was gained, although the pious means spread through France, Italy, and Austria for a long time. The movement bears the name of Cornelis Jansen, although others did more than he to instill and spread this impassioned devotion. Jean Duvergier de Hauranne converted the old Cistercian nunnery of Port Royal into a popular center of pietism for both men and women, with a branch in Paris proper, and he was the main superintendent of souls during his lifetime. Members, associates, and friends were attracted to the nunnery by the desperate devotion and rigor of the abbess (from 1602 to 1630 and again from 1642 to 1654), Jacqueline Marie Angélique Arnauld, called Mère Angelique.

There was a certain desperation in the perpetual adoration to which Mère Angélique's nuns dedicated themselves, for it consisted in perpetual penance for the indelible stains of original sin. There was desperation in the dependence of Port Royal and the entire Jansenist movement on the Arnauld family, whose members Angélique shut out of the abbey when in her eyes they were not good enough for it. There was desperation in the Solitaires, those Messieurs de Port Royal who, except when they taught school, stayed in seclusion for their constant penance and penitence. There was desperation in Jansen's closeting himself with Duvergier for five years, trying to memorize all the tracts Augustine wrote against those who dared question the ravaging effects of original sin upon mankind. There was desperation both in Duvergier's own insistence that a valid absolution depended on the penitent's perfect contrition and in his seeking spiritual renewal by abstaining from the holy communion. Indeed, there was desperation in Pascal's risking little to win infinitely in his wager that God exists, in his lifelong need for an effective conversion from "as-if" to heartfelt belief, and in his ability to produce only bits and pieces of what he conceived as a definitive case for Christian belief against systematic doubt. This quality of desperation drove Heer to call Port Royal a spiritual "concentration camp."[17]

But if the Jansenists took personally everything Christians had learned about human misery, they also individualized what Christians had taught about the grandeur of humanity. The Jansenists' kind of pendulum piety discovered that the profundity with which one lamented the wounds of Christ regulated the ecstasy with which one delighted in the salvation those wounds procured. Through the Jansenists this sad-glad spirituality maintained a grip on European Catholics that no Jesuit theological faculty and no pope could shake. Jansenism reappeared all the stronger forty years after Innocent X condemned it (in 1653) as heresy. Damned again (in 1713), it was flourishing (in the 1780s) in Austria, dominating the church in Tuscany, and surviving in France down to Napoleon's concordat (of 1801) with the papacy.

The movement's vigor throughout our period indicates the need of religious virtuosi to take with utmost seriousness the spiritual system of sin, guilt, penance, forgiveness, and communion. The official church, of course, taught that this system was entirely too much to bear without the assistance of automatically effective sacraments and a highly authoritative priesthood. In defiance of all that, the Jansenists doubted all ecclesiastical and hierarchical assurances that their souls were saved and they looked to their own feelings or inner states of mind about religion for indications of their spiritual condition. Typical pietists that they were, the Jansenists literally took to heart the religious transactions that traditionally took place in the church.

English pietists knew the sinfulness of man as well as the Jansenists, but instead of deploring it with penitential self-punishment they analyzed it with dramatic subtlety. The master analyst was John Bunyan, who knew all the pendulum swings between sadness and gladness of heart. "Of all tears, they are the best that are made by the Blood of Christ; and of all joy, that is sweetest that is mixt with mourning over Christ," he wrote.[18]

The rude tinker who framed that thought was born (in 1628) only five years after the birth of Pascal. Bunyan achieved the intense assurance of his own salvation that eluded the brilliant scientist. Pascal looked to patently religious acts as the occasions for testing and reconfirming his personal certitude of holiness, while Bunyan found those occasions in everyday life. The language as well as the crucial message of the Bible impressed itself on Bunyan, who wrote from jail (in 1666) perhaps the most distinguished spiritual autobiography produced in a century that is distinguished for that genre. Moreover, no book in English has more determined the character of personal religion than *The Pilgrim's Progress,* an artful allegory exploring the hazards that befell pious Christians and showing how every danger they avoided, every trial they overcame, brought deeper strength to the virtuosi. This "profound statement about the crafting of a life," in Milo Kaufmann's phrase, evidences the virtuosity at once of the writer, of the plain persons in and out of prison whose lives he personally guided, and of the enormous readership he has taught over three centuries.[19]

The first and essential lesson of his piety was to avoid moralism. In the city of Morality, commended to the pilgrim named Christian by Worldly Wiseman, dwelt Mr. Legality and his son Mr. Civility, who would be able, Wiseman promised, to lift Christian's burden of sin. Christian was told he could send back for his wife and children, because in Morality good houses rented cheaply and good provisions could be bought cheaply. There honest neighbors abounded. In this city set upon a hill Worldly Wiseman went to church. But Evangelist warned Christian that the city of Morality was the city of spiritual death, that Worldly Wiseman was an alien, that Legality was a cheat, that Civility was a hypocrite. Only by avoiding the allure of Morality could a Christian enter the Wicket Gate on the pilgrimage to the Celestial City.

The tribulations that befall Christian en route reinforce that lesson, for they make a grand design of events stripping him of every hint of his own worthiness or merit. Ignorance, who is worldly wise but unacquainted with saving grace, avoids the narrow gate and climbs over the wall to begin his fated journey. Ignorance crosses the river of death not on faith but in the ferryboat of Vain-hope, and at last the Shining Ones throw him through the door bypassing heaven and going straight to hell. The search for morality leads religious pilgrims to the self-confidence and self-esteem that damn their souls.

Having learned this lesson by reading about Christian's pilgrimage, his wife and children and their friends, figures of the whole church, took a relatively easy and safe journey through similar pitfalls in the guidance of Mr. Great-heart. Mr. Great-heart led the women and children throughout their pilgrimage, and without him the likes of Feeble-minded and Despondency could never have reached the river. But Mr. Good-will was only the gatekeeper where the pilgrimage began, unable even to lighten Christian's load. The pietists' religion was religion of the great heart, not that of the good will.

Bunyan's autobiography attests richly to the heart as the organ upon which Christ stamped the warnings and promises of scripture. While Satan was tempting the newly converted Bunyan, "Yet God did bear me up, and keep my heart upon this word, from which I had also for several days together very much sweetness and comfortable hopes of pardon" (191). A doubt arose, and "Now began my heart again to ake, and fear I might meet with disappointment at the last" (196). Again the refreshing "Scripture came into my heart" (198). Indeed, "that Scripture fast[e]ned on my heart" (201). Bunyan was freed from affliction and temptation when "I also saw moreover, that it was not my good frame of Heart that made my Righteousness better, not yet my bad frame that made my Righteousness worse: for my Righteousness was Jesus Christ himself" (229). To fill his heart with Christ was the aim and the reward of Bunyan's practice.

Bunyan knew Christ in a simple-minded yet orthodox way. The god-man's divinity gave Christ a righteousness he did not need in order to be god; he had no need of righteousness to make him human because he was perfect man; "therefore, he can spare it, a justifying righteousness, that he for himself wanteth not, and therefore he giveth it away." In the allegory, although Christiana's "heart was lightful and joyous before" Christ came to be her righteousness, her heart was "ten times more lightsome and joyous now. And . . . if the most burdened man in the world was here and did see and believe, as I now do, 'twould make his heart the more merry and blithe."[20]

If tears measured spiritual burdens and if assurance of salvation made a blithe heart, the blithest and most burdened of Christian pietists was Count Nikolaus Ludwig von Zinzendorf. Already at age six his tutor's concern for his soul drove the boy (in 1706) to uncontrollable weeping over his savior's sufferings. There and then he dedicated his life to the love and service of the wounded Jesus. Already he was composing love letters to his elder brother Jesus. By age ten he could preach about and pray to Jesus both effectively and affectively.

Zinzendorf was reared by his grandmother and schooled at Halle under her pietistic friends, whose leader, Francke, disliked him. Then legal training at Wittenberg prepared him for the grand tour of Europe, and he spent a few years in public service to the Saxon government. At his majority he came into considerable wealth and bought, near his grandmother's home, an estate surrounding the village of Berthelsdorf. Then he proposed marriage to Erdmuth Dorothea von Reuss, a countess in her own right, on condition that they dedicate their lives to winning souls to Christ. They entered a union between Christian warriors (*Streiterehe*) that was designed to mirror Christ's marriage to the church. Countess Erdmuth aptly managed finances while Count Nikolaus majestically executed campaigns for Jesus.

From his youth Zinzendorf liked to enlist friends into fraternities cultivating prayer and personal religiousness. As a young adult he gathered his pastor at Berthelsdorf, a neighboring minister, and a friend into the Covenant of the Four Brethren. Each pledged at all costs to promote holiness in himself and in one another and in everybody else. On the estate there settled Moravian Protestants fleeing religious coercion and others drawn by the piety of the village and of its Lutheran pastor. As the Moravians were busy building their settlement, the lord of the manor was busy settling disputes between them and members of the established church.

Zinzendorf constituted (in 1727) the Renewed Moravian Church at Herrnhut into a commune within the Lutheran parish of his estate. His religious fraternity had grown into a denomination and a body politic; he was chieftain of both. Soon after the insight came to him (in 1734) that the sacrificial death of Jesus pumped Christianity's only heartblood, he became a minister-missionary. Later ordained a bishop, he eventually headed a church stretching to England and the Baltic, to Greenland and

Pennsylvania and the Virgin Islands, to South Africa and Persia.
Until his death (in 1760), the Count wrote compulsively and
impulsively, always straining for a compelling statement of the
single emotion that impelled his salvation—his overpowering
and erotic affection for the bleeding Jesus who took as spiritual
wife the souls that fell in love with his suffering humanity. The
rambling lectures, sermons, discourses, homilies, letters, hymns,
diaries, polemics, etc., that made this simple point now fill eighteen stout volumes. The religiousness to which they testify was
indeed simple. It was singular for its unrelieved appeal to sexual imagery and uncomplicated by either theological technicali-
ties or ethical applications. To be sure, Zinzendorf considered
himself faithful to basic Lutheran doctrine and he shared the
Brethren's upright living, but everything hinged on being saved.

This experience of salvation could be reliably measured. The
test was "simply this: to receive, to receive the Saviour, to feel an
inclination within oneself: I want to have Him! If I only had
Him! He is coming! Welcome! When these thoughts are united
—He is coming! Welcome, a thousand times welcome, dearest
Lamb! Come, do come soon, my Bridegroom—then salvation is
real and incontestable."[21] For all the emotion, Zinzendorf made
objectively valid the experience wherein "for a moment the
Saviour becomes present to him in person" and the saved one
"comes into the circumstances in which the apostles stood when
they saw Him" (144-45; 80).

To be sure, these lush phrases come from the so-called "sifting
period" (from 1743 to 1750) in Zinzendorf's career, which a
Moravian church historian has said were marked by "a morbid
concentration and wordplay upon the blood and wounds of the
crucified Christ and a simulated irresponsibility of behavior supposed to be a demonstration of childlike faith."[22] But the very
themes that came to their richest experience and expression in the
man's prime were motifs in every phase of the life from early
childhood until death. Moreover, when Zinzendorf tried to check
the excessive childishness, he still clung to the notion "that in

order to enjoy all the blessings purchased by the death of Jesus, we must become children in the bottom of our hearts." He regretted neither the idea nor its embodiment in the fraternity he called the Order of Little Fools, ruing only the fact that "what was at first a small circle of men, who really had the spirit of children, soon grew into a large society and in a few years greatly degenerated."[23]

Zinzendorf was the quintessential pietist who dreamed of reuniting all Christians on the religion's one fundamental principle, the passionate love of the human heart to the Lamb of God bleeding on the cross. Whatever increased or expressed that love belonged to Christianity and whatever failed of direct involvement with it was not only optional but also inconsequential. That was "the inmost result and center of that religion so universally received, and deriving its name from Christ," as well as "that object, which . . . all the desire of the soul" ought to "employ itself upon," both here and in the hereafter; " 'tis no other, than to view that transaction and posture of our God, when he bled to death for our sins' sake upon the cross." In a nutshell, "The tenderest connection with our redeemer, burying our corruption and misery in his death, is the great affair, and other things are regarded only for and according to the habitude they bear to this."[24]

Precisely and only this heart-religion—*Herzensreligion,* Zinzendorf's favorite term—could cleanse the filth of personal sinfulness in the lavatory of Jesus' blood. Zinzendorf's savior would make no "public showing" of himself (*seine Parade*) that did not display clearly his wounds, which were "His sign" (*sein Zeichen*). Zinzendorf told of Satan's appearance to a bishop in the guise of a majestic, splendid savior; the ruse failed with the bishop's question, "If you are Christ, where are your wounds?" (51; 28).

To behold this crucified person merely from historical curiosity "would make but a horrible figure. Yet to the heart it is really beautiful: those torn, bloody, death-pale, and stiff limbs, with which he hung before God, men, and angels, as a most abominable sight, scorned, spat upon, and sorely distressed. These are indeed and in truth they which alone still pierce and wound the hearts of all poor sinners to this very day, and these my heart is captivated with too."[25] Most languages misrepresented things by saying that a person whose heart was smitten by this beautiful, suffering Jesus became a Christian (*Christianer*), but "in our German alone one says, *ein Christ,* and that is the right word" (138; 77).

Louis Antoine Noailles, cardinal archbishop of Paris, saw in the young Zinzendorf such a Christ and joined his fraternity. John Wesley's first but by no means lasting impression of Zinzendorf, who received him at Marienborn (in 1738), was of one so "encompassed . . . of Christ" that "his behaviour was not unlike that of his Master . . . when He took the little children in His arms and blessed them."[26] When outward Christians undertook as their chief duty "to carry the death and the bloody sacrifice of their redeemer continually within their heart," they became inward Christs.[27] Then they lived "in this life as if we were already risen again; and thus . . . death . . . becomes a delicacy [*eine Delicatesse,* "a dainty"] for our heart" (37; 20).

The difference between being a Christian and being a Christ appeared plain and measurable to Zinzendorf. But because the agency causing the transformation was divine, the process by which "Jesus Christ with his five wounds is formed in us" was at once so "secret, sudden, unknown . . . , hidden," and varied so from person to person, "that it can never be described" (53; 29, 28-29). Certainly neither the process nor the test of the fact could be cast in any moral terms, for the pietist who became a Christ remained a sinner.

Such freight of meaning Zinzendorf loaded onto the indefinite article distinguishing *a* christ from *the* Christ. Of the former, "None for his little good is better, and none for his many enormities worse," for all were sinners. The transaction by which *the* Christ made one *a* christ took place in the heart instead of the conscience, for "Concerning our outward life and behavior, we oftentimes do nothing else, but what other people do, but with a childlike, loving, and cheerful heart towards God and man."[28]

Thus the union with Jesus that Zinzendorf experienced and bore witness to was conjugal like Bernard's, a bridegroom-bride relation in which the wife took the name and virtue of the husband. Beyond that general resemblance the two differed entirely. For Zinzendorf the union took place on earth and in worldly time; for Bernard both time and place were ethereal. Zinzendorf's bridegroom was the wounded Jesus who "obtained His bride with His blood"; and the "bride-hearts" were steady companions, not souls mated in momentary rapture, for they "day and night live, eat, drink, sleep, and get up with the Saviour" (57; 31). Bernard's union was that of a bride on her wedding night, Zinzendorf's that of a housewife throughout marriage. Bernard's experience involved refining the carnality of his love so it would be perfected for the union, while Zinzendorf's found plain, effusive, human affection the appropriate vehicle by which Christians "love unutterably; they are all deeply in love with Him. His soul has risen up in all their minds in full, sweet love; the bones of all of them are united with God through Him. Thus a Christian, a child of God, the very least beginner, cannot be venerated enough" (97; 54).

For Zinzendorf, as for Bernard, the human soul was feminine in grammatical gender. For the German it was also female in actual sex, "and any other thought would be the greatest spiritual absurdity; the human creature in a congregate sense is its creator's bride," and the lovers of Jesus' wounds actualized that relation to him. Male Christians or men-christs bore the special charge of Christ to work "blessed effects on the sisters entrusted to them." This temporal modeling of Christ's marriage with his creatures "clothes afterwards all particular incidents with a holiness suitable for redeemed sinners, and with a liturgical awe, namely the begetting, bearing, and educating of children, which is all done in the light of faith and grace."[29] God the Father and the maternal Holy Spirit begat Christ the son, who in turn created mankind and married faithful souls, making possible what

Zinzendorf called "congregation-marriage" in which the human father, mother, and children re-enacted the mystery of the divine trinity.

So far as conjugal and familial imagery convey the notion of exclusive union, however, they belie the primal egalitarianism of Zinzendorf's religiousness. He dreamed that his brotherhood would permeate and purify all denominations and unite all Christians in a spiritual kinship and amity that would remove the strife of ecclesiastical allegiances. As he labored to make converts from every race and nation, their varying circumstances called for varying strategies. He claimed America for the Lamb's blood, but thought religious freedom there, particularly in Pennsylvania, obviated the need for anything as highly organized as the Moravian church. In Europe the role of that church was to seek and spread religious toleration. When a new ruler of Wetteravia required (in 1750) the Brethren to declare full allegiance to one of the two legitimate churches, one thousand Moravians accepted the costly alternative of abandoning the village they had built and of resettling in other Moravian communities.[30]

Although Zinzendorf launched the modern Protestant missionary movement, he did not think of making humankind Moravian. It was the privileged duty of those in love with the wounded Jesus to tell his name abroad so others might be sanctified. Moreover, Jesus' revealed plan, according to Paul, was to await the conversion of the Jews before harvesting all the gentiles. Meanwhile, Moravian missionaries were to convert a few members of each race and nation as first fruits.

This scheme led Zinzendorf (in 1747) to commission John Valentin Haidt to make for the chapel at Herrnhaag a painting of Christ exposing his wounded left side to the people from all nations who surround him, representatives of the Moravians' first converts—American Indians, blacks from Surinam and the Virgin Islands, South African Hottentots, Eskimos from Greenland, and the rest. Sinners all, they dance blithely before the wounded Christ who has forgiven them and whose face is that of Zinzendorf, himself *ein Christ*.[31]

PERFECTIONISTS

John Wesley formed his first impression of Zinzendorf as *ein Christ* surrounded by holy Moravian apostles; their heart-religion glowed so warmly. When Wesley learned that they measured piety simply by its heat and held good works suspect as indicating salvation, he denounced this quietism in favor of gauging faith by the degree to which Christians lived disciplined lives expressing love in action. Later, Zinzendorf called the Methodists absurd for paying attention to the (to him utterly mysterious) process by which persons were spiritually reborn (53; 29).

The high Anglicanism in which the young Wesley steeped himself never dissipated, and his mature zeal for spreading religion combined the moralism of that tradition with Moravian pietism by making each impulse cancel out the other's extreme expression. Several features of Wesley's spirituality reveal the distinct way he trained in both modes of virtuosity—his penchant for autobiography, his liking for disciplinary rules, and his attainment of "Christian perfection."

As autobiographer, his pious dependence on Christ saved him from egocentrism, and his moral discipline spared him from emotionalism. From young manhood throughout his very long life, Wesley recorded how he used each hour of the day, and from these diaries he published the extracts that we know as his extensive journals. A huge correspondence recounting his doings adds details, and many sermons draw upon his own experiences. Wesley tells us in writing more about how he felt, what he did, how he felt about what he did, and what he did about how he felt than any other Christian on record.[32]

Wesley's feeling and doing, his blending of piety with morality, aimed at the fullest possible practice of Christianity. All his voluble speaking and voluminous writing invited or directed others to the same practice. All one needed to begin was the desire to be saved from sin, a desire that Wesley made the sole condition of membership in the bands, or classes, that made up his United Society. A class consisted of twelve members from a neighborhood, meeting punctually at least once each week for

prayer and frank conversation about the state of their souls.
Members watched after one another. The class leader guided
their daily lives and kept in touch with the larger movement.
Heartfelt desire to be saved was evidenced by the avoidance of
specific evils (e.g. buying, selling, or drinking spiritous liquors),
by the performance of particular good deeds (e.g. giving food to
the hungry), and by the observance of religious duties (e.g. going to church and reading the Bible). By the trenchant, mutual
examination of these evidences the early Methodists' desires for
saving faith became apparent—and urgent.

The sense of urgency prepared one for the gift of faith. By
being saved through faith Wesley meant that the newborn soul
was given an eye to see Christ, an ear to hear Christ, a palate to
taste Christ. "It is the feeling of the soul whereby a believer
perceives . . . both the existence and the presence" of Christ
"and indeed the whole invisible world, the entire system of
things eternal" (386-87). The result was that the convert "is
saved from doubt and fear and sorrow of heart, by a peace that
passes all understanding; from the heaviness of a wounded spirit
by joy unspeakable; and from his sins of whatsoever kind they
were, from his vicious desires as well as words and actions—by
the love of God and of all mankind then shed abroad in his
heart" (392).

The practice that issued from this faith differed only in temper
and degree, not in kind, from the practice that evidenced a desire for it. In faith the selfsame avoidances, performances, and
observances became joyful, delightful, sweet, even easy. Wesley
himself and throngs of his followers perfected that practice. Of
course, he never claimed he or anybody else could be wartless,
flawless, perfect in status. Rather he practiced warmhearted religion under stern discipline so consistently and constantly that he
achieved moments of a genuinely lived-out, and in that sense perfect, Christianness of desire and deed. Albert Outler put it theo-
logically: "There is something quite distinctive in Wesley's vision of the Christian life as an organic fusion of justification *and*
sanctification as reciprocals" (222). Shifting to the discourse of

religion, the man joined piety and morality, being holy and being good, into a relation in which the practice of each improved the practice of the other to the point that the practitioner attained perfect skill in spiritual means, as when training and pleasure reciprocate in the tennis player's or golfer's "perfect stroke." In this entireness of religious virtuosity Wesley erased the polarity implied by the "isms" in "pietism" and "moralism" and achieved a moral piety that fully concurred with his pious morality. He modeled the achievement for millions.

What Wesley epitomized as a Protestant virtuoso was equaled by his contemporary Catholic virtuoso, Alfonso Maria dei Liguori. Both lived long lives that nearly spanned the 1700s. Had they known one another, their disagreement would have been complete in respect to ecclesiastical allegiance. They were theological aliens but they were religious brothers to the bone. Each initiated a movement disturbing to the church he loyally served. The Neapolitan founded the Redemptorist order of monks and nuns, the Englishman the Methodist movement. Both spread devotion among the poor who were unreached by the normal apparatus of their churches. Each devised a discipline and a sanctity whose very attainability offended many. Each preached a blunt and direct message of religious affection and duty as the essence of Christianity. Both tested piety by morality and morality by piety.

Seen through his devotional writings, especially the tender and sometimes cloying effusions of fondness for the Virgin Mary and her savior-son, Liguori looks for all the world like Zinzendorf dressed in the garb of a humble Italian bishop. "Amiable Redeemer!," he cried, "the only Love of my soul! . . . I wish to be entirely yours, and for your love I wish to suffer every thing you please."[33] Would, he prayed, that the crown of thorns could expand to enclose his own head next to that of the dying Nazarene, that the nails could pierce his sinful hands instead of Jesus' innocent ones. Mary was so worthy a goddess that the more she was praised the more praise she deserved. He addressed her, "O my most sweet Lady and Mother Mary," for in her, after Jesus, he has placed his "entire hope of salvation." With her "most sweet hand" she has "drawn me from the world and delivered me from hell." Christ was the head from which source all grace flowed, but Mary was the single "neck through which it flows."[34] Such passages survived the corrections of his books, under orders, to mute his regard for Mary's divine status.

But this Liguori is also the man *The New Catholic Encyclopedia* calls "the prince of moral theologians." As noted, he shied as far from laxity as he did from rigor in settling cases of conscience that involved probable opinion in favor of liberty against law. In earlier writings against Jansenists he agreed with the Jesuits' justification of the less probable opinion to guide the doubtful. Then he devised the all-time compromise of "equiprobabilism." In cases of doubt one may choose between equally or nearly equally probable obligations.

Liguori's moralism came from his having been trained as a lawyer, for he was applying to religious duties a distinction between criminal and civil law. Criminal judgments must go beyond doubt to moral certainty, but that rule, if applied to civil cases, would be paralyzing. Civil cases could be decided on nothing more certain than the probable weight of evidence. The Jesuits, using the criminal model, had said that one reasonable doubt about the rightness of an act could justify another act, even one containing another reasonable doubt. Liguori decided cases by questioning the rightness of a moral law even when the weight of evidence supported it. He allowed choice only when the probabilities balanced one another. Therefore, each case had to be reasoned out on its own merits. By decree Catholic confessors were authorized (after 1831) to follow any decision made by Liguori, regardless of his reasonings in the particular case.

From this side, then, Ligouri looks for all the world like an Ames or a Taylor, if from the other like a Zinzendorf. The twin resemblances of his virtuosity make him the Catholic Wesley and Wesley the Protestant Liguori. Both enriched religious moralism with pietism and, of course, vice versa. Both achieved a religiousness that combined the moral and the pious impulses into a reciprocal and interdependent relation. Liguori put his definitive work on moral theology through nine editions, and the twelve decades following his death (in 1787) saw sixty more before the definitive edition appeared. He wrote several detailed manuals instructing confessors in how to apply his moral theology. Simultaneously with this stream came a flood of manuals of devotion centered on the passion of Jesus and the sorrows of Mary. It is not too much to say that Liguori combined these modes of religious practice into his own brand of Christian perfectionism, devising guides to salvation and sanctification, to righteousness and holiness, appropriate to the stations in life of monks, secular priests, and laity.

The moral works centered on practice. So did the pious ones. *Practica di amar Gesù Cristo* appeared in English as *The Love of the Lord Jesus Christ Reduced to Practice.* Rules of Christian behavior existed to be practiced, and the art of confessors was to render them practicable. Liguori's cleansed conscience remained contrite, sorry for having offended Jesus yet resolved all the more to love Jesus, with the favor and intercession of Mary. Acts of affection and devotion promoted the desire and ability to do only what Jesus willed. All led to the simple goal. "I wish to become a saint at any sacrifice"—not Liguori's private ambition, but a prayer for everybody to say.[35] This brief devotional manual quoted no fewer than seventy saints, theologians, and popes, many of them frequently, at once telling how to attain sainthood in practice and showing that attaining sainthood was practicable. To exercise one's capability or faculty for being religious led to steady improvement in the skill of loving Jesus with head and hand and heart. When the exercise combined so that duty and devotion were their own rewards, perfection in practice conferred sainthood. Liguori himself succeeded, for within one generation after his death he had a local cult, and within two generations a universal cult was authorized to honor him as Saint Alphonsus.

The breakup of united Christendom into territorial monarchies, each with its enforced ecclesiastical allegiance, evinced in European Christians a quest for individual, personal, and religious virtuosity. At first, two distinct modes appeared. Piety focused upon inspiration, affection, blessedness, happiness, bliss. Morality sought obligation, duty, goodness, justice, contentment. Pietists welcomed the wounded, bleeding, pitiable Jesus as a worker of miracles, particularly the miracle of bleaching the stain of sinfulness and conferring holiness. Moralists knew Jesus as teacher and legislator of precepts from which one could adduce the good (i.e. the godly) course to take, whatever choice presented itself, and thus Jesus conferred righteousness. Both required practice. And the practice of both in combination, by the end of the period, conferred that perfection by which holiness and righteousness became a single skill, the training for and performing of which turned discipline into delight and delight into discipline.

VI

AUTONOMY

Activists and Apologists

in the Modern Nations

1806-1945

The cultural crises that befell modern Europe with and after the French Revolution were summed up in two remarkable sentences in Meyer Abrams' remarkable book on Romanticism: "The Romantic era was one of technical, political, and social revolutions and counter-revolutions—of industrialization, urbanization, and increasingly massive industrial slums; of the first total war and postwar economic collapse; of progressive specialization in work, alterations in economic and political power, and consequent dislocations of class structure; of competing ideologies and ever-imminent social chaos. To such a world of swift and drastic change, division, conflict, and disorder, the inherited pieties and integrative myths seemed no longer adequate to hold civilization together."[1]

The event that thrust modernity upon Europe was not so much the French Revolution itself as the initial disappointment and the subsequent aspirations that its failure generated. Hopes that Europeans might by revolution create a new heaven and new earth within a new social order had been raised high by the relatively easy success of the American Revolution. But that endeavor was quite unlike the French experience. The Americans had fought to recover certain traditional liberties of Englishmen that a German king of Great Britain was abridging. Yet they grounded their nation in the rights, at once God-given and natural, of all people everywhere to be free and equal. Rights long ago prophesied by John Locke (in the late 1600s) were concretely declared (in 1776) and soon thereafter actualized by many Americans. The fact that these Europeans abroad had initiated the world's "first new nation" inspired Europeans at home to renovate the world's old nations. That effort in France placed faith in liberty, pinned hope on equality, and cast charity in the role of fraternity. The stubborn defense of human rights in America, however, contrasted sharply with the fervent pursuit of human ideals in France.

In the English tradition as well as in the French tradition, privilege had been enjoyed by the nobility and the clergy. For

Americans this privilege, embodied in persons across the wide ocean, had only to be diluted and distributed among the nation's adult males who were white and propertied. The French nullified the prerogatives of their privileged classes whose status symbolized and stabilized social order. Sacred privileges brook change and transfer, but by their very nature they tend to defy clean erasure. The revolutionaries in France thus exiled or imprisoned and then slew some members of the exempted estates, as the bourgeoisie became privileged.

The French Revolution veered into the Reign of Terror. As liberty became license, equality inequity, and fraternity hatred, many who had at first yearned for freedom through external change of the social and political structures now sought a different freedom through internal change of the human consciousness. One of the earliest of these, the German philosopher Johann Gottlieb Fichte, chose the French Revolution as the model for his new system of thought, "the first system of freedom." Fichte decided to repudiate all traditional philosophy in order to establish man "in his first principle as an autonomous being [*als selbstständiges Wesen*]."[2]

Quickly this capacity for human self-liberation permeated politics, poetry, art, philosophy, theology. Somewhat more slowly it transformed the social and the natural sciences. But quickly or slowly, all arenas and dimensions of experience were revalidated by human consciousness, a mode of awareness that made personhood both the chief subject and the main object of concern. Autonomous persons learned that they could simultaneously exist, exist consciously, and be self-conscious about existing and existing consciously. In more epistemological terms, moderns think, they think critically about what they are thinking about, and they then think critically again about the process of their own critical thinking about what they are thinking about.

They make into a human transaction what their forebears had reserved to the deity, namely the grounding and actuating of their own existence. For the preceding European form of humanity, everything was because it was taken into the awareness of God

and thereby made to be. Moderns learned to certify their own existence by taking themselves into their own awareness. They do,
they watch or smell what they are doing, and they watch or smell
themselves watching or smelling what they are doing.

Further steps into autonomy, such as that of watching the
watching of the watching of the doing, would lead to a regres-
sive bog. For when humans have taken over the primary function
of deity in relation to themselves, they render it useless to invade
the divine being's own inner existence, which the initial arrogation has already turned into a mere human construct. Ramified
into all realms of thought and action (a distinction that tends to
recede among moderns), this arrogation establishes the autonomy
of being human. This new humanity makes history; the old was
made by it.

The same holds for religion. By this thought-action moderns
harmonize themselves with their own realms of thought-action
and thus become their own father-creator, their own christ-re-
deemer, their own providential spirit guiding history toward the
end they choose for it. The reason for thus speaking of Christian
forms of deity is that Europeans (after 1800) arrogated to themselves the functions not of all divinities, but of the particular
deity of Christianity.

The result of this audacious thought-action was not to dispel
or to forfeit everything sacred but rather to regulate and invoke
the sacred's entry into the modern. When attempts have been
made flatly to exclude all manifestations of the sacred, its oblique
and usually unrecognized irruptions in the western world have
typically taken the forms initially of racism and ultimately of
genocide. Put another way, men and women liberally took over
the divine functions of the creation and redemption and mastery
of their history. So long as they followed the lead of most early
Romantics they did so in the name of all humanity. But when
they tried to exhaust the sacred by further arrogating the divine
role of judgment over the welfare and existence of other peoples,
the result in the west has been colonialism, slavery, and, most
rampantly, Holocaust. The secular imperium initiated by Napo-

leon Bonaparte thus presaged that borne by Adolf Hitler. The early Romantics had engaged in a "metaphysical process," Abrams wrote, that "does not delete but simply assimilates the traditional powers and actions of God, as well as the overall pattern of Christian history."[3] Hitler took unto himself the power and action of God in judging the nations.

In line with the preceding chapters, the period now under consideration, from Bonaparte to Hitler, is bounded by two rulers. By military conquest each briefly brought most of Europe under his self-appointed dictatorship. Each created his own empire, conferred upon himself total authority over the peoples he ruled, and undertook to determine the process and aim of history.

This chapter first shows how external and internal revolutions transformed the several dimensions of human experience, asserting an independence of the human spirit that enabled men and women to assimilate to themselves the transactions previously assigned to Christianity. Second, it assesses the depletion of traditional Christian authority through successive assaults upon fundamental elements in the inherited religious world view. Third, it briefly delineates the main ways in which Christians have built for themselves religious refuges from self-reliance by arbitrarily assigning final spiritual authority to pope and to Bible, to creed and to cult, and by buttressing that authority through foreign missionary activity.

Mainly, and at greater length, the chapter describes the two styles of religiousness by which certain exemplars christianly expressed their modernity. Activists, the first of these, learned to articulate their Christian concern through dedication to various programs of social justice, finding Christ newly incarnate in or present among the poor and the oppressed. Apologists, also accepting their own modernity, in several ways analyzed the modern sensibility such that it needed to be re-Christianized and enriched from the religious heritage; they looked to a Christ who belonged to and perfected self-substantiating consciousness and culture.

ACHIEVEMENTS

The men who made the French Revolution were dubbed "scribblers and puny philosophers" by Friedrich Heer, who granted nevertheless that they "succeeded in shattering the old France, convulsing the world and setting a question mark for ever over an order which had held for more than a thousand years."[4] There is no squaring accounts with these men by Jules Michelet's improbable excuse that behind wretched leaders stood worthy followers. Pregnant with twins, the Revolution first delivered a dead, misshapen fetus and forthwith gave birth to the cultural and spiritual revolutions that characterized subsequent European history.

Political convulsions allowed Napoleon to seize power until his defeat during the counterrevolution and the restoration of the monarchy. Another revolution (in 1830) ended that restoration, and similar movements (in 1848) excited France as well as Germany and Italy. A milder revolution increased the power of the English bourgeoisie through parliamentary reforms. Revolutions made independent nations out of Spanish and Portuguese colonies in the Americas. The Russians, marching to their own drummer, waited (until 1917) for their upheaval. The Industrial Revolution, both spurred by and spurring several technological revolutions, changed the form and pace of European life from that of the village to that of the city. Other revolutions transmuted science, exploding old chronologies of the earth and of humanity's career on it. Then the new sciences of history and ethnology identified and described many quite different forms of personal and social experience over time and space, indeed many distinct humanities.

Each of these movements articulated in its own way the basic revolution of the human spirit elicited by the failure of the French Revolution. Abrams again put it in a nutshell: the traditional Christian "faith in an apocalypse by revelation had been replaced by faith in an apocalypse by revolution, and this now gave way to faith in an apocalypse by imagination or cognition."[5]

But by no means did this last move simply replace the intermediate one. Rather, external revolutions that failed generated successful internal ones, while the internal ones that succeeded generated still more external ones. The Revolution that failed to create a new France begat a new Europe and a new version of the human enterprise.

Many names have been conjured for this humanity and its stance and aspect, its sensibility and accomplishments. It is so much shared by the contemporary western world (of the late 1900s), that no name quite describes it. Was it Romantic? post-Christian? critical? secular? modern? natural-supernatural? existential? The fact that several names partly fit and partly misfit signals that plural experience has characterized modern Europeans, experience in which the experiencer is the only available unifier of the experiences, all of which can never be fully unified. Autonomy—better, a network of mutually reinforcing autonomies—underlay the plural features of this form of human existence. Friedrich Nietzsche wrote that life no longer consisted in the whole because the whole was no longer whole.

These new Europeans fashioned national governments that reduced the privileges of institutional Christianity by means of blatant state control over the churches. The notion that the state should be neutral about religion crossed few European minds and boggled many of those. Napoleon charted this nationalism, particularly in relation to the church, in his concordat (of 1801) with the papacy. At the end of the period the papacy was still making concordats of essentially this sort with Hitler and Benito Mussolini and Francisco Franco. The French state, no longer adversary to the church as it was during the Revolution proper, now doled out favors to church and clergy as a matter of patronage for a price instead of privilege.

Bonaparte crowned himself the emperor of France (in 1804) and then crowned his Joséphine the empress. Abolishing the Holy Roman Empire (in 1806), he began building a grander imperium than had any European predecessor—the entire continent excepting Britain, Sweden, Portugal, Turkey, and Russia.

Although the Treaty of Vienna (1815) dismantled his realm, the Corsican stamped on each of the pieces the mark of nationalism that ever since has been at once the boon and the bane of Europe.

States expressed their populaces' genius, embodied in rulers who steered nations toward their destinies. The *raison d'état* became simply *l'état* with Napoleon, who (in a phrase ascribed to Louis XIV) called himself the state (*"l'état, c'est moi"*). Even where constitutional measures checked and channeled political power, the traditional functions of deity were arrogated by states created by their peoples, redeemed by their peoples' genius, and managed by their peoples' governors.

The decade dominated by Napoleon was peopled by harbingers of autonomy in arenas other than the political. Demonstrating that each human being stood for and measured itself, Europeans in the new century looked on children not as miniature adults but as persons in their own right with their own stages of development, problems, and levels of expectation and performance. Outstanding women rose to prominence in certain fields of endeavor. Madame de Staël, a contemporary but no admirer of Bonaparte, appointed herself arbiter of high culture and enlisted literature in the service of social institutions. She heralded the German culture, whose intellectual revolution (of the 1790s) warned Europe of the outburst of autonomy that the new century would soon bring. Her *On Literature* (in 1800) and *On Germany* (in 1810) frame the decade that is famous for rejecting absolute norms in favor of a humanity ready to measure itself by itself. If an insular lawyer's son could become dictator of Europe, why not grant autonomy to everybody?

On its face the proposition that all European souls could win their way to personal self-sovereignty seems ludicrous. Taken quantitatively, it is just that. Pertinacious souls autonomized, one by one, each dimension of human endeavor so that some element of the autonomy touched "everybody," at first subtly but then openly. Their success in placing a sovereign human consciousness within reach encouraged almost everybody to reach somewhat for it. What Napoleon did in politics, G. W. F. Hegel did in philosophy, Ludwig van Beethoven in music, William Wordsworth and Samuel Taylor Coleridge in literature—all within the century's opening decade. (Johann Wolfgang von Goethe's *Faust,* Part I, begun much earlier, was completed and published in 1808.) All modeled a daring spirituality for a long list of articulate men and women who ever since have been pressing the enterprise forward, downward, upward, inward, outward, onward.

Bruno Bauer, Max Stirner, Ludwig Feuerbach, Victor Cousin, Friedrich Jacobi, Thomas Carlyle, Karl Marx, Charles Darwin, and Friedrich Nietzsche—to say nothing of Pablo Picasso and Samuel Beckett and Jean-Paul Sartre—all suggest that this chapter must choose only a few figures to illustrate the cultural crisis of modernity and then choose only a few persons to illustrate the religious responses that were characteristic of the era. The first case rests mainly with the first decade's achievements, which implied most if not all of what followed. Attention turns first to thought, then to music, then to poetry.

Hegel published *The Phenomenology of Spirit* (in 1807) only a year after Napoleon consigned the Holy Roman Empire to its own annals. More than a decade earlier, Hegel had written a life of Jesus (published only in 1906), depicting the founder as a human teacher whose genius had been to live so that he merged his finite consciousness into infinite consciousness. What Hegel saw Jesus as having done he himself proceeded to do even more definitively as he relocated "the world of divine intellect [*die Intellektual-Welt*] in the mind of man, so that 'one can see, know, and feel in one's own consciousness everything that formerly was beyond.' "[6] To be sure, Hegel was elevating human experience of the divine mystery to a prominence over the doctrines that described it. He was also opening the way to humanizing deity and to divinizing humanity.

The steps are actually simpler than Hegel's involved philosophizing about them: Consciousness begins by relying on the senses but then can find no permanence in objects outside itself. Self-consciousness remedies that need but fails to find permanence in its own selfhood. Then reason discovers the rationality of the world and of the human soul, making both reliable, but reason can find no solidarity of human endeavor. That feat is accomplished at the level of spirit, the lowest rung of concrete (as opposed to the earlier levels of abstract) consciousness. Spirit gains inspiration but falls short of the reflection that can free one from social convention. That becomes the task of religion. But religion subserves an imperfect notion of the divine, which can be purified only by absolute knowledge in which the spirit knows itself as spirit and also knows divine being as spirit; the two coalesce. Thus in a few brilliant, dialectical moves Hegel's humanity is autonomous, the measure of itself, and even the arbiter of the divine.

Let Eric Voegelin comment. Hegel "has never identified God and man; he has only philosophically identified both their natures as 'self-consciousness.'" Divine being is spirit, and spirit is self-consciousness, and self-consciousness is both divine being and spirit. "The game is rigged; you can't win once you let yourself be sucked into accepting Hegel's language," wrote Voegelin.[7] Indeed, the human imagination and attitude of much of western Europe were gladly "sucked in." The "game," however rigged, emboldened philosophers and other intellectuals to join the chorus of politicians and poets, composers and scientists, preachers and publicists, who were singing the genius and the freedom of the human species.

Little wonder that tradition-recovering Christians from Søren Kierkegaard to Karl Barth have idolized Wolfgang Mozart, the master of music "concerned with honouring God and delighting the heart of man." Their *bête noir* has been Beethoven, who initiated "Music which holds the universe in thrall, which reflects ideas in the form of feeling, which aims at expressing and awakening the passions, which as feeling for life addresses itself in a mysterious way to the feeling for life."[8] The new creative power of musicians exploded in Beethoven's symphonic *œuvre,* first with the Third, or Eroica (of 1804), in praise of Napoleon, then (in 1808) with the Fifth and the Sixth, or Pastoral. And it is no accident that his great Ninth, or Choral, symphony in its last movement set to music the ode to joy by Friedrich von Schiller, who declared that "The right art is that alone which creates the highest enjoyment. But the highest enjoyment is the freedom of the spirit in the living play of all its powers."[9] Mozart had epitomized and perfected the classical development since Palestrina that Chapter V noted. Beethoven pointed ahead to the radically liberated music of Arnold Schönberg and Alban Berg.

Autonomous humanity irrupted through politics in France, through philosophy and music in Germany, and through poetry in England with Wordsworth and Coleridge (and in Germany with Goethe). Coleridge recorded how he and Wordsworth planned to exploit in a new way poetry's power to arouse and rearrange the reader's sensibilities, both "by a faithful adherence to the truth of nature, and . . . by the modifying colors of imagination." They dared use supernatural agents for natural purposes, that is, to stir the affections by placing the divine in relations to the reader such that the reader would suppose the relations real. "And real in *this* sense they have been to every human being who, from whatever source of delusion, has at any time believed himself under supernatural agency," wrote Coleridge. These poets also treated commonplace subjects in ways that evoked the same sense of supernatural presence. The secret, Coleridge recalled, was to depict persons and places and powers "so as to transfer from our inward nature a human interest and a semblance of truth sufficient to procure for these shadows of imagination that willing suspension of disbelief for the moment, which constitutes poetic faith."[10]

Whether or not their collaboration on *Lyrical Ballads* (1798) achieved this ambitious program, any doubt that Wordsworth succeeded in *The Prelude* (written 1805) has been erased by the careful work of Abrams, who suggests that Coleridge also succeeded in *Dejection: An Ode* (written 1802); these poets, like a host of others after them, reversed the old divine-human relation into a human-divine relation. For being grasped by deity through its own theophany they substituted grasping deity through human "autophany" or self-revelation. They subjected the divine mind to summons by human minds. In the traditional language, they put the "creator" at the beck and call of the human "creature" and of course in doing so rendered such language obsolete.

Belief gave way to something that sounds like it but is wholly different, the "willing suspension of disbelief for the moment." In other words, religious faith merged into poetic faith. Now nature was perfected not by grace but by the poetic imagination. In fact, Wordsworth and Coleridge depicted nature with an effect previously assigned only to the grace of conversion—the effect of newly arousing and rearranging human sensibilities. Moderns receive their new frames of mind and heart not from the divine redeemer, but from poetry, especially narrative poetry, and particularly from the novel and its audio-visual rendition in cinema.

It was all self-consciously conceived and executed. Wordsworth shifted the task of theodicy from that of justifying the ways of God to man to his announced "intent to weigh/ The good and evil of our mortal state." Indeed, once the divine function had been assimilated by the human mind and imagination, to do that weighing became equivalent to the traditional task of theodicy. Abrams calls it "a secular theodicy—a theodicy without an operative *theos*." (An "anthropodicy"?) Less somberly, he quoted a critic's best definition of Romanticism as "spilt religion" —not *split, spilt!*[11]

To cast the outburst of human boldness in terms of politics, philosophy, music, and poetry underscores the fact, noted in each of these chapters, that the cultural crises of Europe brought new ways of justifying and organizing and exercising power. All the earlier modes of earthly sovereignty, however else they differed, acknowledged the divine as the ultimate fount of power and the final judge of power's use or abuse. Moderns broke from that consensus by locating power in the people. Of course, democracy is but one of many schemes for organizing popular power into administrable forms. Hitler, Franco, and Mussolini each took the title not of king but of the leader (*der Führer, El Caudillo, Il Duce*) of the people who granted them dictatorial powers.

Human autonomy has profaned the powers that had once been given and received as holy. The desacralized imperium in Europe furthered the desacralizing of other functions previously assigned to deity, such as the revealing of truth, the conferring of grace and salvation, the endowing of nature with beauty and utility, the adjudicating of economic activity, and the directing of history. Put very simply, Europeans singly and collectively became their own do-it-yourself deities. But because their culture, tradition, and language were Christian in form, they specifically became do-it-yourself christs.

The sovereign consciousness of Europeans took over roles once reserved for Christ because, in part, churches during the epoch of ecclesiastical allegiances had parodied the divine in their doctrines. When polemical theologies cast the numinous into lead-soldier molds of Catholic, Lutheran, Reformed, and Anglican scholasticism, pietists warmed their hearts and moralists salved their consciences through personal rapport with Christ. The modern move from heart and conscience to autonomous consciousness was at once a new step and a synthesizing of the older life-patterns. The deity of the former epoch had made demands that religious practitioners "perfectly" met. Moralists and pietists who had "perfected" their practice had only to become autonomous and they could take over the functions of a doctrinally shrunken and highly personalized divinity.

RESPONSES

Moderns have employed their personal and cultural autonomy in a wide variety of responses to their Christian heritage. Some challenged the tradition at its roots. Others erected new schemes of religious authority to replace crumbling ones. Still others adapted the religion to the modern spirit. The adaptations made by activists and apologists involved a religious invention whose

boldness becomes clear only when it is set against the other options, summaries of which are in order.

Scientific and historical investigations drew gauze curtains
across the four chief vistas of the Christian world view that had
framed European life since the fall of Rome; one could see them
still, but only as indistinct scenes. They may be summarized as
follows. First, the earth and its inhabitants came into being
uniquely, by divine fiat. Second, the human race received a unique
character as bearer of God's image which, however marred, remained indelible. Third, the divine hand guided human history
toward a divinely appointed consummation. Fourth, Christ alone
bore the status of god-man and his followers alone enjoyed salvation.

The period from Napoleon to Hitler is also the period from
Claude Saint-Simon's socialistic to Sigmund Freud's psychoana-
lytic debunkings of these four self-understandings. Their veracity fell under profound doubt as scientists in many fields rendered each vision at worst false and at best quaint. Those to
whom these visions became false tried to replace them with veri-
fiable explanations about the earth and its human beings, about
history and its religions. Perhaps most people cherished them as
quaint—at once strange to contemporary life and pleasant for
suggesting the customs and manners of bygone generations.

Put another way, these four constitutive myths of European
Christianity became so radically differentiated that the force they
had carried as compact myths gave way to the near impotence of
legends. All myths tend toward differentiation when people use
them to answer causal questions about human affairs. The differentiation of these myths was radical because the people who asked
causal questions took themselves and nature to be the efficient
causes of human affairs. The process, often called secularization,
may be illustrated by briefly tracing what happened to each of the
four myths.

The myth of unique creation and mission forcibly entered the
new century, altered only slightly by the deistic proposition that

God had made a cosmic clock and set it running on its own. Europeans received the basic myth, of course, from Genesis, but Christians had fit it into a salvation-drama beginning in Eden, climaxing in Christ, and ending in heaven. Coleridge, on the testimony of his *Confessions,* found the Bible inspiring and for that reason alone inspired. This literary view of scriptures enabled Henry Hart Milman to undercut the notion of an old covenant preparatory to the Christians' new covenant. Milman studied the Hebrew Bible simply for the cultural and religious history of an ancient, Oriental tribe. Around his *History of the Jews,* first published anonymously (in 1829), swirled a storm of criticism. He had bypassed the two elements for which Christians prized the Old Testament. First was the myth of God's unique creation of the world through six days in a given year; James Ussher's calculation of the 4,004th year before Christ's birth led the field. Second was the mythic prophecy of and preparation for the coming of Christ as sole savior.

As the ink dried on Milman's book, Charles Lyell began publishing (in 1830) the three volumes of his *Principles of Geology.* Rather than attack the notion of catastrophic and relatively recent creation, Lyell persuasively demonstrated the formation of the earth over aeons of geologic time. His work implied that the human animal, although ancient against the old scale of sixty centuries, actually appeared in a mere yesterday of twenty thousand centuries ago, since the oyster's career spanned five million centuries. Although Lyell and his important forerunners did not set out to challenge the Christian view of creation and humanity, their unintentional subversion was even more devastating than the direct but weak attacks of the rationalists.

The displacing of the particular creation-myth itself pales in importance beside the change in human self-awareness that was involved in stretching their planet's age from a mere sixty centuries to many millions of centuries. Lyell showed that science must explain the past by unchanging laws that had operated during all those centuries and that remained in continuous operation into the present and would so remain in the future.

Only gradually did Lyell adopt the evolutionary scheme earlier advanced (in 1800) by the Chevalier de Lamarck in his inaugural address on the invertebrates. Lamarck posited (in 1809) the evolution of all living creatures by adaptation to environment and by the inheritance of acquired characteristics, thus linking all forms of life into a single, incessant, biological chain. Honest minds tried to salvage the myth that man and woman were special bearers of God's image, but scientific work left "the historicity of the Creation stories in Genesis difficult for honest men to maintain."[12] Then Darwin's epoch-making *Origin of the Species by Means of Natural Selection* (of 1859) and *The Descent of Man* (of 1871) made fables of the notion of human uniqueness and the story of the animals in Noah's ark. Put crudely, humanity bore the image of the ape—*creatio in imago simii*. Ground had been prepared for Darwin by Robert Chambers' popular book, *Vestiges of the Natural History of Creation* (of 1844; eleven editions by 1860), suggesting that ongoing evolution would improve on *Homo sapiens*.

Eventually more important than both Lamarck's and Darwin's explanations of how living organisms developed over time was the work of an Austrian botanist and abbot of the Augustinian monastery in Brünn (now Brno, Czechoslovakia), Gregor Johann Mendel. He demonstrated that members of a given species differed genetically, and he published (in 1866) his findings from his research on heredity in garden peas. A generation passed before his work was appreciated. By that time the theory that each animal embryo recapitulated the evolution of its ancestors, together with the classification of all animal life in one developmental chain, had been set out (in 1899) by Ernst Heinrich Haeckel, professor of zoology at Jena, in *The Riddle of the Universe*.

Further tracing of advancements in biology would only reinforce the point that Europeans, who had entered the century sure of their uniqueness among creatures because of their unique relation to the creator, exited from the century aware of their linkage to all living things by evolutionary laws and genetical patterns.

Most of the century's scientists, including Darwin, sensed the tension between the conclusions their data implied and their personal attachments to the traditional sense of human uniqueness. Even Haeckel wrote a book (in 1892) reconciling religion and science under monistic philosophy. These scholars could neither retain nor entirely forfeit the old, secure world view.

Human society's development and reorganization also came under scientific mastery. A prophet who early urged this move was Claude Saint-Simon, and a designer who early charted it was his understudy, Auguste Comte. They and successors in the social sciences that they founded—perhaps most ominously Marx and Friedrich Engels—discovered within the historical processes certain principles by which to explain and to renovate history. For providential guidance of societies they substituted human manipulation and for a divinely decreed eschaton they devised utopias where egalitarian distribution of wealth and privilege among productive people would replace class strata and elect souls. Recognizing the trend of his times (the early 1800s), Saint-Simon based human solidarity in socially beneficial work, both practical and theoretical. He subjected the known past to empirical, positive, scientific analyses that would illumine the present and determine the future. The lack of honor he eventually received in his own country confirms his prophetic role.

It matters little that some of Saint-Simon's most interesting programmatic publications can now be attributed to Comte. Both unraveled the myth of providence and both made men and women the victims until then and the victors thereafter of their own history. Comte cut neater divisions among the theological, the metaphysical, and the scientific or positive epochs of human experience. Saint-Simon had proposed that renovated society should embody Christianity's sole truth, namely that all men and women were sisters and brothers, while Comte translated features of Catholic myth and ritual into a practicable religion of humanity. Both heralded the new age of autonomous history, beginning (like Hegel) with themselves.

Marx, then, took but a short step when he declared that "Religion is the sigh of the oppressed creature, the heart of a heartless world and the soul of soulless conditions. It is the opium of the people."[13] His scheme of social change, at once more historically determined and more politically revolutionary than Saint-Simon's or Comte's, resembled theirs in that all three served an ideology meant to supplant the inherited Christian vision of divine sovereignty over history and society. Social consciousness during the era of human autonomy made order in the world the creature of human designers and assigned meaning in history to progress, either automatic or aided by human effort.

In parallel developments, then, each main feature of the Christian horizon was redrawn. Nietzsche (by 1900) disrespectfully buried the deity that hallowed this world view—in a grave alongside that of the form of humanity that could know or use such a god. With the myths of special creation, human uniqueness, and providence radically differentiated, what was left for Christians to learn from their Bibles? Very much indeed, but only so long as the myth that cast Christ and his church in unique roles as savior and saved remained intact. This myth above all had enthralled the European imagination by conveying at once its own historical reliability and its own achievement of salvation.

There is little reason here to summarize the eclipse of this main myth's luminosity, an eclipse that Hans Frei has precisely traced and documented. Critical study of the Bible had long occupied scholars of rationalistic bent (since the late 1600s)—in England since Locke and in Germany since Baruch Spinoza. German Protestants had long placed great stock in the inspiration and verbal accuracy of the biblical texts. Scholars became increasingly curious about the individual books' literary history as well as the reliability of their reports.

Since the figure of Jesus Christ dominated Christian belief, the accounts of him, especially those in the first three Gospels with their historylike narratives, naturally drew keenest attention. "Friends and enemies of inherited Christian belief," Frei wrote, "alike came to agree that that belief stood or fell with the historicity of the reports concerning the chief events of Jesus' life."

Inevitably, a disciplined and sustained tradition of critical thinking generated skeptical thinking. Skepticism appeared full-blown in David Friedrich Strauss's *Life of Jesus* (of 1835-36), in which "the most important of these supposed fact claims" about Jesus' birth, teachings, death, and resurrection "turned out . . . to be myths instead."[14]

Since then, the extent to which the Christ of faith is congruent with and verified by the Jesus of history has obsessed Christian thinkers. Some have answered, not at all. Most have found some discordance or remainder. Many have ducked the question under the doctrine of verbal inerrancy. There has developed no steady consensus on the subsidiary but pressing question of how much dissonance it takes between fact and faith to make faith untenable—and at what points.[15]

The European Christian world view stood before autonomous humanity bereft of a special and dateable creation, bereft of a unique human race, bereft of a providential history, bereft of a certifiable historical founder bearing the unique status as god-man needed to confer unique status on his followers who alone were truly saved. The curtaining of these old vistas on self and world at once summarized and magnified the cultural crisis that brought it about.

As the four scenes were being blurred, Europeans had certain options. They could see creation, humanity, and history as determined by physical laws, as manipulated by an arbitrary and wonder-working deity, or as developing according to an immanent power at once natural and supernatural. They could have a historical Jesus determined by or conflicting with their Christ of faith, or they could make Christ a paradigm of the humanity about which people archetypally dreamed and which they yearned to attain. The predicament was not one of having to reject everything that the old world view included but rather one of having to choose whether and how to re-envision what had simply and distinctly stood in the old view. And options tend to reduce world views to opinions.

These choices first arose for botanists and social scientists, philosophers and politicians, clergymen and teachers, scholars and publicists. They spread through education. What about the ordinary men and women who received only the barest education? The inarticulate majority of any bygone epoch is an elusive quarry for the historical hunter, save as the articulate minority shaped their lives and minds. It seems safe to say that these theories and opinions and mythic differentiations bore less on the common round of living than did the Industrial Revolution. First in Britain and then in Germany, increasingly everywhere as the period wore on, that movement was turning peasants into proletarians and villagers into urbanites.

While sophisticated humanity was being reconceived in the image of the ape, common humanity was being recast in the image of the machine. The churches, by and large, could hardly have lost in the city the folk they had never won in the countryside. The activists who will be described in this chapter evidence strenuous efforts to win them as and after they became urbanized. Certainly the Christian world view was proffered them with diminishing confidence that it corresponded with the real world. Just as certainly, not all Christian beliefs were expunged from the minds and lives of religious people. But gradual erosion eventually cuts deeper canyons than does sudden excavation.

Religious belief stridently affirming the inerrancy of a miscellaneous assortment of interwoven and overlaid writings was hardly the same as religious life proceeding unself-consciously under the power of certain myths told in those writings. Religious belief denying human cousinhood with simians can hardly be compared with religious life straightforwardly delighting in brotherhood with a god-man. Religious belief trying to hold Christ in the status of a redeemer differed from religious life humbly serving an incarnate and resurrected savior.

Then, too, the churches' defenders wavered. In each country there were religious professionals who in varying ways conceded what the liberal Anglicans acknowledged in *Essays and Reviews* (of 1860). Science had cooked the goose of the Pentateuch's cosmogony. Historical criticism had discovered legends enveloping the historical Jesus with divinity. From the churches' trumpets came uncertain sounds. Christian self-understandings continued to appeal to simple as well as educated men and women. But the appeal became more and more nostalgic, the self-understandings more and more personal and private.

To the extent that Europeans have participated in the autonomous form of humanity, whether hailing or deploring it, their spirituality has become private instead of public, optional instead of compelling, voluntary instead of vocational, and plural instead of unitary. Even the intensest devotion has taken essentially personal forms very different from the older public expressions, emphasizing sentimental attachment more than overarching allegiance to the religion. The act of becoming and remaining Christian became deliberate, a matter of choosing rather than of being chosen. Maintaining the right to choose to be Christian involved defending others' rights to choose to be non-Christian or anti-Christian. This defense undercut Christian claims to possessing universal truth. However religious persons may have been able to unify their lives, the old, inherent unifying force of Christianity had been exchanged for the self as its own unifier.

The autonomous spirit learned how to place the religious realm of its experience under an externalized authority, thereby insulating that realm from modernity. That is, autonomous people have placed certain arenas of life under authoritarianism, most obviously the arena of religion. Modern Protestants typically chose scripture as their refuge of religious authority, while modern Catholics typically chose the papacy. The contrast, of course, goes back to the Reformation, but the situation changed when later Christians elected to re-establish these once self-validating authorities. The main difference between the alternatives seems to be that popes asserted their infallibility in matters of faith and morals far more explicitly than did scriptures. But this difference is more apparent than real, since the effectiveness of both kinds of authority depended not on their claims, but on how people regarded them. Pius IX and his near predecessors were being accorded infallibility by Catholics long before the first Vatican

Council so declared and Pius so decreed. And scripture was held to be the unique, exclusive word and record of God and his acts long before neo-orthodox and fundamentalist Christians worked out the particular systems of doctrine and practice that were validated solely by "the Word of God."

After the declaration of papal infallibility (in 1870-71), Pius IX gladly accepted his role as sole definer of Catholic faith and morals. The Council said the pope's definitions in those areas were infallible and universal; they actually became so when Pius decreed that they had always been so. Then Pius X bound Catholics to certain traditional notions about the authorship of biblical books long after serious scholars had refuted and abandoned those ascriptions. In all things touching on religion Catholics were to follow whatever popes dictated, since each pope "was" tradition. But the neo-orthodoxy associated with the work of Barth and the neo-traditionalism associated with Pius IX and Pius X arose in distinct ways. Those popes detested modernity and sought to isolate their flock from it, while Barth had admired it and its liberalism until the catastrophe of World War I drove him to find more secure ground. Barth condemned all religion while exempting true Christianity from the genus; in his secure position only Jesus Christ, and not Christian religion, whether a religion about him or the religion of him, manifested the divine reality. For the Piuses that reality had always been embodied where they intended to keep it, in the papacy.

Despite those differences, the Catholic and Protestant authoritarianisms functioned in much the same way. The operative agency of papal authority was the cult, especially the mass that was kept sacrosanct (until Vatican II) by the rule that it must be said or sung in Latin, nobody's common language. The authority of scripture functioned by the agency of its interpretation—that is through doctrines that decreed the proper meanings of texts and then used the same passages as proof-texts of the doctrines. In fact, papal authority rested in a sacerdotal power that, as more than one Catholic has said, exceeded the spiritual power of the Virgin Mary to the order that she made Christ palpable only once while every dutiful priest did so thousands of times. Analogously, biblical authority derived from believing the doctrine that the Bible was God's message whose saving power became manifest when people generated it by accepting this doctrine.

The shades and gradations within each of these two major forms of authoritarian Christianity are many and need not detain us. For in all versions of both syndromes the procedure is for modern men and women autonomously to exempt the religious arena of their lives from the autonomy pervading the other arenas of life. One of the fascinating features of the modern spirit has been its readiness, even while taking into human consciousness the traditional functions of the Christian deity, to keep open the option of holding a formal sphere of religious assurance immune to the acids of modernity.

This autonomous religion made heroes of foreign missionaries. The black, yellow, brown, and red people whom they went abroad to evangelize were neither modern nor pre-modern. They lived on their own time scales until missionaries and colonizers, aided by ethnologists, began to westernize them. The missionaries themselves shared the autonomy characteristic of the age, to the extent that they arrogated the divine functions of saving souls and of judging other races to be less noble forms of humanity than their own. So far as they identified the relief of hunger, ignorance, and disease with the cause of Christ they resembled activists. So far as they affirmed the cultures to which they went and enriched them with Christian values they resembled apologists. But more than either of these, and usually without realizing they were doing so, they reaffirmed a religious authority that was waning back home by proving its appeal abroad.

To summarize and to anticipate. This chapter has reviewed the internal and external revolutions through which an autonomous form of humanity erupted in Europe. It has traced the erosion of the authority traditionally exerted and of the truth traditionally proclaimed by Christianity. It has also noted two ways in which moderns typically have erected for themselves bastions of religious authority and truth that they chose to keep in isolation from the modernity that pervades other areas of their life.

The chapter now turns to the two modes of expressing Christianity by and through a fully autonomous humanity and therefore of bringing Christianity to terms with modernity. One uses thought-*action,* the other employs *thought*-action. Activists expressed their Christian autonomy by finding arenas of popular justice and welfare in which to perform christianly. Apologists (the term is here given a particular sense, not that of apologetics or apologetic theology) expressed their modernity christianly by identifying arenas of autonomous experience which they could interpret as needing Christian improvement and fulfillment. In both cases, special attention is paid to the adaptation of Christ to these styles of life.

ACTIVISTS

Exemplary apologists and activists candidly expressed autonomous humanity christianly after secularism and nationalism splintered the cultural and religious life of Europe. Few exemplars of these modes of religiousness rose to pan-European or even international eminence. The last section of this chapter will treat several apologists who attained such prominence, beginning with Friedrich Schleiermacher and Samuel Taylor Coleridge, then paying closer attention to John Henry Newman, Søren Kierkegaard, and Albrecht Ritschl. This section selects for treatment outstanding activists, beginning with Hugues Félicité Robert de Lamennais in France. Then the section quickly surveys programs of social activism under Catholic and Protestant auspices on the Continent and in England. It concludes with Dietrich Bonhoeffer in Germany. (Were the book concerned also with the United States, several of the most eminent activists would be women, perhaps beginning with Catharine Beecher and certainly including Jane Addams.)

Lamennais' career, unlike the careers of those American women, ran from promise to prominence to lonely isolation.

From his uncle he received a wide-ranging, disjointed education that invited original thinking. Led to espouse Christianity (in 1804) by his elder brother, with whom he soon collaborated on two major books, he drifted (in 1816) into ordination to the priesthood. As prophet of the revolution (of 1830) he led many of the finest minds in the French church to join issue with the public affairs of the day. When the pope gently silenced him, he at first took his lumps humbly and then struck back with one of the most influential political pamphlets of his generation. Under harsh papal condemnation he quietly retired from formal religion. Membership in the Constituent Assembly after the revolution (of 1848) impressed him as ineffectual. He died (in 1854) without the last rites of the church, asking to be left in the peace of solitude. The man, born to a minor title and once hailed by leading intellectuals and churchmen as their chieftain, asked to be and was laid to rest, in a pauper's grave, by proletarians.

Throughout, his underlying vocation was to reform politics and society. What he read in the signs of his times impelled him to find in social action the deepest channels of religious commitment. Seen in this light, Lamennais' career was of a single piece, although changing circumstances made for seeming vacillations between defending and denouncing the church, between conservative ecclesiastical centralism and radical political socialism, between obeying and defying popes, even between espousing and rejecting formal Christianity. The man's integrity rested in his readiness to accept his own modernity and to express it christianly by working out increasingly subtle relations between religion and society and between divine and human justice.

The three French revolutions through which Lamennais lived stamped his consciousness with the inevitability of social upheaval and riveted his conscience to the worth of the oppressed masses. He was recording this almost apocalyptic preoccupation in letters (from 1825 to 1827) well before the restored monarchy fell. "I think we are reaching the catastrophe of this terrible drama." Again, "We are at the beginning of an immense revolution which will end either with the death or with the rebirth of the people." Once more, "I have long been persuaded that a general revolution is inevitable, and that all the efforts of good men should be directed to the future. . . . It is folly to count on the governments. . . . We must work with the people . . . until the time set by God for the consummation of things."[16]

When he realized (about 1827) that neither pope nor bishops would free the church from national control so that Christianity might rejuvenate society, he urged Catholics to promote revolution as the most concrete enactment of their religion. Nor did he focus his attention only on France, where his predictions of social and political upheaval came true twice during his lifetime. He warned that all of Europe would face such cataclysms until there came a religio-socio-political renovation based on a common reason that the divine creator had implanted in mankind—particularly the masses.

This early, basic commitment never wavered. For half his career he begged churchmen to translate their religion, which presupposed and perfected the common sense of the people, into the regeneration of history. When instead the church repudiated him, signaling that it cared more for privilege under the old order than for responsibility to the new, he appealed directly to the masses for the same regeneration. Through shifting circumstances he steadfastly identified the fundamental significance of Christianity with social and political reform. Social activism defined the religiousness he advocated and practiced. Politics always excited him because politics made concrete the excitement of religion. Human autonomy meant revolution. Revolution needed religion. To be Christian meant to be religiously revolutionary.

Appreciating Lamennais' early career within the church, *The New Catholic Encyclopedia* naturally hailed him as contributing to apologetics, particularly in his essay analyzing and attacking religious indifferentism.[17] That fact does not make him an apologist as the term is used in this chapter. For his regrounding of religious certainty in the common mind of mankind (*sensus communis*) depended on making the spiritual and political realms at once distinct from and dependent upon one another. Both were certified by human consensus, by natural reason, by Christian revelation, and by social tradition.

The first volume of his attack on religious indifference thrust Lamennais into the center of attention for all kinds of French literates. The pope thought of making him a cardinal. The reviewer who epitomized the book's central message in the phrase, "there is nothing more liberal than religion and nothing more religious than liberalism," captured what Lamennais was all about and predicted that the church would become too confining for him.[18] Lamennais identified Christianity with the social virtues arising from the liberal and revolutionary movements of his time—the extension of suffrage, economic equality, social solidarity and fraternity, political liberty, freedom of education, an unfettered press, and separation of Church and State. As his articulation of this program grew more popular and more strident, the more suspicious became the bishops and the pope. When aggressive supporters began to organize protests, to conduct fundraising campaigns, to form local committees against governmental abuse, and to publish with Charles Montalembert a journal called "L'Avenir," or "The Future" (October 1830–November 1831), the papacy silenced the leader.

Lamennais had earlier summarized the program in these words: "Society cannot be cured by ordinary means; . . . an entire, absolute dissolution is inevitable and . . . necessary to the renewal of life. . . . When a certain number of men . . . will unite among themselves, then the seed of a new society will exist. . . . Hence liberty, possessed or sought, is today the first need of the people and the indispensable condition of salvation. . . . Therefore everything must be done by the people, that is, by a new people, gradually formed under the influence of a better conceived Christianity, amid the nations in ruins."[19] Such a program was hardly silenceable even by the pope, to whom Lamennais submitted himself for religious discipline as a priest. But no pope could command his political and social conscience, which erupted and startled the world with the writing (in 1832) and publishing (in 1834) of the apocalyptic *Words of a Believer* (*Paroles d'un croyant*). The church had condemned his central idea that Christ lived contemporaneously in and for the masses. Like many later activists, Lamennais summoned the masses to become the new, noninstitutional embodiment of Christianity. This appeal arose from the conviction that God had bypassed the institutional church. The argument gained cogency when the pope, on the urging of the Austrian prince von Metternich, explicitly condemned the book and its author.

In a vision that anticipated Dostoevsky's legend of the Grand Inquisitor, Lamennais beholds seven men, wearing crowns and cursing Christ for having "restored liberty to the earth." They plot to undo Christ's work and to "stifle liberty." One proposes to "abolish the religion of Christ." All agree. Others suggest abolishing learning and thought, the press, even human concord. One declares, "The executioner is the prime minister of a good prince." Yet another wants to "exhaust strength, and energy, and courage by corruption." Their *coup de grâce* is to bribe the priests of the church to teach that God willed peoples' subjection under tyranny. In the next vision these rulers turn into anguished shades, for Christ has won. "Faith and thought have broken the chains of the people . . . and . . . emancipated the earth." Oppression has united the people against tyranny. The rulers chant, "Christ has conquered; cursed be he!"[20]

To be sure, Lamennais' Christ reigned divinely as the only master worthy of the masses' allegiance because he had suffered and died humanly for them. "His heart did beat with the hearts of the people, and the hearts of the people beat with his heart." He offered salvation to all, for "He hath shed for each of us a drop of blood." Those who ruled on earth were foiling his purpose; as humans Christ had saved them, but as rulers they recrucified him wherever they wielded power over instead of on behalf of the people.[21]

In allegiance to Christ—"the saving Christ, the liberating Christ, the Christ who pities the poor, the weak, the miserable, and who breaks the sword over their oppressors"—Lamennais was justifying power in keeping with the spirit of his age, just as Gregory the Great and other predecessors had.[22] Autonomous modern societies embodied sacred imperium in the equality of the people. "All men are born equal; no man upon entering the world, brings with him the right to command." All humans had the same God for their father, the same Christ for their sole master. As for those who exercised power in the world, "If they are righteous, they are your servants; if they are not righteous, they are your tyrants."

Righteousness, however, consisted in dedication to the will of the people. The remedy for the sins of princes was for the people to choose "one or more" of their own "whom they believed to be the most righteous, to protect the good against the wicked; and that the weak might live in peace."[23] No other power could be legitimate because God on behalf of the masses had lodged authority in those whom the people elected to administer their power.

No institutional church could actualize this essential Christianity, Lamennais eventually conceded. But the spirit of Christ as the exemplar of divine compassion for mankind lived on in reform, in liberty, in revolution, in the people. The church that expelled this advocate of the common people without ever excommunicating him could not rid the world of his Christ, who became present wherever there was human liberty. For Lamennais popular liberty incarnated divine reality as the historical Jesus had done. The locus of the contemporary Christ was popular liberty. A Christian's activity on behalf of popular liberty was the truest service to Christ.

Lamennais' equation of a just, harmonious society with true, applied Christianity commended itself to many in France, Belgium, England, Italy, and Scandinavia. The identity of the movement, variously called Christian socialism or social Christianity or religious socialism, is recognizable whether in Catholic or Protestant or other dress. So far as activism was a Christian mode of life responsive to autonomous humanity living in urban-industrial-commercial societies, Lamennais is rightly regarded as its inaugurator and great exemplar.

Throughout the stormy history of modern France, the official church strove to protect its privileges and exemptions. Even during the Second Republic (1848-52) and well into the Third (after 1871), it coveted past glories. Only disestablishment (in 1905) threw the French church back on its own merits and released its latent spiritual power. All this time, Catholic activists in France resorted to varied stratagems to avoid Lamennais's path of repudiating the church.

His disciple Philippe Gerbet eventually renounced social activism and helped draft Pius IX's *Syllabus of Errors*. Others attacked the ills of industrialism from high public office and kept their Catholicism private. Philippe Buchez, at mid-century France's leading Christian socialist, worked within the Catholic frame of reference without becoming a practicing churchman. He strove to make Catholics revolutionary and revolutionaries Catholic, enlisting support from such divers sources as organized labor and the archbishop of Paris. A socialist advocate of Fourieristic improvement, Hippolyte de la Morvonnais, returned, under Lamennais' influence, to the faith he had earlier rejected, and as a liberal Catholic he equated harmonious social relations with applied Christianity. The official church blinked at this layman's deviations from orthodox doctrine. The bishop of Langres greeted the February Revolution (of 1848) by claiming that liberty, equality, and fraternity were the profoundest and the exclusive ideals of Christianity.[24]

Socialist priests organized a banquet in Paris (in 1849) for workers to hail the Second Republic. The revelers toasted Jesus Christ as the father of socialism. But not all activism fell on the liberal side. The bishop of Chartres saw the revolution (of 1848) lighting fires of reform all over Europe, and in a pastoral letter he denied that the Second Republic began on Mount Calvary and that Christ favored any sort of political liberty. Conservatives tried to relieve poverty and misery through programs of charity instead of schemes of reorganization. This kind of activism persisted in France beyond the Second Empire and into the Third Republic.

As soon as Pius IX condemned the whole idea of bringing Catholicism to terms with modernity, Émile Keller published an influential book (1865, republished as late as 1909) to persuade workers and the poor that the only hope for improving their lot arose from a mighty church run by absolute popes. The revolutionary doctrine of popular sovereignty, in Keller's view, encouraged usurpers to despotic rule over the people, whose social and political welfare the church had always guarded. Conservative activists in France strove to employ the spirit of autonomy expressed through religion as the agent for emancipating the populace from bondage to the spirit of autonomy expressed through power and wealth. Workingmen's clubs and Catholic industrial employers promoted the corporate welfare against a revolutionary individualism that they believed weakened the workers and the society. This conservative social movement prompted Leo XIII to issue (in 1891) the encyclical *Rerum novarum,* assigning natural right to the organizing of laborers and instructing clergy to form associations for social and economic improvement. He also grounded private property and class distinctions between rich and poor in natural right.

These fundamental disagreements over what was good for society are instructive about Christian activists, who throughout our period served different and even opposing causes and ideologies. On every great, modern, social or political question were found people who gave contradictory Christian answers while christianly serving their causes. National socialism under German and Italian dictators rallied Christians in support and Christians in opposition. When Soviet influence spread over central and eastern Europe after World War II, many Christian activists comfortably allied themselves with the new doctrines and new régimes, while fellow Christians resisted or fled "godless" communism.

The anomaly of opposite programs arising from the impulse of what had been (and many thought still was) a single religion disturbed leading Christian socialists in England. Although English society was industrialized earlier and more thoroughly than was French, the only harbinger of religious activism to appear in

Britain before mid-century was Thomas Carlyle. In his famous *Sartor Resartus* (of 1833-34), Carlyle made plain his impatience with doctrine and theology because they mislocated the religious principle in the minds of the learned instead of the hearts of the good. Carlyle "thundered against the doctrine of *laissez-faire,* and he made a deep impression upon Maurice and Kingsley, but the real impetus" of the Christian socialist "movement came from Ludlow."[25]

That is tantamount to saying it came from France, for John Malcolm Forbes Ludlow received his education and imbibed socialism there. He accorded Lamennais a place among religious reforming geniuses near Bossuet and Luther—somewhere between Savonarola and Fénelon.[26] In France he learned Louis Blanc's social theory and admired Louis Meyer's *Société des Amis des Pauvres.* Witnessing Paris in the immediate aftermath of the February Revolution impressed upon him the need for worldwide socialistic reform. He, like Buchez, resolved to christianize socialism and to socialize Christianity.[27]

The same thought was coursing through the mind of lawyer Ludlow's acquaintance and soon-to-be friend, a lawyer-turned-preacher named Frederick Denison Maurice. The English upper classes feared that the Chartist movement would prey upon turmoil among workers after the economic crisis (of 1847) and erupt into revolution. Ludlow, Maurice, Charles Kingsley, and others feared not so much the introduction of socialism as the failure of Christians to channel England's socialism. Maurice from the pulpit, Ludlow through the periodical called *Politics for the People,* Kingsley through open letters, and all of them through workingmen's colleges and associations identified the essence of Christianity as social improvement.

That is not to say they agreed on a single ideology of reform. Kingsley wanted changed hearts, commending the Bible for its single thought, "justice from God to those whom men oppress, glory from God to those whom men despise"; the Bible issued "the poor man's comfort, and the rich man's warning."[28] Maurice adhered to theological principles proclaiming Christ as head of the human race and brother to each of its members; he envisioned a kind of idyllic British empire spreading over the world under the kingship of Christ. Ludlow remained practically concerned to publicize and ameliorate the awful living conditions of the downtrodden. Maurice's animus against parties and partisanship helped him avoid embracing any ideology that might conflict with the ideologies of other Christian socialists. This attempt at comprehensiveness also left the movement vague and short-lived. In the end it was religiously ineffectual. The effective practitioners of Christian activism in urban and industrial England (down to the 1930s) were neither the nonconformists nor these mellow Anglicans, but the Anglo-Catholics who formed quasi-monastic guilds and sisterhoods dedicated to working for and among the poor. Among Roman Catholics in England, Henry Edward Manning lent his prestige as archbishop of Westminster (after 1865) to many programs of social betterment and espoused many workers' causes. Manning, who mediated the London Dock Strike (in 1889), took for his mentor another Catholic activist, the pioneer French sociologist Frédéric Le Play.

The foremost Christian activist of England (in the 1930s and 1940s) was William Temple, who during World War II became archbishop of Canterbury. Nobody better understood or more plainly faced the enigmatic fact that Christians embraced no clear, unified, agreed-upon, comprehensive, workable plan for dealing with autonomous humanity in autonomous societies. Of all the activists he most prized a pragmatic approach. The official church should never "interfere in a particular issue, such as . . . an actual trade dispute which has broken out." The church "has its own witness to give; and if this were heeded, no dispute would arise." Instead, "It is very seldom that Christianity offers a solution of practical problems; what it can do is to lift the parties to a level of thought and feeling at which the problem disappears." Conflicting interests among parties to a controversy posed an insoluble problem. "If, on the other hand, all could be brought to love their neighbours as themselves, there would be no problem. It would not be solved; it would be abolished."[29]

Only lately did Italy and Germany join the ranks of autonomous nations. The February Revolution in France, to be sure, sparked brief uprisings in both areas, but each took time (until the 1870s) to gain political unity. Stirrings toward a united Italy can be traced back to Bonaparte's occupation of the peninsula, but activists undertook religious programs to improve the autonomous Italian state mostly in the new century. The succession of leadership passed from Giuseppe Toniolo and his fellow corporatists before World War I through the liberal Romolo Murri and his Christian Democrats down to Luigi Sturzo who, after a long exile (from 1924 to 1946), "participated in the triumph . . . of the Christian democratic party which was the popular party revived and expanded."[30]

Both Protestant and Catholic Germans grappled with social issues late in the century. Baron Wilhelm Emmanuel von Ketteler of Mainz (bishop 1850-77) strove to rid modern industrialist-capitalist society of what he contended were slave-market practices that made living christianly impossible. He established the basis of the Catholic Center Party, and followers kept alive his program. Among German Protestant activists, Adolf Stoecker formed a political party (in 1878) to practice gospel and anti-capitalist principles. When Stoecker died in 1908, he was a chief spokesman for pure German blood and for anti-Semitism. Friedrich Naumann helped found the nationalist Socialist Party (in 1903) and the German Democratic Party after World War I. The Zurich pastor Hermann Kutter, among others, spread into southern Germany a program of identifying movements for social justice outside the church as signs of divine activity in the world. Leonhard Ragaz combined into his activism influences from Coleridge, Kutter, and Count Leo Tolstoi, seeing signs of the kingdom of God in socialistic success.

On the whole, the more conservative activists' programs for society coincided with official church policies. But the coincidence tended to be accidental. Activists have typically distinguished between their loyalty to the Christian religion in its institutional forms and their allegiance to the christianly formed conscience in matters political and social. That distinction became plainly operative with Lamennais and persisted down to Murri and Sturzo in Italy, to Temple in England, to the German religious socialists after World War I, and to the French worker-priests led by Georges Michonneau after World War II.

The tension created by this distinction reached near the breaking point in the career of Dietrich Bonhoeffer when he christianly engaged in a conspiracy to assassinate Hitler. The brilliant, energetic, young theologian turned activist with his conversion (in 1931) to personal and fervent religiousness. He then, at a conference in Cambridge, became youth secretary of the World Alliance for Promoting International Friendship through the Churches. The activist style of life enticed him ever more compellingly. He was nearly the first, maybe the very first, German Christian to speak out (in 1933) against Nazi oppression of the Jews—less because they were Jews than because they were Germans and his Germany was treating them unjustly. The next year he joined the Confessing Church to protest against state control of German religion. The next year he founded a commune to train pastors in practical Christian living and social action. The next year he was forbidden to exercise his lectureship at the University of Berlin. The next year (in 1937) the Nazis closed his seminary. On the eve of World War II (in 1939) he went to New York City, where he refused offers of exile. Returning to Germany that summer, he soon became a double agent. Using the cover of being a pastor, he worked in Munich as a civilian in counterespionage for the military intelligence wing of the armed forces' high command while plotting with the underground first to overthrow and then to kill Hitler.

The first two attempts on Hitler's life (in March 1943) misfired. A month later, Bonhoeffer was arrested and imprisoned, not because he was suspected of being complicit to the plot, but to be interrogated about various interests of his army command. "The Gestapo," wanting to control military intelligence, "had no idea that, with this arrest, they had in fact made a direct hit at the heart of the conspiracy."[31] When his involvement in the almost successful plot (of July 1944) came to light, he and nearly five thousand others were executed. He was hanged (on April 9, 1945) with five other plotters, only three weeks before Hitler's suicide and four weeks before Germany's surrender. Fame came not with Bonhoeffer's death, but with the publication (in 1951) of his writings in prison. Two or three decades after he died he ranked among the most famous European Christians of his generation.[32]

His own career led from auspicious beginnings, to protest, to duplicity, to crime, to imprisonment, to humiliation, to execution. Religiously he proceeded from a boyhood vocation to the ministry, through theological training, to conversion, and to protest against the main-line church, and eventually to a solidarity with Christian and non-Christian conspirators that made him forfeit any solace first in his identity as a pastor and then even in his identity as a Christian. The recollection of him runs ironically in the opposite direction, from humiliation and execution to fame and praise and more fame and to veneration as a saint.

Bonhoeffer's cause increasingly became a just society in Germany. That cause precluded his self-exile on the eve of war. It drew him back to Germany in the knowledge that he must protest against the Nazi régime by seeming to serve it in order to subvert it. When he failed in his attempts to negotiate terms of surrender favorable to Germany on the promise of then getting rid of Hitler, the only responsible step by his lights was to get rid of Hitler forthwith and to hope for a just Germany in the future under acceptable terms of surrender.

In his posthumous *Ethics,* Bonhoeffer wrote that "that which is Christian is to be found only in that which is of the world, the 'supernatural' only in the natural, the holy only in the profane, and the revelational only in the rational." He himself actually found it ethically responsible to commit crimes. He continued, "The unity of the reality of God and of the world, which has been accomplished in Christ, is repeated, or, more exactly, is realized, ever afresh in the life of men."[33] Bonhoeffer did not identify what was Christian with what was worldly, but rather he newly conjoined the two so that what was done christianly could be done only in the worldly arena.

For previous forms of humanity the Christian religion had consisted in depending upon and serving an all-powerful, transcendent deity. For Bonhoeffer autonomous humanity's Christianity consisted in identity with a Christ who united him with God by remaining the powerless, humbled man who exemplarily suffered for others. This is the nub of Bonhoeffer's now-famous sayings such as "the world come of age," "religionless Christianity," "the nonreligious interpretation of biblical concepts," "Jesus the man for others," "worldly responsibility," "living with and for others," and "The church is the church only when it exists for others." Alasdair MacIntyre put succinctly Bonhoeffer's religiousness: "The Christian way of life consists not in any reliance either on ecclesiastical forms or on divine power but in a life of worldly powerlessness, lived totally for others."[34]

The activists expresed their Christianity through their autonomous humanity by doing christianly whatever they did, by finding their arenas for activity in autonomous spheres such as revolution, charity toward the poor, by organizing laborers to demand their rights, by socialistic reform—or, as epitomized by Bonhoeffer in response to Hitlerism, by conspiracy in assassination done christianly. Since he was hanged not for being a Christian but for being a conspirator, Bonhoeffer, if he was a martyr, was a martyr for his witness not to Christ but to a just society in his beloved Germany—and beyond. His was a witness borne christianly because he found his identity with Christ in the cause of social justice in Germany (and beyond) and in his own living and dying in what he took to be the way in which Christ lived and died for others.

From Lamennais to Bonhoeffer, then, all over western Europe, there were Catholic, Protestant, and Anglican activists who responded to their autonomous humanity by attending a Christ who identified with and therefore could be found only among the people. In one of Bonhoeffer's now popular phrases, since Christ was the man for others, those who followed him should christianly be for others. In fact, they followed him and worshipped him supremely and normatively by christianly being for others the way he had been for others.

APOLOGISTS

As noted above, Lamennais took the common mind of humanity to be the source and arbiter of religious certitude and he looked to the church's teachings to perfect that consensus. So far, he early reflected the style of an apologist, but he directed this concern into a career of activism. The two persons who most influentially chartered the way for modern Christian apologists were Coleridge in England and Schleiermacher in Germany. This section first shows briefly how each found in human autonomy certain features that, christianly considered, corresponded with and culminated in certain features of a revamped Christian ideology. Then the section examines three apologists who each identified a distinct mode of experience as the basis for christianly interpreting human existence. All three took as given the modern form of humanity and adapted the Christian world view to an aspect of it.

John Henry Newman in Oxford and Birmingham expanded the capacity of self-conscious people for assenting to and apprehending a complex of Christian doctrines whose development he traced back to the original, simple idea of Christianity evoked by Christ's incarnation.

Søren Kierkegaard in Copenhagen depicted subjective selfhood as the appropriate imitator of a humbled Jesus Christ who reached into the present to save the individual from despair.

Albrecht Ritschl in Göttingen construed humans gathered into ethical communities as working out Christ's guidelines for the kingdom of God on earth.

These three exemplary apologists undertook careers of advocating Christianity to and in the modern condition; they took appointment as ambassadors of Christ to the foreign realm of autonomous humanity, affirming the post-Christian or ex-Christian condition of modernity while showing how to be re-Christian or neo-Christian within that condition. They based their apologies, respectively, on assent and historical development, on the plight of individual personhood, and on the quest for human community, thus making specific the more general apologies of Schleiermacher and Coleridge.

Coleridge disallowed any difference in kind between ordinary language and religious language, holding the latter to be more emphatically "symbolic, tensional, and stereoscopic" in order to show that ordinary language shared these characteristics to lesser degrees.[35] In other words, everybody by virtue of being human had the capacity and the inclination to exercise the imagination, particularly what Coleridge called the Secondary Imagination, because it made sense of what in the Primary Imagination remained direct and immediate. Thus everybody tended to receive and reflect the ultimate reality that was God, who had facilitated matters by appearing as man in Christ. Thus Christianity amounted simply to truth operating as life. Foundational to it was "The sense, the inward feeling, in the soul of each Believer of its exceeding *desireableness*—the experience, that he *needs* something, joined with the strong foretokening, that the Redemption and the Graces propounded to us in Christ are *what* he needs." Moreover, Coleridge experimentally tested the validity of Christianity. In almost his own words, "In order to [have] an efficient belief in Christianity, a man must have been a Christian."[36] Insiders knew that the religion fit their human condition.

Schleiermacher took another tack to reach the same harbor. Almost exactly Coleridge's contemporary (both died in 1834), he affirmed that human experience was naturally religious, that moral monotheism was a higher type of religion than polytheism, and that Christianity was distinct in that it related everything to the redemption that Jesus of Nazareth had accomplished. Like Coleridge, Schleiermacher made a splash among and through intellectuals. The ripples of both men's ideas spread far and wide.

Schleiermacher's famous discourses (of 1799) on religion to its cultured despisers sketched the fundamentally new approach to Christianity that his later writings detailed. This approach grounded religion in humanity's taste and feeling for the divine, later expressed as a sense of absolute dependence upon the infinite. His attributing this taste, feeling, or sense for the divine to being genetically human was a characteristic of his own being modernly human.

For Schleiermacher was sensitive to differing and changing forms of human experience—to the significance of Napoleon for Germany and Protestantism and to his own break from and return on a higher plane to the Moravian piety in which he was raised. He starkly realized "the fatefulness for the individual of the unity as well as of the diversity of human nature." In a dialogue on Christmas (written 1805) he symbolized conversion by male propensity for change, sanctity by the female inclination to spontaneous fidelity, the believing community by the natural family, and Christlikeness by the innocence of childhood. This dialogue, according to Richard R. Niebuhr, "contains Schleiermacher's first projection of the argument to the existence of an historical founder of Christianity from present religious experience."[37]

In short, Schleiermacher studied piety, both corporate and individual, as the index to what aspects of Christianity appealed to his own era and culture. The appropriateness of moderns and Jesus Christ to one another arose because for him Jesus bore fundamental resemblances to autonomous humanity. The crux of the matter is that Schleiermacher, along with Coleridge, rearranged the features of the inherited religion to match the features of contemporary human experience.

That is not to say they collapsed religion into intuition as a means of knowing or into emotion as a means of feeling. Rather, those faculties became the receptors of what remained relevant and viable in the figure of Jesus and in the religion he founded. An earlier chapter of this book described the medieval form of humanity as one whose nature was both corrected and perfected by grace. The apologists affirmed the modern form of humanity as one whose nature implied and pursued and could attain grace.

Their Jesus Christ embodied in his own time a humanity that for them in their time exemplified what their humanity could and ideally ought to become.

In Carlyle's pithy phrase, Coleridge "knew the sublime secret of believing by 'the reason' what 'the understanding' had been obliged to fling out as incredible."[38] If Coleridge guarded the secret for a few full-fledged Romantics, Newman announced it to the world and by so doing altered the thing announced. For Coleridge the reason or imagination allowed a willing suspension of disbelief, while for Newman the dogmas of revealed religion invited everybody to apprehend their truth and not merely to accept them as opinions. Newman urged people to realize that their daily lives proceeded not by accepting neat, notional propositions that logically produced scientific conclusions but rather by assenting to a vast series of probabilities that concretely presented themselves as the reality and truth of the world.

Revealed religion invited such assent. Newman knew that many honest persons would decline. Here was no Anselm welcoming the expanded power of human reason to ask questions, then enlisting it in the service of Christian doctrine, then demonstrating those doctrines' reasonableness without appeal to scripture or tradition. Rather, Newman showed that men and women of cultivated consciences whose whole, almost subconscious, personal history equipped them for religion could assent quite reasonably to religious probabilities. Natural needs aroused desires for the religious probabilities in persons inclined toward religion. Other persons whose quite natural, moral, mental, and psychological inclinations leaned toward disbelief acted reasonably in disbelieving, but theirs was a narrower reasonableness.

Newman did not hold that disbelievers must believe to be rational. He held that believers believed more rationally than disbelievers disbelieved rationally. There were two crucial features of this apology. On the side of the believer there was the power of what Newman called "the illative sense," of believing what could be fairly inferred from what was already firmly believed. On the side of things believed there was what might be called "the illative development," the orderly expansion of doctrines from less explicit doctrines. Both processes were needed to certify assent and to validate what was assented to.

Assent for Newman characterized daily, concrete living and acting, while critical doubt and scientific proof worked only for theoretical, abstract propositions. Whatever might be said of natural religion, revealed religion belonged to daily and concrete living. In Newman's words, written (in 1841), long before *Grammar of Assent* was published, "Many a man will live and die upon a dogma: no man will be a martyr for a conclusion. A conclusion is but an opinion; it is not a thing which *is,* but [one] which *we are 'quite sure about';* and it has often been observed, that we never say we are sure and certain without implying that we doubt. To say that a thing *must* be, is to admit that it *may not* be."[39] In matters of imagination or speculation people suspended disbelief to affirm a certitude that embraced doubt. In matters of assent people acted upon inferred probabilities that were so forcible as to command action.

Because religion consisted in concrete living (a blend of believing and worshipping and enacting), the proper means to it was real assent or faith and not notional assent or opinion—not, in the later idiom of Michael Polanyi, explicit knowledge, but personal, tacit knowledge. Newman did "not contemplate" religion "in conclusions drawn from dumb documents and dead events, but by faith exercised in ever-living objects, and by the appropriation and use of ever-recurring gifts" (371). Thus Christianity consisted in a living idea planted and perpetuated by Christ both in history and in the minds of believers, yet growing and adapting itself to human sensibilities that were also growing and adapting.

The idea of Christianity in its modern development was graspable by moderns, who could then show what they grasped to be orderly developments of the original idea—in history and in their minds. "At this very day its rites and ordinances are continually eliciting the active interposition of that Omnipotence in which the Religion long ago began. First and above all is the

Holy Mass, in which He who once died for us upon the Cross, brings back and perpetuates, by His literal presence in it, that one and the same sacrifice which cannot be repeated." This Christ actually entered, "soul and body, and divinity, into the soul and body of every worshipper who comes to Him for the gift, a privilege more intimate than if we lived with Him during His long-past sojourn upon earth." This Christ personally lived in the churches of his followers. "Such is the profession of Christianity, and . . . its very divination of our needs is in itself a proof that it is really the supply of them" (371-72). Once again, insiders knew with perfect certainty that the religion fit their human condition.

The critic is dead right who wrote that "Newman always wants to tell us the story of Newman."[40] His own religiousness— a living, growing, developing idea and act—proceeded from an evangelical upbringing through the Anglo-Catholicism of the Oxford Movement to the embracing of Roman Catholicism and eventually to a disaffection from that church's declaration of papal infallibility and its repudiation of doctrines of development. It is not too much to suggest that his *Apologia Pro Vita Sua* summarized in the first person the essays on development and on assent. The two themes thus ran together in Newman's own life. Assent consisted in a developing sense of the way he acted on probabilities. Christianity consisted in a development of the original idea of itself. Newman's life consisted in developing assent to developing Christianity. Thus the *Development of Christian Doctrine* illustrated the principles of exfoliation by working from earlier to later statements. But the book's real story line worked from Newman's assent to Catholicism back toward the initial idea of Christianity. What had come to be a vastly ramified and differentiated set of myths and doctrines stood, he insisted, in continuity with the original idea.

Genuine developments were tested by seven notes: preservation of the type, continuity of principles, power of assimilation, logical sequence, anticipation of the future, conservative action upon the past, and chronic vigor. Any church might exhibit one or more of these marks, but only Roman Catholicism possessed them all. Only his own theory of development, he claimed, could explain the validity of heretical baptism, disagreements and contradictions among the church fathers, the canon of Scripture, the sinlessness of the Virgin Mary, the early church's confused language (before 325) about the trinitarian deity, the doctrine of indulgences, and the eucharistic sacrifice. But even his theory was hard put to explain papal infallibility.

The Christianity that this modern modernized for moderns stood in continuity with the original idea that the apostles received from Jesus Christ and at the same time adapted itself to changing forms of humanity. Newman acknowledged the religion's remarkable adaptability throughout European history, then by his own historical reconstruction of it demonstrated its continuity.

It is too simple but not totally off the mark to say that for Newman people began by believing everything and discarded only what became unbelievable. He appreciated the integrity of nonbelief and even of disbelief. Yet he did convert David Hume's program of systematic doubt into a program of systematic belief. "Belief is a state of mind," he wrote; "belief generates belief; states of mind correspond to each other; the habits of thought and the reasonings which lead us on to a higher state of belief than our present, are the very same which we already possess in connexion with the lower state."[41]

Instead of grasping religion by the willing suspension of disbelief, Newman grasped it by disbelieving only what he could find good reason for not believing—that is, by the willing expansion of belief. The man's modernity lies in the fact that he grasped Christianity, not it him. Having done so, as Powell has written, "Newman explained the power and influence of Christianity in the history of the world as a function of the imprinting of the image of Christ by Christ Himself in the minds of His followers individually."[42] He embraced Christianity so avidly that he felt it return the embrace.

Søren Kierkegaard regarded the idea of Christianity and its

doctrinal development as the antithesis of authentic Christianity. He rendered truly being Christian (or purity of heart) available only to the solitary individual struggling with the existential possibilities and radical choices of personal life. This struggle, when undertaken with utter seriousness, prepared the self to imitate the humble life of Jesus. To be sure, Kierkegaard wrote more about Christianity's antitheses than about its authenticity. A vast literature (mostly from the 1900s) has calibrated his angles of attack on the religion prevailing while he lived (mid-1800s) in Denmark. He came at traditional and institutional Christian religion obliquely and directly, obtusely and acutely, almost always disapprovingly. Far more important, Kierkegaard plumbed individual solitude to its depths where it became torn between self-affirmation and self-denial, between self-possession and self-sacrifice, between commitment to others and utter loneliness. He described and commended what he himself had appropriated through painfully self-conscious living. Aesthetic delight yielded ennui. Ethical resolve generated guilt. Outward religion produced self-righteousness. Inward religiousness ended in humiliation.

This hunchback, who was inordinately attached to the person and companionship of his father, developed a learned literariness and an irrepressible wit that cloaked a tormented spirit. He was haunted and hounded by the knowledge that he had been begotten by Michael Kierkegaard, who as a shepherd-boy had once cursed God, and his servant-girl Ane Lund, and had been born four months after Michael's first wife died. Michael amassed a small but comfortable fortune by which Søren lived and studied and published his books. He broke his engagement (to Regine Olsen) under a mysterious divine vocation to self-sacrificial, inward loneliness. Outwardly he cut the figure of a *bon vivant* in Copenhagen until the editor of a scandal sheet Kierkegaard had attacked made him the butt of popular ridicule. Eventually he wrote blistering accusations that the Danish church and all its members were devoid of the Christianity found in the New Testament and in the person of Jesus. He died (in 1855) in his early forties, at peace with his savior and isolated from his church whose last sacrament he had spurned.

From Kierkegaard's pen, over a profusion of pseudonyms and sometimes above his own name, came a varied effusion of treatises, discourses, meditations, sermons, instructions, and polemics, all cast in the dialectical paradoxes he needed to convey his intense sensitivity to the ambiguities and conundrums encountered by autonomous, individual selfhood. That to which the self committed itself in fundamental choice determined all the self's relations—to God and to others and to itself. One's relation to the absolute, then, dictated one's relation to the universal, not vice versa, as had been the case for Enlightenment humanity. Kierkegaard's own commitment was anything but that of claiming to be a model, modern Christian. To make that claim would prove the opposite!

Rather, he committed himself to honesty about the intolerable demand of authentic Christianity for the imitation of Christ in purity of heart and in works of love. All human commitments, then, led to despair. But despair enabled the self to recognize its basic sinfulness. Only in such a realization could one accept the contradiction of the broken man Jesus in his true status as God.

That culminating, objective paradox of suffering deity issued in another, subjective paradox: The profoundest despair adjoined the highest hope. The deep water that threatened to drown became by a leap of faith, the water buoying up the swimmer. Such faith allowed one to imitate Christ and gain inward freedom for the self. It also incurred other persons' and society's outward rejection by which one could measure one's inward freedom.

A few of Kierkegaard's sentences lend flavor to any description of his life-style. "If thou dost behold in a winter's storm one who is clad in the lightest summer garments, not even he is so painfully exposed as he who wills to be a solitary man in a world where all persons are in connexion, and consequently require, with the selfishness characteristic of connexion, that one must hold together with them, until the individual secures himself against several connexions by entering into one connexion, whereas the solitary individual, as soon as it has become evident that he will hold with none, has against him (grandiose connexion!) all connexions united in one connexion."

Again, "And this is Christian piety: to renounce everything in order to serve God alone, to deny oneself everything in order to serve God alone—and then to have to suffer for it, to do good and have to suffer for it." Note, however, that the renunciation, the self-denial, the suffering, remain wholly inward. "The highest thing is: while being absolutely heterogeneous with the world by serving God alone, to remain in the world and in the midst of reality, before the eyes of all, directing upon oneself the whole attention of all—for then persecution is unavoidable."[43] Service to God equaled imitating Christ's humiliation.

Kierkegaard's Christ invited people to follow him not as some historically reconstructible figure from the past, but as the god-man whose lowliness always shone forth from his illegitimate birth to his ignominious death. This figure became to Kierkegaard the eternal contemporary, given to presenting himself across time and space in the humbled, crushed manhood that paradoxically at once offended and invited followers. Only by accepting the offense could one imitate Jesus' lowliness, accept his invitation, and thereby recognize and glorify his divine exaltation, which was coincident with his suffering.

For this special existential crisis of despair and hope Kierkegaard invented a special existential language, replete with paradoxes like that of Jesus' being the eternal contemporary. Kierkegaard's rhetoric was intended to repudiate all conventional Christian discourse and to lead its readers toward being genuine persons, perhaps even true Christians. By his insistence upon the naked individual as the only authentic religious subject he intended to unmask the hypocrisy of institutional religion and to help people face themselves and their redeemer. His analysis showed how autonomous, individual subjectivity in all its relations drove persons to sense their spiritual need; he encountered Jesus Christ as the one who provided the profoundest imaginable revelation of and remedy to that need. The modern human condition thus begged for its fulfillment in Christianity.

The fact that Kierkegaard's writings swelled to vast influence beyond Denmark only (after 1920) when they were nearly a century old, underscores his aptness as apologist for a form of personhood that he early and sensitively manifested. He is a giant of one century (the 1900s) who happened to write in another (the 1800s); he is the exemplary apologist of individualism. He faced head-on the autonomy of individual personhood, exploring all the twists and turns of the various life situations that such persons have been able to choose and commit themselves to. Each led to the dead end of despair.

But the dead ends were only apparent, for in fact they were also alive beginnings to persons who accepted the invitation of Kierkegaard's Christ to come heavy-laden and receive rest. He made being a Christian at once the intensification and the fulfillment of being an autonomous individual, whether its life pattern be the aesthetic or the ethical or the outwardly religious. In doing so he drove Christianity so deeply within the individual that he had to denounce the Danish church and with it all public Christianity.

Albrecht Ritschl and his disciples down to Ernst Troeltsch singled out human community as seeking fulfillment by Christ's kingdom of God. Ritschl studied theology at Bonn, Heidelberg, and Tübingen, then taught at Bonn (from 1851 to 1864), and then (from 1864 to 1889) at Göttingen. Holding that religion could neither be reduced to nor explained by other modes of experience, he rejected metaphysics in favor of basing theology in human community and especially religious community. His history of German pietism condemned all individualism for truncating the Christianity that in its genuineness had to do with communal experience.

Ritschl tested the reality of religious experience by the value judgments made and maintained by religious groups. Thus, religion consisted fundamentally in a way of living, or "life-style" (*eine Weise des Lebens,* or *Lebensführung*). "What distinguishes Christianity from every other religion," Barth wrote about Ritschl, "is that it answers the questions all religions ask. . . . That is the meaning of an apologetics of Christianity: to demonstrate this significance of Christianity for the realization of the ideal human life."[44] This (for Ritschl) highest possible religion embodied the community of neighborly love to which all human societies aspired. This loving community manifested the kingdom of God on earth that Jesus inaugurated. For though they fall short of the ideal kingdom, people were consoled by divine forgiveness. In yearning and striving for it they were encouraged by the example of Jesus' vocation of love and obedience.

It has been written that "for Ritschl, the Church was the Kingdom on its knees with hands folded in prayer, and . . . the Kingdom was the Church on its feet with tools for work and weapons for warfare in its hands."[45] In Ritschl's own terms, the "divided and naturally conditioned existence" of people in groups called for what "the personal example of Christ himself" proffered them, namely, "sonship with God and dominion over the world" as well as "the ethical functions of dutiful action in one's particular vocation and the development of ethical virtues." What people needed and what Christ provided met in "autonomy from every particular authority."[46] Once again, "the *first* group of virtues—self-control and conscientiousness—makes for autonomy and honorableness of character" (66). The Europeans' quest for personal and communal autonomy led to a spiritual pot of gold in the kingdom of God at the end of Jesus' rainbow.

For Ritschl and his liberal followers Christianity actualized what all human communities needed and what other religions projected as desirable and potential. The communal life-style that Jesus bestowed correlated precisely with what humanity wanted and needed. What human societies were obligated to achieve coincided precisely with what Christianity forgave them for falling short of achieving and then enabled them to achieve. The supranatural fraternity and sorority of humankind equaled the supra-

mundane kingdom of God on earth. "This destiny . . . is realized by men only in their union with the community of their lord
Jesus Christ" (13). Natural, narrowly ethical groups were too
limited to express the love of neighbor, which was the highest
value to which communities could aspire. The people of Israel
formed community "as the union of subjects bound together by
righteous conduct" under God (7). Only the supranatural community or the kingdom of God fulfilled in actuality the destiny
of Christian justice.

Ritschl broke with Ferdinand Christian Baur, his teacher at
Tübingen, for Baur's being overly abstract and underly historical.
Ritschl himself proceeded to ground Christianity in the historical
figure of Jesus from whom the history of western Christianity
had flowed. Then Ritschl generalized the value of Christianity
by making it the desire of all religions and the destiny of all
communities. The Ritschlians took this historical program with
increasing seriousness, right down to Adolf von Harnack, who
distilled Christianity into the essence of Jesus' historical message
—"the kingdom of God and its coming," "God the Father and
the infinite value of the human soul," and "the higher righteousness and the commandment of love."[47]

Troeltsch at first agreed. But later he found that by historical
study he could abstract no such essence. Christianity consisted
entirely in its own history and was whatever it became. "Thus
the essence of Christianity can be understood only as the productive power of the historical Christian religion to create new interpretations and new adaptations. . . . In this sense the essence
of Christianity differs in different epochs, and is to be understood as something involved in the totality of its active influence."[48]

Troeltsch realized that Christianity thus became the fulfillment
of western aspirations. The religion's universal claims must be
withdrawn. As Europeans, he wrote, "We cannot live without a
religion, yet the only religion that we can endure is Christianity,
for Christianity has grown up with us and has become a part of
our very being." However, "this does not preclude the possibility

that other racial groups, living under entirely different cultural conditions, may experience their contact with the Divine Life in quite a different way" and practice their own religion; "they may quite sincerely regard this as absolutely valid for them."[49] Apologists who identified modes of modern western experience as aspirations that Christianity fulfilled met a Jesus Christ who redeemed modern Europeans. When fully historicized, this redeemer redeemed *only* the modern Europeans who chose him. Nobody else.

ENIGMAS

The choice of Newman, Kierkegaard, and Ritschl to exemplify the way of life of apologists shows the variety of features in the experience of autonomous humanity that have been made the bases for additive Christianity. Intellectual and historical development, the self-consciously individual person, and voluntary community have been constitutive characteristics of autonomous human experience. Apologists showed each of them to be christianizable. In a similar pluralism, seen above, activists espoused many and sometimes opposite social programs, yet remained Christian because they christianly espoused them.

In conclusion it is natural to ask if even that most arrogant feature of autonomous humanity, people's taking unto themselves the traditionally divine function of judging the nations, could itself be construed to need and be fulfilled by neo-Christianity. Were modern colonialism, racism, and genocide possible arenas for thinking and acting christianly? Could these social programs be the objects of Christian activism and the bases of Christian apologies? Put the question with respect to the superiority of western European civilization to T. S. Eliot and Christopher Dawson. Put the question with respect to Italian Fascism and German Nazism to Eugenio Pacelli, both before and after he was Pius XII, and to Emanuel Hirsch. Put the question with respect to the slaughter of Jews to Adolf Stoecker and Alfred Rosenberg. The answers are clear. They are affirmative.

Autonomous European humanity assimilated the divine functions of the Christian deity only to find it could not eliminate what it had devoured. Thus the current term, "post-Christian," expresses a longing more than it describes an achievement. More accurate may be "ex-Christian," understood in apposition to "ex-lover," denoting a *status quo* indelibly marked by the *status quo ante,* connoting an ambivalence between spurning and yearning, referring at once to a theonomous tradition that cannot be forgotten and an autonomous condition that cannot be escaped. The protagonist in an American novel was made to say it rather well: "To be Christian was impossible, to be pagan also. That left you-know-what."[50] The statement is poignant precisely because you do *not* know what.

The activists affirmed human autonomy as capable of being christianly reformed in the interest of social and political justice for the masses, among whom Christ was present. The apologists affirmed autonomous culture by identifying its features that were susceptible to being christianly advanced to new fulfillments by Christ's blessing. It is too simple to distinguish these expressions merely as stressing deeds or ideas, action or thought, although the activists did share a mood with the moralism and the apologists with the theodicy of earlier times. Separating these modern ways of life from all predecessors is their endorsement of the autonomous form of human experience. The activists strove to christianly reform autonomous society. The apologists strove to christianly transform autonomous culture.

Chapter I

1. For an amplification of this point and a more general discussion of the historiography of religion see William Anthony Clebsch, "History and Salvation; An Essay in Distinctions," in *The Study of Religion in Colleges and Universities,* ed. Robert Paul Ramsey and John Frederick Wilson (Princeton: Princeton University Press, 1970), pp. 40-72.

2. Richard Hofstadter, "History and the Social Sciences," in *The Varieties of History From Voltaire to the Present,* ed. Fritz Stern (New York: Meridian, 1956), pp. 414-15.

3. Eric Voegelin, *Order and History, 4, The Ecumenic Age* (Baton Rouge: Louisiana State University Press, 1974), p. 243. Voegelin's book has informed much of the discussion at hand, and its citation here and in notes to the main chapters only begins to indicate my intellectual debt to him. On the subtle questions surrounding the identity of Jesus Christ I am privileged to have conversed and corresponded over many years with Hans Wilhelm Frei, whose writings on this topic have instructed me with such broad force that detailed influences and borrowings can no longer be traced. See Frei, "Theological Reflections on the Gospel Accounts of Jesus' Death and Resurrection," *The Christian Scholar,* 49 (Winter 1966), 263-306, and, in that issue, the comments on Frei's article by Amos Niven Wilder, Daniel Day Williams, and Ian D. Kingston Siggins. See also Frei, *The Eclipse of Biblical Narrative; A Study in Eighteenth and Nineteenth Century Hermeneutics* (New Haven: Yale University Press, 1974); and Frei, *The Identity of Jesus Christ; The Hermeneutical Bases of Dogmatic Theology* (Philadelphia: Fortress, 1975). My acknowledgment of these heavy debts does not imply, of course, that my creditors approve my use of the loans.

4. Bruce Bennett Lawrence of Duke University showed me this passage and allowed me to copy his translation from p. 39 of his typescript, "Notes from a Distant Life; The Major Features of Sufi Literature in pre-Murghal India (1206-1526 A.D.)," citing *Amsār al-asrār* as quoted by ᶜAbd al-Ḥaqq, *Akhbār al-akhyār,* pp. 131-32; this short title is more fully referenced in Lawrence's bibliography as ᶜAbd al-Ḥaqq Muḥaddith Dihlawī, *Akhbār al-akhyār fī asrār al-abrār* (Delhi, 1705).

5. Irenaeus, *Adv. Haer.,* 5, pref., P.G., 7, 1120: "solum autem verum et firmum magistrum sequens, Verbum Dei, Jesum Christum Dominum nostrum: qui propter immensam suam dilectionem factus est quod sumus nos, uti nos perficeret esse quod est ipse."

6. See Robert Clark Gregg and Dennis E. Groh, "The Centrality of

Soteriology in Early Arianism," *Anglican Theological Review,* 59:3 (July 1977), 260-78.

7. Voegelin, pp. 56, 332, *et passim.*

8. *Ibid.,* p. 268; Henri Focillon, *The Year 1000* ([1969]; New York: Harper & Row, 1971), p. 23.

9. See William Hugh Clifford Frend, *Martyrdom and Persecution in the Early Church; A Study of a Conflict from the Maccabees to Donatus* (Oxford: Basil Blackwell, 1965), and Robert McQueen Grant, *Augustus to Constantine; the Thrust of the Christian Movement into the Roman World* (New York: Harper & Row, 1970), for the period's interest in martyrs and monks.

Chapter II

1. Caesar Augustus Octavianus, *Res Gestae Divi Augusti,* 6:34, tr. Frederick William Shipley, Loeb Classical Library ([1924]; Cambridge: Harvard University Press, 1967), pp. 398-401.

2. Mikhail Ivanovitch Rostovtsev (Rostovtzeff), *Rome,* ed. Elias Joseph Bickerman, tr. James Duff Duff (London: Oxford University Press, 1960), p. 163.

3. Charles Norris Cochrane, *Christianity and Classical Culture; A Study of Thought and Action from Augustus to Augustine* (London: Oxford University Press, 1944), p. 3.

4. Rostovtsev, p. 216.

5. Robert McQueen Grant, *The Sword and the Cross* (New York: Macmillan, 1955), p. 57; cf. Robert McQueen Grant, *Augustus to Constantine; the Thrust of the Christian Movement into the Roman World* (New York: Harper & Row, 1970), pp. 78-83.

6. Peter Robert Lamont Brown, *The World of Late Antiquity from Marcus Aurelius to Muhammad* (London: Thames and Hudson, 1971), p. 67.

7. See Eric Robertson Dodds, *Pagan and Christian in an Age of Anxiety; Some Aspects of Religious Experience from Marcus Aurelius to Constantine* ([1965]; New York: W. W. Norton, 1970); Eric Voegelin, *Order and History, 4, The Ecumenic Age* (Baton Rouge: Louisiana State University Press, 1974), p. 315.

8. See Grant, *Augustus,* p. 55.

9. Anon., *The Epistle to Diognetus,* 5:1-2, 4-5, 9-12, Kirsopp Lake, tr., *The Apostolic Fathers,* Loeb Classical Library, 2 vols. (London: William Heinemann, 1913), 2, 359-61.

10. See Grant, p. 62.

11. See Eusebius Pamphili, *The History of the Church from Christ to Constantine,* 1:1, 3:1, tr. Geoffrey Arthur Williamson (Baltimore: Penguin, 1965), pp. 31, 107; Origen, *Gen. comm.,* 3:24, P. G. *12,* 91-92. See Grant, p. 63n.35.

12. Herbert Anthony Musurillo, tr. and ed., *The Acts of the Christian*

Martyrs, Oxford Early Christian Texts (Oxford: Clarendon, 1972), includes texts and translations of the twenty-eight best-authenticated *acta;* parenthetical numbers in the remainder of this section refer to pages in this work. Some one hundred and fifty named persons appear in these stories and some fifteen more are enumerated or alluded to; one-sixth were women; at least six, possibly many more, were soldiers. As nearly as dates can be assigned, none died before 155 and about half died after 295. For the *acta* of several late Egyptian martyrs, see Eve Ann Elizabeth Reymond and John Wintour Baldwin Barns, eds. and trs., *Four Martyrdoms from the Pierpont Morgan Coptic Codices* (Oxford: Clarendon, 1973). A popular dictionary of saints, Donald Attwater, *The Penguin Dictionary of Saints* (Baltimore: Penguin, 1965), gives the names of more than two hundred persons, a few of them admittedly legendary, who attained sainthood by martyrdom during our period; for the next 1500 years there are some seventy martyrs' names in this catalogue. Eusebius and early chroniclers who relied on him leave the impression of innumerable martyrs, a tradition considerably qualified since the 1600s. Henry Dodwell (in 1684) drastically reduced earlier estimates, but Thierry Ruinart (in 1689) held to the immense numbers. Recent estimates of Ludwig Freiherr von Hertling are close to 10,000, but Henri Grégoire counted a tenth that number. See "Martyr," *New Catholic Encyclopedia,* where the date of Dodwell is in error.

13. See Grant, p. 167; Cyprian, *Letters,* 61:2, tr. Rose Bernard Donna, Fathers of the Church, *51* (Washington: Catholic University, 1964), 197.
14. See Eusebius Pamphili, *Life of the Blessed Emperor Constantine in Four Books from 306 to 337 A.D.,* 1:37, tr. anon. (London: Samuel Bagster, 1845), p. 31; and Eusebius Pamphili, *History,* 8:12, tr. pp. 342-43; see also Giuseppe Ricciotti, *The Age of Martyrs; Christianity from Diocletian to Constantine,* tr. Anthony Bull (Milwaukee: Bruce, 1959), pp. 118-19.
15. See Reymond and Barns, pp. 157-58.
16. Grant, p. 231.
17. See Rosemary Rader, The Role of Celibacy in the Origin and Development of Christian Heterosexual Friendship (unpubl. diss., Stanford University, 1977), pp. 49-63; cf. Mary R. Lefkowitz, "The Motivations for St. Perpetua's Martyrdom," *Journal of the American Academy of Religion, 44* (September 1976), 417-21.
18. See Brown, pp. 106-7.
19. See Herbert Anthony Musurillo, ed. and tr., *The Acts of the Pagan Martyrs: Acta Alexandrinorum* (Oxford: Clarendon, 1954).
20. See Reymond and Barns, pp. 151-84.
21. Eusebius, *History,* 6:42, tr. p. 279.
22. *Ibid.,* 10:5, tr. p. 402.
23. Eusebius, *Constantine,* 1:21; the following paragraphs contain parenthetical numbers referring to books and chapters of this work.

24. Robert Austin Markus, *Christianity in the Roman World* (New York: Scribner, 1974), p. 101.
25. Peter Llewellyn, *Rome in the Dark Ages* (New York: Praeger, 1970), p. 23.
26. John Cassian, *Institutes,* 11:18, in *Works,* tr. Edgar Charles Sumner Gibson, *NPNF, 11,* 279. On Ammonius see Palladius, *The Lausiac History of Palladius,* 11:2-4, tr. William Kemp Lowther Clarke (London: Society for Promoting Christian Knowledge, 1918), pp. 64-65.
27. Brown, p. 106.
28. See William Hugh Clifford Frend, *Martyrdom and Persecution in the Early Church; A Study of a Conflict from the Maccabees to Donatus* (Oxford: Basil Blackwell, 1965), p. 462.
29. Palladius, 32:8-10, tr. p. 115.
30. Athanasius, *Life of St. Anthony,* 5, 6, tr. Mary Emily Keenan, *Early Christian Biographies,* ed. Roy Joseph Deferrari, Fathers of the Church, *15* (n.p.: Fathers of the Church, 1952); parenthetical numbers in the following paragraphs refer to chapters in this work.
31. Anon., *The Life of Pachomius (Vita Prima Graeca),* 120, tr. Apostolos N. Athanassakis, Society of Biblical Literature Texts and Translations, 7 (Missoula, MT: Scholars Press, 1976); the two following parenthetical references are to paragraphs in this work.
32. *Apophthegmata Patrum,* Poemen 184, P.G. *65,* 567; see Derwas James Chitty, *The Desert a City; An Introduction to the Study of Egyptian and Palestinian Monasticism under the Christian Empire* (Oxford: Basil Blackwell, 1966), p. 71. Evagrius Ponticus, *Chapters on Prayer,* 124, and *Praktikos,* 81, in *The Praktikos; Chapters on Prayer,* tr. John Eudes Bamberger, Cistercian Studies Series, 4 (Spencer, MA: Cistercian Publications, 1970), 76,36.
33. Evagrius Ponticus, *Praktikos,* 43, 55, tr. pp. 28, 31.
34. 'Anān-Īshōᶜ of Bēth 'Abhē, comp., *Stories of the Holy Fathers; being histories of the anchorites, recluses, monks, coenobites and ascetic fathers of the deserts of Egypt,* tr. Ernest Alfred Thompson Wallis Budge (London: Humphrey Milford, 1934), pp. 375, 377.
35. Evagrius Ponticus, *Praktikos,* 12, 28, tr. pp. 18, 19, 24.
36. See Wilhelm Frankenberg, *Euagrius Ponticus,* Abhandlungen der Akademia der Wissenschaften in Göttingen, Philologisch-Historiche Klasse, n.F. *13:2* ([1912]; Kraus Reprint, Göttingen: Vandenhoeck & Ruprecht, 1970), 521-31.
37. See Cassian, *Institutes,* 10:24, tr., *11,* 274-75, and *Life of Pachomius,* 6.
38. Brown, p. 102.
39. Frend, p. 548; for these references see "Martyr," *New Catholic Encyclopedia.*
40. See Palladius, 3:3-4, tr. p. 51.
41. Anon., *The Life and Works of Our Holy Father, St. Daniel the Stylite,* 92, 96, Elizabeth Anna Sophia Dawes and Norman Hepburn

Baynes, trs., *Three Byzantine Saints; Contemporary Biographies translated from the Greek* (Oxford: Basil Blackwell, 1948), pp. 65, 68.

42. Athanasius, 60; for other references, see Hans Lietzmann, *A History of the Early Church, 4, The Era of the Church Fathers,* tr. Bertram Lee Woolf (2nd ed., London: Lutterworth, 1953), p. 156n.4.
43. *Life of Pachomius,* 1.
44. John Cassian, *Conferences,* 10:6, *NPNF, 11,* 403.
45. *Idem.*
46. Palladius, 22:11-13; numbers in parentheses in this paragraph refer to chapters and subdivisions in this work.
47. See Chitty, p. 76.
48. Athanasius, 60.

Chapter III

1. Arnaldo Momigliano, "Christianity and the Decline of the Roman Empire," in *The Conflict between Paganism and Christianity in the Fourth Century,* ed. Arnaldo Momigliano (Oxford: Clarendon, 1963), p. 1; cf. pp. 1-6.
2. See William Carroll Bark, *Origins of the Medieval World* (Stanford: Stanford University Press, 1958).
3. See *ibid.,* pp. 54-55.
4. See Edward Arthur Thompson, "Christianity and the Northern Barbarians," in Momigliano, ed., pp. 56-64.
5. Bark, p. 77.
6. Friedrich Heer, *Charlemagne and his World* (New York: Macmillan, 1975), p. 11.
7. Momigliano, p. 9; see Archibald Ross Lewis, *Emerging Medieval Europe, A.D. 400-1000* (New York: Alfred A. Knopf, 1967), p. 28.
8. Momigliano, p. 12.
9. Eric Voegelin, *Order and History, 4, The Ecumenic Age* (Baton Rouge: Louisiana State University Press, 1974), p. 93.
10. *Ibid.,* p. 172.
11. Anicius Manlius Severinus Boethius, *The Consolation of Philosophy,* tr. Richard Hamilton Greene (Indianapolis: Bobbs-Merrill, 1962), pp. 91, 104-5, 117.
12. Helen Marjorie Barrett, *Boethius, Some Aspects of His Times and Work* (Cambridge: Cambridge University Press, 1940), p. 2, citing Hastings Rashdall and John Burnet.
13. Friedrich Heer, *The Intellectual History of Europe,* tr. Jonathan Steinberg ([1953]; Cleveland: World, 1966), p. 28.
14. Reprinted in William Anthony Clebsch and Charles Roth Jaekle, *Pastoral Care in Historical Perspective* ([1964]; New York: Jason Aronson, 1975), pp. 124-35.
15. Howard Rollin Patch, *The Tradition of Boethius, A Study of His*

Importance in Medieval Culture (New York: Oxford University Press, 1935), p. 42.

16. *Ibid.,* p. 120.

17. "But the expression 'God is ever' denotes a single Present, summing up His continual presence in all the past, in all the present, . . . and in all the future." But, "Our present connotes changing time and sempiternity; God's present, abiding, unmoved, and immoveable, connotes eternity," Anicius Manlius Severinus Boethius, *De Trinitate,* 4, *The Theological Tractates,* ed. and tr. Hugh Fraser Stewart and Edward Kennard Rand, Loeb Classical Library ([1912]; Cambridge: Harvard University Press, 1962), pp. 16-17.

18. Anicius Manlius Severinus Boethius, *Contra Eutychen et Nestorium,* 3, *Theological Tractates,* pp. 84-85; see Karl Barth, *The Doctrine of the Word of God,* tr. G. T. Thompson (Edinburgh: T. & T. Clark, 1962), *1:1,* 409.

19. James Westfall Thompson and Edgar Nathaniel Johnson, *An Introduction to Medieval Europe 300-1500* (New York: W. W. Norton, 1937), p. 121.

20. Paulus Diaconus, *De gestis Langobardorum,* 2:4, P. L. *95,* 480-81, William Dudley Foulke, tr., *History of the Langobards by Paul the Deacon* (New York: Longmans, Green, 1907), pp. 57-58.

21. See Helen Margaret Gardner, *Art Through the Ages* (3rd ed., New York: Harcourt, Brace, 1948), pp. 258-63.

22. Procopius, *Buildings,* 1:1:29-30, Henry Bronson Dewing and Glanville Downey, trs., *Procopius,* Loeb Classical Library, 7 vols. ([1940]; Cambridge: Harvard University Press, 1971), 7, 16-17.

23. Peter Llewellyn, *Rome in the Dark Ages* (New York: Praeger, 1970), p. 78.

24. Gregory the Great, *Dialogues,* 2:15, tr. Myra L. Uhlfelder (Indianapolis: Bobbs-Merrill, 1967), p. 22; see Llewellyn, pp. 72-73; the quotes that follow in this paragraph are from Llewellyn, pp. 77, 85, 85, the last citing a letter (of 580) from Pelagius II to Bishop Aunacharius of Auxerre. The third chapter gives rich detail of Gregory's life and administration; the most exhaustive treatment of Gregory in English remains Frederick Homes Dudden, *Gregory the Great; His Place in History and Thought,* 2 vols. (London: Longmans Green, 1905).

25. Llewellyn, p. 93; Charles Forbes René de Tryon de Montalembert, *The Monks of the West from St. Benedict to St. Bernard,* ed. Francis Aidan Gasquet, 6 vols. (London: Nimmo, 1896), 2, 59.

26. See *The Rule of St. Benedict,* in Owen Chadwick, ed. and tr., *Western Asceticism,* Library of Christian Classics, *12* (Philadelphia: Westminster, 1958), 291-337.

27. Walter Ullmann, *The Growth of Papal Government in the Middle Ages* ([1955]; 3rd ed., London, Methuen, 1970), pp. 36, 37, 37n.5. For Voegelin's phrase, see note 9 above.

28. Ullmann, p. 39.

29. *Ibid.,* p. 46.
30. *Ibid.,* p. 48.
31. Gregory the Great, *Regulae Pastoralis Liber, S. Gregory on the Pastoral Charge,* tr. Henry Ramsden Bramley (Oxford and London: James Parker, 1874), 1:1; parenthetical numbers in the following paragraphs refer to chapters and paragraphs in this work.
32. Heer, *Intellectual History,* p. 31; the source italicized the first quotation.
33. See Dudden, *1,* 296-305.
34. See Llewellyn, pp. 127-28, 97, 139-40.
35. Dudden, *1,* 319, quoting Gregory the Great, *Epistles,* 5:35; for many more details see Dudden, *1,* 311-20.
36. See Gregory the Great, *Epistles,* 7:13, *NPNF, 12,* 216.
37. Gregory the Great, *Dialogues,* 4:14, tr. Odo John Zimmerman, Fathers of the Church, *39* (New York: Fathers of the Church, 1959), 205-7.
38. Dudden, *2,* 42.
39. *Ibid., 2,* 340.
40. Gregory the Great, *Moralia,* 6:58, 33:24, P. L., *75,* 762, *76,* 687.
41. See Dudden, *1,* 276, 276n.2.
42. Heer, *Charlemagne,* p. 29.
43. Llewellyn, p. 124.
44. Heer, pp. 146-47, citing Alcuin to Charlemagne, June 799.
45. *Ibid.,* p. 139: *"Carolo augusto, a Deo coronato, magno et pacifico imperatore romanorum, vita et victoria."*
46. *Ibid.,* p. 176.
47. *Ibid.,* p. 225.
48. David Knowles, *The Evolution of Medieval Thought* ([1962]; New York: Vintage, 1964), p. 72, citing, respectively, a capitulary (of 789), the Council of Chalon (in 813), and an instruction of Theodulf, abbot of Fleury and bishop of Orleans.
49. Patch, pp. 59, 60. See F. Anne Payne, *King Alfred & Boethius; An Analysis of the Old English Version of the Consolation of Philosophy* (Milwaukee: University of Wisconsin Press, 1968). See also Henry Sweet, tr., *King Alfred's West-Saxon Version of Gregory's Pastoral Care* (London: Early English Text Society, 1871-72). The literature about King Alfred's books is copious.

Chapter IV

1. Paul Johnson, *A History of Christianity* (New York: Atheneum, 1976); Part 4, pp. 189-264, is called "The Total Society and its Enemies (1054-1500)." Note also the phrase's context in this passage: "the old medieval Church, the total society dating from Carolingian times," p. 267.
2. Henri Focillon, *The Year 1000* ([1969]; New York: Harper & Row, 1971), pp. 59-60, 69.

3. See Richard William Southern, *The Making of the Middle Ages* (New Haven: Yale University Press, 1953), pp. 16-17.

4. See Friedrich Heer, *The Holy Roman Empire*, tr. Janet Sondheimer (New York: Frederick A. Praeger, 1968), pp. 27-28.

5. Richard William Southern, *Western Views of Islam in the Middle Ages* (Cambridge: Harvard University Press, 1962), p. 3.

6. Heer, p. 45.

7. See Walter Ullmann, *The Growth of Papal Government in the Middle Ages* ([1955]; 3rd ed., London: Methuen, 1970), pp. 240, 247. For a portrayal of Otto as divine and imperial see Roland Herbert Bainton, *The Horizon History of Christianity* (New York: American Heritage, 1964), pp. 168-69.

8. Heer, plate 23; see also plates 21, 27.

9. Sylvester II (Gerbert of Aurillac), *The Letters of Gerbert with His Papal Privileges as Sylvester II*, tr. Harriet Pratt Lattin (New York: Columbia University Press, 1961), no. 221, p. 284.

10. Southern, *Making*, p. 98.

11. John Thomas McNeill and Helena Margaret Gamer, eds. and trs., *Medieval Handbooks of Penance* (New York: Columbia University Press, 1938), p. 147.

12. Henry Charles Lea, *A History of Auricular Confession and Indulgences in the Latin Church*, 3 vols. (Philadelphia: Lea Brothers, 1896), *2, 6,* citing Alexander of Hales, "Summae P. IV Q. XVII. Membr. ii. Art. 1§6; Art. 2§2; Membr. vii.—Astesani Summae Lib. V. Tit. ix. Art. 1-4."

13. Edward Cuthbert Butler, *Western Mysticism, The Teaching of Augustine, Gregory and Bernard on Contemplation and the Contemplative Life* ([1922]; 3rd ed., London: Constable, 1967), pp. 124-25 *et passim,* drew a sharp distinction between Bernard and later Latin mystics in that Bernard paid no attention to the negative steps that preoccupied the Victorines and others who based their schemes on pseudo-Dionysius. Notwithstanding, Bernard grounded both the first degree of love to God and the first step in humility on contrition. This feature set Bernard off from Augustine and Gregory the Great, who had distinguished the active from the contemplative life, commended the latter, and noted certain psychological and spiritual benefits of contemplation. Butler linked Bernard with these earlier writers in other important respects; *ibid.,* pp. 19-198.

14. Bernard of Clairvaux, *The Steps of Humility and Pride,* 7:21, tr. Mary Ambrose Conway, *Works, 5 (Treatises II),* Cistercian Fathers Series, no. 13 (Washington: Cistercian Publications, Consortium Press, 1974), p. 49-50.

15. See *ibid.,* 10:28—21:56, tr. pp. 57-82.

16. Bernard of Clairvaux, *Sermones super Cantica Canticorum,* ed. Jean Leclercq, C. H. Talbot, and Henri M. Rochais, 2 vols. (Rome: Editiones Cisterciensis, 1957-58), *9:*2. In several paragraphs that follow, numbers in parentheses in the text refer to sermons and sections of

them in this edition. See Bernard of Clairvaux, *On the Song of Songs*, pt. 1 (sermons 1-20), tr. Kilian J. Walsh, *Works, 2,* Cistercian Fathers Series, no. 4 (Spencer, MA: Cistercian Publications, 1971).

17. Bernard of Clairvaux, *On Precept and Dispensation,* 54, tr. Conrad Greenia, *Works, 1 (Treatises 1),* Cistercian Fathers Series, no. 1 (Spencer, MA: Cistercian Publications, 1970), p. 144.

18. Watkin Wynn Williams, *Studies in St. Bernard of Clairvaux* (London: Society for Promoting Christian Knowledge, 1927), p. 2.

19. Ullmann, p. 430.

20. Richard of St. Victor, *Benjamin Minor,* 76, P.L., *196,* 54.

21. Hugh of St. Victor, *De Anima,* 4:10, P.L., *177,* 181.

22. See Hilda Charlotte Graef, *The Story of Mysticism* (Garden City, N.Y.: Doubleday, 1965).

23. See Steven Edgar Ozment, *Mysticism and Dissent; Religious Ideology and Social Protest in the Sixteenth Century* (New Haven: Yale University Press, 1973).

24. Edmer, *The Life of St Anselm, Archbishop of Canterbury,* 1:7, tr. and ed. Richard William Southern (London: Thomas Nelson, 1962), p. 12.

25. Anselm, *Cur Deus Homo,* 1:7, Sidney Norton Deane, tr., *St. Anselm: Basic Writings* (2nd ed., Lasalle, IL: Open Court, 1962), p. 187; see Southern, *Making,* p. 236.

26. Anselm, *Proslogion,* 1, tr. p. 7.

27. Edmer, 1:19, tr. p. 29.

28. John of Salisbury, *Metalog.,* 3:4, P.L., *199,* 900, quoting Bernard of Chartres; see Eugene Rathbone Fairweather, ed. and tr., *A Scholastic Miscellany: Anselm to Ockham,* Library of Christian Classics, *10* ([1956]; New York: Macmillan, 1970), p. 21n.21.

29. *Ibid.,* p. 31.

30. Gertrud Schiller, *Ikonographie der christlichen Kunst,* 3 vols. (Gütersloh: Gerd Mohn, 1966-71), *1,* 166.

31. Hans Preuss, *Das Bild Christi in Wandel der Zeiten* (Leipzig: H. Voigtländer, 1915), plates 15, 14.

32. *Ibid.,* plates 42, 43, 53.

33. The depiction at Santa Catarina in Pisa was made by Francesco Traini (active 1321-63); see Lodovico Ferretti, *San Tommaso d'Aquino,* Arte Sacra Italiana, Collezione Iconografica (Rome: Società Editrice d'Arte Illustrata, 1923), p. 11, plate 1, and for similar depictions plates 5, 13, 16, 17, 21. For a photograph of the Traini picture see Bainton, p. 195.

Chapter V

1. Richard Slator Dunn, *The Age of Religious Wars, 1559-1689* (New York: W. W. Norton, 1970), p. 29.

2. See William Anthony Clebsch, *England's Earliest Protestants, 1520-1535* (New Haven: Yale University Press, 1964), pp. 151, 160-61.

3. Friedrich Heer, *The Holy Roman Empire,* tr. Janet Sondheimer (New York: Frederick A. Praeger, 1968), p. 188.

4. Dunn, p. 82.

5. Alfred North Whitehead, *Science and the Modern World, Lowell Lectures, 1925* (New York: Free Press, 1967), p. 46.

6. *New Catholic Encyclopedia, 9,* 1133, citing Bartolomeo Medina, *Comment. in 1a, 2ae, ST* 19.6.

7. See Fred Ernest Stoeffler, *The Rise of Evangelical Pietism,* Studies in the History of Religions (Supplements to *Numen*), *9* (Leiden: E. J. Brill, 1971), 66-67.

8. Richard Baxter, *Autobiography (Reliquae Baxterianae),* ed. and abr. Joseph Morgan Lloyd Thomas (London: J. M. Dent, 1931), p. 7.

9. Thomas Wood, *English Casuistical Divinity during the Seventeenth Century With Special Reference to Jeremy Taylor* (London: S.P.C.K., 1952), p. 103.

10. See Wood, pp. 59n.1, 60-61, 106-7; p. 60n.2 gives the title of the first English translation (in 1657) as *Les Provinciales: or the Mysterie of Jesuitisme. Discover'd in certain Letters, written upon occasion of the present Differences at Sorbonne, between the Jansenists and the Molinists. Displaying the Corrupt Maximes and Politicks of their Society.*

11. William Ames, *The Marrow of Theology,* 1:1:8, tr. John Dykstra Eusden (Boston: Pilgrim, 1968), p. 78.

12. Hugo Visscher, "William Ames His Life and Works" (Haarlem: J. M. Stap, 1894), tr. Tjaard Georg Hommes and Douglas Horton, in Douglas Horton, tr., *William Ames by Matthew Nethenus, Hugo Visscher, and Karl Reuter* (Cambridge: Harvard Divinity School Library, 1965), p. 70; Karl Reuter, "William Ames, the Leading Theologian in the Awakening of Reformed Pietism" (Neukirchen: Neukrichner, 1940), tr. Horton, *ibid.,* p. 179.

13. Ames, 1:2:4, 1:1:12, tr. pp. 80, 78.

14. Jeremy Taylor, *The Whole Works,* ed. Reginald Heber, rev. Charles Page Eden, 10 vols. (London: Longman, Brown, Green, and Longman *et al.,* 1847-52), *9,* xxi. All citations from Taylor are from this edition; volume and page numbers are given parenthetically in the text. The most frequently cited individual works, with the numbers of their volumes, are *The Great Exemplar, 2; Holy Living, 3; The Worthy Communicant, 8;* and *Ductor Dubitantium, 9* and *10.*

15. These three paragraphs on chastity summarize and paraphrase passages from *Holy Living, 3,* 55-68, 111-13.

16. Charles James Stranks, *The Life and Writings of Jeremy Taylor* (London: S.P.C.K., 1952), p. 96.

17. Friedrich Heer, *The Intellectual History of Europe,* tr. Jonathan Steinberg (Cleveland: World, 1966), p. 344.

18. John Bunyan, *Grace Abounding to the Chief of Sinners,* ed. Roger Ian Sharrock (Oxford: Clarendon, 1962), conclusion, par. 5; num-

bers in the text of the section on Bunyan refer to paragraphs in the body of this work.

19. U. Milo Kaufmann, *The Pilgrim's Progress and Traditions in Puritan Meditation* (New Haven: Yale University Press, 1966), p. ix.

20. John Bunyan, *The Pilgrim's Progress,* ed. Frank Raymond Leavis (New York: New American Library, 1964), pp. 194, 195.

21. Nothing is gained in translation. Zinzendorf wrote, "Ich habe von einem *Supposito* geredt, meine Freunde! in dem man selig wird, und dasselbe heißt: Annehmen, den Heiland annehmen, eine *Inclination* bey sich spüren: Ich will Ihn Haben! hätte ich Ihn doch! Er kömmt! willkommen! Wenn die *Idé*en beysammen sind: Er Kommt! tausendmal willkommen, willkommen allerliebstes Lamm! komm, komm nur bald, mein Bräutigam! so ist die Seligkeit richtig und *incontestabel.*" Nikolaus Ludwig von Zinzendorf, *Hauptschriften,* ed. Erich Beyreuther and Gerhard Meyer, 6 vols. (Hildesheim: Georg Olms, 1962-63), 6 (1), 123. The translation is Nikolaus Ludwig von Zinzendorf, *Nine Public Lectures on Important Subjects in Religion Preached in Fetter Lane Chapel in London in the Year 1746,* tr. and ed. George Wolfgang Forell (Iowa City: University of Iowa Press, 1973), pp. 68-69. Where the following paragraphs cite these London Lectures, references are given parenthetically in the text, first the page number in *Hauptschriften, 6* (1), then that in Forell.

22. John Rudolf Weinlick, *Count Zinzendorf* (New York: Abingdon, 1956), p. 198.

23. *Ibid.,* p. 205, citing Eugène Victor Félix Bovet, *The Banished Count; or, The Life of Nicholas Louis Zinzendorf,* tr. John Gill (London: J. Nisbet, 1865), p. 251; the passage is unreferenced in the original, Bovet, *Le Comte de Zinzendorf* (3rd. ed., Paris: Libraire Française et Étrangère, 1865), p. 352.

24. Nikolaus Ludwig von Zinzendorf, *Maxims, Theological Ideas and Sentences, out of the Present Ordinary of the Brethren's Churches. His Dissertations and Discourses From the Year 1738 till 1747,* ed. John Gambold (London: J. Beecroft, 1751), p. 257 (capitalization and spelling modernized).

25. Nikolaus Ludwig von Zinzendorf, *Sixteen Discourses on the Redemption of Man By the Death of Christ. Preached at Berlin . . . Translated from the High Dutch* (London: James Hutton, 1740), p. 111 (capitalization and spelling modernized).

26. John Wesley, "Utph" [Westphalia?], July 6, 1738, to Susanna Wesley, *The Letters of the Rev. John Wesley,* ed. John Telford, 8 vols. ([1931]; London: Epworth, 1960), *1,* 250.

27. Zinzendorf, *Sixteen Discourses,* p. 41.

28. *Ibid.,* pp. 19, 190.

29. Zinzendorf, *Maxims,* p. 157.

30. See Weinlick, p. 205.

31. The painting is reproduced in Erich Beyreuther, *Zinzendorf und die*

Christenheit, 1732-1760 (Marburg/L.: Francke, 1961), facing p. 272. A contemporary portrait of Zinzendorf was reproduced in Weinlick, frontispiece.

32. See Albert Cook Outler, ed., *John Wesley,* A Library of Protestant Thought (New York, Oxford University Press, 1964), p. 37. Wesley's works exist in many editions, and yet another is in progress, promising to be definitive. Outler's is the best brief, accessible compend, and the following references made parenthetically in the text are to it.

33. Alphonsus Liguori, *The Love of our Lord Jesus Christ Reduced to Practice . . . Addressed to Those Souls That are anxious to secure their Eternal Salvation, and to advance towards Perfection,* tr. anon. (Baltimore: F. Lucas, Jr., n.d.), p. 143.

34. Alphonsus Liguori, *The Glories of Mary,* rev. Robert Aston Coffin ([1750]; London: Burns, Oates & Washbourne, 1868), pp. 1, 2, 4.

35. Liguori, *Love,* p. 264.

Chapter VI

1. Meyer Howard Abrams, *Natural Supernaturalism; Tradition and Revolution in Romantic Literature* ([1971]; New York: Norton, 1973), pp. 292-93.

2. Johann Gottlieb Fichte, April? 1795?, to Baggesen?, Briefe no. 231, *Briefwechsel,* ed. Hans Karl Schulz, 2 vols. ([1930]; Hildesheim: Georg Olms, 1967), *1,* 449. See Abrams, p. 349.

3. Abrams, p. 91.

4. Friedrich Heer, *Europe, Mother of Revolutions,* tr. Charles Kessler and Jennetta Adcock (New York: Praeger, 1972), p. 12.

5. Abrams, p. 334.

6. Georg Wilhelm Friedrich Hegel, *Vorlesungen über die Geschichte der Philosophie, 3:3:*1, Jubiläumsausgabe, ed. Hermann Glockner, 20 vols. (Stuttgart: Friedrich Frommann, 1965), *19,* 330; see Eric Voegelin, *Order and History, 4, The Ecumenic Age* (Baton Rouge: Louisiana State University Press, 1974), p. 173. See also Eric Voegelin, "Response to Professor Altizer's 'A New History and a New But Ancient God?,' " *Journal of the American Academy of Religion, 43* (December 1975), 765-71.

7. Voegelin, *Ecumenic Age,* p. 264.

8. Karl Barth, *Protestant Thought: From Rousseau to Ritschl,* tr. Brian Cozens (New York: Harper, 1959), pp. 48, 62. Much earlier, Eugène Delacroix, *The Journal of Eugène Delacroix, a Selection,* ed. Hubert Lindsay Wellington, tr. Lucy Norton (London: Phaidon, 1951), p. 109, wrote on Feb. 7, 1850: "At this concert and the following one, I compared the two Beethoven overtures with the overture to the *Magic Flute,* and to so many others by Mozart; in the latter, what an assemblage of every quality that art and genius can

combine to produce perfection! and in the former, what strange, undisciplined imagination!" William Hardman Poteat called this reference to my attention.

9. Johann Christoph Friedrich von Schiller, *Die Braut von Messina,* Vorrede, *Sämtliche Werke,* ed. Otto Güntter and Georg Witkowski, 20 vols. (Leipzig: Hesse & Becker, 1910), *20, 252;* see Abrams, p. 433.

10. Samuel Taylor Coleridge, *Biographia Literaria,* ed. John Shawcross, 2 vols. ([1907]; London: Oxford University Press, 1967), *2,* 5-6.

11. William Wordsworth, *Prospectus,* quoted in Abrams, p. 466; *ibid.,* pp. 95, 68.

12. Charles Earle Raven, *Natural Religion and Christian Theology* (Cambridge: Cambridge University Press, 1953), p. 171.

13. Karl Marx, *Critique of Hegel's "Philosophy of Right,"* tr. Annette Jolin and Joseph James O'Malley, ed. Joseph James O'Malley ([1844]; Cambridge: Cambridge University Press, 1970), p. 131.

14. Hans Wilhelm Frei, *The Eclipse of Biblical Narrative; A Study in Eighteenth and Nineteenth Century Hermeneutics* (New Haven: Yale University Press, 1974), p. 222.

15. The consternation aroused by Strauss persists today among Christians. The article on Jesus Christ in *The Oxford Dictionary of the Christian Church* (2nd ed., 1974) weaves and waffles: "The Gospels contain such facts as it was held important for a Christian to know about His earthly life and therefore often fail to satisfy a purely biographical curiosity. Moreover, being written for and by believers, they interpret as well as record, but their aim is to make plain what actually happened, i.e. they are concerned with historical truth as well as with theological interpretation" (p. 736). The far bolder proposal that the notions, the Jesus of history and the Christ of faith, framed a wrong-headed question came from Voegelin, pp. 243-44: "To invent a 'critical history' that will allow us to decide whether Incarnation and Resurrection are 'historically real' turns the structure of reality upside down; it flies in the face of all our empirical knowledge about history and its constitution of meaning." But this resolution itself forfeits the Christian sense of Christ's unique, definitive, normative agency of divine presence, for Voegelin found Plato and Paul agreeing "that the reality of history is . . . the In-Between where man responds to the divine presence and divine presence evokes the response of man" (p. 242). On this level view Plato's theophany becomes quite as important to the meaning of history as Paul's, but to concede that point is to discard a cardinal tenet of traditional Christian doctrine (and the recurrent theme of traditional Christian devotion) to the effect that Christ is not only the god-man for Christians but also the only god-man.

16. Peter N. Stearns, *Priest and Revolutionary; Lamennais and the Dilemma of French Catholicism* (New York: Harper & Row, 1967), pp. 155-57, citing Félicité Robert de Lamennais, April 30, 1825, to

the Marquis Charles Louis Alexandre de Coriolis d'Espinousse; March 18, 1826, to Comte de Senfft-Pilsach; May 2, 1827, to Comtesse de Senfft von Pilsach. Stearns selected and translated important letters from *Lamennais: Correspondance,* ed. Paul Émile Durand Forgues, 2 vols. (Paris, 1864).

17. Félicité Robert de Lamennais, *Essai sur l'indifférence en matière de religion,* 3 vols. (Paris: Tournachon-Molin et Seguin; Lesage, 1817-23). Alexander Roper Vidler, *Prophecy and Papacy; a Study of Lamennais, the Church, and the Revolution* (New York: Scribner, 1954), pp. 68-69, distinguished the elements of Lamennais's thought as apologetic traditionalism, ecclesiological ultra-montanism, and political liberalism, and he granted that eventually Lamennais integrated these elements. Vidler then (chaps. 3, 4) proceeded to deal separately with Lamennais's "New Apologetics 1817-1824" and "New Politics 1825-1829." Vidler refused to regard Lamennais as a Christian activist because his mature commitment to social Christianity came after the pope considered him to be apostate; indeed, Vidler transferred Lamennais's significance from church history to secular history as of 1836, "when the publication of *Affaires de Rome* sealed his rupture with catholicism" (p. 11). See Alexander Roper Vidler, *A Century of Social Catholicism, 1820-1920* (London: S.P.C.K., 1964), p. 7. The following paragraphs show that Lamennais's significance as the inaugural exemplar of activism for the subsequent history of Christianity in Europe grew to be enormous; he influenced the religion more after than before 1836.

18. Vidler, *Prophecy,* p. 84, citing Charles Loyson, review in *Le Spectateur politique et littéraire* (1818).

19. Stearns, pp. 158-59, citing Lamennais, January 11, 1829, to Friedrich Christian Ludwig Senfft von Pilsach.

20. Félicité Robert de Lamennais, *Words of a Believer, translated from the French of F. de la Mennais* (New York: Charles de Behr, 1834), pp. 65-75.

21. *Ibid.,* pp. 126-27.

22. Stearns, p. 165, citing Lamennais, December 15, 1832, to Comtesse de Senfft von Pilsach.

23. Lamennais, *Words,* pp. 91-92.

24. See Vidler, *Century,* pp. 9-10, 13-17, 21-23, 34.

25. Alexander Roper Vidler, *The Church in an Age of Revolution 1789 to the Present Day,* The Pelican History of the Church, 5 (Baltimore: Penguin, 1961), 95.

26. Torben Christensen, *Origin and History of Christian Socialism 1848-54,* Acta Theologica Danica, 3 (Aarhus: Universitets-forlaget, 1962), 38n.11, citing John Malcolm Forbes Ludlow, Diary, June 5, 1839.

27. *Ibid.,* p. 61n.11, citing Ludlow, *Autobiography,* chap. 18.

28. Charles Kingsley, *Charles Kingsley: His Letters and Memories of His Life, Edited by His Wife,* 9th abr. ed., 2 vols. (London: C. Kegan Paul, 1881), *1,* 126.

29. William Temple, *Christianity and Social Order* (New York: Penguin, 1942), pp. 21-22.
30. Vidler, *Century,* p. 163; see also pp. 152-62.
31. Eberhard Bethge, *Bonhoeffer: Exile and Martyr,* ed. John W. De Gruchy (London: Collins, 1975), p. 127. This little book brings into interpretive focus the massive detail of the definitive biography, Eberhard Bethge, *Dietrich Bonhoeffer, Man of Vision, Man of Courage,* tr. Eric Mosbacher *et al.* (New York: Harper & Row, 1970).
32. *The Oxford Dictionary of the Christian Church* (1957) first gave Bonhoeffer neither an entry nor even mention in entries about organizations and movements he influenced. The revised edition (1974) accorded him a full column, as much as Albert Schweitzer and more than William Temple. During the two decades after publication of the prison writings, an article on Bonhoeffer appeared at the average rate of one every fortnight, to say nothing of a spate of brief books, and the five slim books he published during his lifetime swelled posthumously into six fat volumes of collected works.
33. Dietrich Bonhoeffer, *Ethics,* ed. Eberhard Bethge, tr. Neville Horton Smith (New York: Macmillan, 1965), pp. 198-99.
34. Alasdair Chalmers MacIntyre, "God and the Theologians," in *The Honest to God Debate, Some reactions to the book 'Honest to God,'* ed. David Lawrence Edwards (Philadelphia: Westminster, 1963), p. 221.
35. Stephen Prickett, *Romanticism and Religion; The Tradition of Coleridge and Wordsworth in the Victorian Church* (Cambridge: Cambridge University Press, 1976), p. 33.
36. Coleridge, *2,* 215-16.
37. Richard Reinhold Niebuhr, *Schleiermacher on Christ and Religion, A New Introduction* (New York: Scribner, 1964), pp. 35, 62. Niebuhr found the germs of Schleiermacher's later and more systematic themes in this rather occasional meditation about Christmas Eve.
38. Thomas Carlyle, *Works, Standard Edition,* 18 vols. (New York: Funk & Wagnalls, 1905), *2,* pt. 2, *The Life of John Sterling,* p. 44.
39. John Henry Newman, *An Essay in Aid of a Grammar of Assent,* ed. Charles Frederick Harrold (New York: Longmans, Green, 1947), p. 71. The following page references in parentheses are to this work.
40. Prickett, p. 174.
41. Newman, p. 314.
42. Jouett Lynn Powell, *Three Uses of Christian Discourse in John Henry Newman: an Example of Nonreductive Reflection on the Christian Faith,* American Academy of Religion Dissertation Series, *10* (Missoula, MT: Scholars Press for American Academy of Religion, 1975), p. 144.
43. Søren Aabye Kierkegaard, *For Self-Examination and Judge for Yourselves! and Three Discourses 1851,* tr. Walter Lowrie (Princeton: Princeton University Press, 1944), pp. 181, 179.

44. Barth, p. 396.
45. Vidler, *Church*, p. 111; Vidler introduced the phrase with, "It has been well said that," but he neither put quotes around it nor referenced it.
46. Albrecht Benjamin Ritschl, *Instruction in the Christian Religion*, in *Three Essays*, ed. Philip James Hefner (Philadelphia: Fortress, 1972), par. 50; in this and the following paragraph, parenthetical numbers in the text refer to paragraphs in this summary of Ritschl's Christianity.
47. Adolf von Harnack, *What Is Christianity? Sixteen Lectures Delivered in the University of Berlin during the Winter Term, 1899-1900*, tr. Thomas Bailey Saunders, 3rd ed. (New York: Putnam, 1904), p. 52, where the phrases are italicized.
48. Ernst Troeltsch, "The Dogmatics of the 'Religionsgeschichtliche Schule,'" *American Journal of Theology, 17* (January 1913), 12-13.
49. Ernst Troeltsch, *Christian Thought: Its History and Application*, ed. Friedrich von Hügel ([1923]; New York: Meridian, 1957), pp. 55, 55-56.
50. Saul Bellow, *Humboldt's Gift* (New York: Viking, 1973, Avon, 1976), p. 10.

INDEX

This index identifies certain persons by the titles of apostle, emperor, empress, king, martyr (till 337), monk (till 910), pope (after 440), and queen. Following each name of a person, the years of birth and (where applicable) of death are given, so far as such years could be ascertained.

A